HAPPY
CHOICES

"Luiz Gaziri has beautifully synthesized research and stories to present a practical guide to a fulfilling life. By choosing to read this book, you are choosing to embark on a journey towards the higher planes of health and happiness."

TAL BEN-SHAHAR, lecturer of the largest class in Harvard University's history, author of *Happier* and *Even Happier*.

• •

"Happy Choices is a vital guidebook for anyone seeking happiness. Luiz Gaziri busts happiness myths and gives us a clear roadmap on how to pursue happiness and use it to fuel success. This compelling book is a must-read!"

MICHELLE GIELAN, best-selling author of *Broadcasting Happiness* and former CBS Morning News anchor.

• •

"Reading *Happy Choices* made me... happy. Luiz Gaziri succeeded in making complicated science approachable and exciting. In this book, the interaction of money, emotions and motivation is explained in a clear and smart way.".

URI GNEEZY, Professor of Economics & Strategy at the Rady School of Management, University of California, San Diego.

• •

"Amidst the costume jewelry of pop psychology, this book shines forth as a true gem. Based on interviews with top scholars and thoughtful analyses of the best contemporary research in psychology, Gaziri provides a roadmap for navigating the seductions and pressures of modern living, and identifies the most reliable pathways to happiness and meaning."

RICHARD M. RYAN, Professor in the Institute for Positive Psychology and Education, Australian Catholic University.

"South America is not known as a hotbed of psychological research. However, Luiz Gaziri has done an excellent job of pulling together research studies from around the world, to show what makes for a truly happy and fulfilling life. His advice is very clear and very accurate, and I am glad to see this information made available to Brazilians and readers of Portuguese. It can change your life!"

KENNON SHELDON, Curators' Distinguished Professor of Psychological Sciences, University of Missouri.

· ·

"Happiness is the one desire that all humans share. Yet we often look for it where we won't find it. Fortunately. Professor Gaziri is here to help elucidate the science of what makes humans happier!"

EMMA SEPPALA, Science Director of Stanford University's Center for Compassion and Altruism Research and Education, Co-Director of the Yale College Emotional Intelligence Project at the Yale Center for Emotional Intelligence, and Faculty Director of the Yale School of Management's Women's Leadership Program, author of *The Happiness Track* .

· ·

"Happiness isn't just something you inherit, it can be cultivated. In *Happy Choices*, Luiz Gaziri uses a deep understanding of science and research to craft an excellent book that shows the power of choice and can be used by anyone seeking greater meaning and well-being for themselves, their teams or their families."

SHAWN ACHOR, NY Times best-selling author of *The Happiness Advantage* and *Big Potential*.

· ·

"How do you make your decisions? Luiz Gaziri will give you the best advice ingeniously extracted from science into a story that will change your life—by supporting you in making better choices. You will also discover what success really means for you and how you can confidently achieve it."

GABRIELE OETTINGEN, Professor of Psychology at New York University and the University of Hamburg.

"Luiz Gaziri reveals the hidden science behind how positive emotions can go viral and impact both our lives and those of the people around us. This book shows how money, recognition and positive thinking can be the villains or the heroes of our happiness. It will change your life goals—for the better".

JONAH BERGER, Professor de Marketing na Wharton School, Universidade da Pensilvânia.

• •

"You must read this book—your happiness may very well depend on it! While most people strive to live happier, healthier and better lives—most people look for it in the wrong places, leading them to feel unfulfilled, anxious and worried. In *Happy Choices*, Luiz Gaziri explains the science of how we can bring lasting happiness into our lives: through our everyday choices. These insights will surprise you and change your thinking which will help you make choices toward happiness in the future."

GRANT DONNELLY, Professor of Marketing at the Ohio State University

• •

"Contrary to conventional wisdom, science teaches us that our happiness doesn't rely on how much money we make, how many prizes we win, or how much positive thinking we do. Luiz Gaziri has read a mountain of studies on the science of happiness. In *Happy Choices*, he explains what he's learned in a clear and engaging language, bringing a rigor to our search for happiness. If you want to be happier (and who doesn't?)—or if you want happier, more engaged employees—this is the book for you."

DANIEL PINK, author of *When*, *Drive*, and *To Sell Is Human*.

• •

"A truly outstanding book that was superbly researched and is presented in an interesting and engaging way. It is full of important findings, all of which are fascinating and some of which are counter-intuitive. Professor Gaziri has done an outstanding job of discussing motivation and well-being, and this work has many applications that can enhance people's lives."

EDWARD L. DECI, Professor of Psychology, University of Rochester, author of *Why We Do What We Do*.

LUIZ GAZIRI

HAPPY CHOICES

Applying the Science of Happiness and Motivation to Take Control of Your Success.

COPYRIGHT © 2019 BY LUIZ GAZIRI

All rights reserved.
No portion of this book may be reproduced, scanned, or distributed in any print or electronic form without permission.

Cover art **OSMANE GARCIA FILHO**
Illustration **WIGO WIGGLES | FIVERR**
Book Formatted by **CRISTIANE SAAVEDRA | CS EDIÇÕES**

To Mariana, Leonardo and Victoria
My biggest sources of happiness.

CONTENTS

Introduction
Myths on Money, Recognition and Positive Thinking 11

PART 1 – MONEY
Chapter 1 – Money, Motivation and Happiness 29
Chapter 2 – Ensuring the Best Profits 61
Chapter 3 – Far Beyond Maslow 81

PART 2 – RECOGNITION
Chapter 4 – Negative, Stressed, Sick and with Fear of Missing Out 103
Chapter 5 – The Advantages of Positive Emotions 109
Chapter 6 – Unrecognizable Recognition 137
Chapter 7 – Being Irreplaceable 149
Chapter 8 – The Results of It All 167

PART 3 – POSITIVE THINKING
Chapter 9 – Being Positive × Thinking Positive 173
Chapter 10 – The Happiness Mentality 187

Conclusion 201
Acknowledgments 205
References 211

INTRODUCTION

Myths on Money, Recognition and Positive Thinking

AN EQUATION WITH UNKNOWN VARIABLES

In the late 1990s, scientists Uri Gneezy, from the University of California in San Diego, and Aldo Rustichini, from the University of Minnesota, made an intriguing discovery, unknown to most people and most corporate circles[1]. They held a scientific experiment in which they observed Israeli students on a traditional Giving Day. The 180 participants were divided into three groups to solicit donations door to door, under the following conditions:

> **Group 1** — was given a short talk on the importance of their work.
>
> **Group 2** — was given a short talk on the importance of their work, plus the information that they would receive 1% of the total donations collected.
>
> **Group 3** — was given a short talk on the importance of their work, plus the information that they would receive 10% of the total donations collected.

Given the conditions for each group, which do you think raised the most money?

Before you answer, you should know what Giving Day is. An Israeli tradition, Giving Days happen a few times a year, and the resources raised are destined to children with disabilities, cancer research and other causes. The dates are announced on television ads and other media, so the whole country is aware of when donations will be solicited, and people are excited to receive the students – responsible for collecting these resources – in the hopes that their donation can make a difference in someone's life. As we can imagine, no effort is required from the students to convince people to give – they don't have to "sell" anything. Therefore, the students' performance **depends exclusively on their efforts**: the more houses they visit, the more they raise.

I should note that participants from Groups 2 and 3 were duly informed that their commissions, that is, the financial incentive for their donations, would be paid by the universities. Therefore, there would be no loss to the beneficiaries of the donations. Also, the groups were not informed about the other groups' conditions, in order to preserve the experiment.

If you ask ten people on the street which group had the best performance, what do you think they would answer?

Based on the intuitive model used by most people, which correlates money, motivation and performance, you might figure that members of Group 3 raised the most resources, after all, the higher the financial incentive, the higher are people's motivations and their performance, right? Also, if we approach meritocracy idea that is common in the corporate environment and take into account that the students' performance depended on themselves only, this conclusion makes even more sense, right?

However, the amounts raised by each group in Israeli New Shekels (₪) were as follows:

> **Group 1** - ₪ 238.60
> **Group 2** - ₪ 153.60
> **Group 3** - ₪ 219.30

Are you surprised that Group 1, which received no financial incentives, had the **best** performance? What caused this? In the paper, published in the *Quarterly Journal of Economics* in August 2000, Gneezy and Rustichini said:

"The main conclusions of these studies were that positive rewards, in particular monetary rewards, have a negative effect on intrinsic motivation."

I'm sure that these results are quite different from what you guessed when I presented the conditions for each group. It seems that the motivation equation brings unknown variables to the general public, and surprisingly, some of them weigh more than money. No doubt money is significant for our motivation on certain occasions—if not, Group 3 would not have had a better performance than Group 2—but the fact that Group 1 had the best result is noteworthy. In any case, you might be wondering: if the commissions were higher than the maximum US$ 1.35 per duo for Group 2, and US$ 13.50 per duo for Group 3, the participants would have better results, right? After all, who is motivated by such low values? To answer that, we'll illustrate with another experiment that tested this hypothesis.

A HUNDRED TIMES MORE = FOUR TIMES LESS

In 2002, researchers Dan Ariely, from Duke University, George Loewenstein, from Carnegie Mellon University, Nina Mazar, from Boston University, e once again Uri Gneezy, from the University of California in San Diego, held an even more interesting experiment in the city of Madurai[2], India. The participants were separated into three groups to perform six different tasks. The financial incentives offered per task, in Indian Rupees (₹), were as follows:

GROUP 1

PERFORMANCE LEVEL	FINANCIAL INCENTIVE
Bad	0.00
Good	2.00
Very good	4.00

GROUP 2

PERFORMANCE LEVEL	FINANCIAL INCENTIVE
Bad	0.00
Good	20.00
Very good	40.00

GROUP 3

PERFORMANCE LEVEL	FINANCIAL INCENTIVE
Bad	0.00
Good	200.00
Very good	400.00

It's important to note what these incentives meant for the participants. At the time of the study, the average monthly wage in rural India was ₹ 495. Therefore, if Group 3 participants reached the "very good" performance level in all six tasks, they could earn the equivalent of **five months' salary**, that is, ₹ 2,400. Similarly, Group 2 participants could earn as much as **two weeks' salary**, and Group 1 could earn approximately **one and a half workday's salary**. Very motivating, don't you think?

Now that these extremely aggressive commission values were offered, can you imagine what happened? As incredible as it may seem, in **five of the six tasks**, Group 3 had the worst performance. Statistically, Groups 1 and 2 had no significant difference in performance, despite the financial incentives of Group 2 being ten times higher than those of Group 1. On average, 25.58% of Group 1 participants reached the "very good" performance level on all six tasks, against 22.21% of Group 2 and just 6.3% of Group 3. This means that the possibility of earning 100 times more caused the number of participants with "very good" performance in Group 3 to be four times lower than in Group 1.

These studies show a very different reality from what most individuals and companies believe to be true about motivation. At this point, you might be thinking that money may not motivate people the way we believe it does, but it surely must produce positive effects on **happiness**. And one answer to this hypothesis comes from a country with a blue, red and white flag, evaluated as **the happiest in the world**. Can you guess the country?

AN EQUATION WITH EVEN LESS KNOWN VARIABLES

In the happiest country in the world, everyone treats each other with respect, has great sleep, smiles and laughs on a daily basis. Its citizens are always learning interesting things, and report that they often feel joy. I've mentioned the colors of the flag—blue, red and white. Now, can you guess the country? A few possibilities may have occurred to you, but I'm sure **Paraguay** wasn't one of them!

You read that right! For the **seventh year in a row**, the population of Paraguay was ranked the happiest in the world, according to *Gallup's Global Emotions Report*, one of the most important and recognized studies on global happiness[3]. It's worth noting that, in the UN's strongest economies rank, Paraguay is at a modest **101st** place, among 211 countries. Behind it on the happiness rank are Colombia, El Salvador, Guatemala, Canada, Costa Rica, Ecuador, Honduras, Iceland, Indonesia, Panama and Uzbekistan. Many believe there's a strong correlation between a country's wealth and the happiness of its population, but such correlation is weak, to say the least. The **United States**, the world's highest GDP, is close to the **40th** position, nearing Brazil, Germany, Luxembourg, Austria, Bolivia, United Kingdom, Mali and South Africa.

A study conducted by researchers from Simon Fraser University, the University of British Columbia and Harvard University proves people's misconception regarding the relationship between money and happiness in a fantastic way[4]. Scientists asked individuals with different incomes to rate, on a scale of 0 to 10, how happy they felt, as well as to give their opinions on the happiness of people divided into ten yearly income ranges (US$ 5,000; US$ 10,000, US$ 25,000; US$ 35,000; US$ 55,000; US$ 90,000; US$ 125,000; US$ 160,000; US$ 500,000 and US$ 1 million). What the study showed was alarming: participants grossly **underestimated** the happiness of low-income people. Those that earned around US$ 5,000 evaluated their happiness at 5.5 in the scale, while the assumption of the other income groups about this group's happiness was close to 2.5. This result shows that **there is** a relationship between higher income and happiness, but a very **modest** one. It's interesting that, regarding those with a higher income, participants got it right, guessing that a big increase in income (from US$ 90,000 to US$ 125,000 a year) does **not** drastically increase happiness. Despite these facts, financial growth is still the ultimate goal of many.

Right now, I'm sure you're not surprised with this result. You certainly had already noticed that money doesn't motivate people in the right way and doesn't bring more happiness. But what do people want, then?

WHAT PEOPLE WANT

By the end of my training sessions, lectures or classes where I present the unknown consequences of money on people's motivation and happiness, somebody always approaches me about this idea. At a certain point in the conversation, the conclusion is no different from what I told you: money doesn't really motivate people. What people want is **recognition**.

REWARDS OR RECOGNITION: WHAT WORKS?

Just like many of us believe that, if offered a great sum of money to perform a task, we'd have increased motivation and, consequently, increased performance, we also believe that, if **recognized** by our work, we will be motivated. In the 1970s, researchers from the Universities of Stanford and Michigan decided to test the impact of recognition on people's motivation, so they created a genius experiment[5].

Children from a Stanford in-campus school, separated into three groups, were told to make a drawing of their choosing, under the following conditions::

Group 1 - Before starting the drawing, the children were told they would get a special prize for their work: a "Good Player Award" diploma to their name, decorated with a big gold star and a bright red ribbon. This diploma would then be placed by the children on the school's "Honor Roll Board", visible to all students. This condition was named **expected reward**.

Group 2 - After finishing the drawing, the children received the same diploma, but as a **surprise**. This condition was named **unexpected reward**.

Group 3 - After finishing the drawing, the children didn't receive any prize. This condition was named **control**.

To determine the participants, two weeks **before** the experiment, the researchers and their team observed 102 school children to assess their interest in the materials that would be used in the study: color markers and special drawing paper—items not usually available in their daily activities. After finding which children were internally moved to drawing, 51 were studied by the research team. Of those, 18 were in the **expected reward** group, another 18 on the **unexpected reward**, and 15 on the **control** group.

With all of the children's drawings at hand, the researchers asked three judges—who were oblivious to the goal of the study—to evaluate their quality. Then, they asked the judges to grade each drawing on a scale of 1 (low quality) to 5 (high quality). The groups were graded, on average, as below:

> **Group 1 - Expected reward: 2.18.**
>
> **Group 2 - Unexpected reward: 2.85.**
>
> **Group 3 - Control (no reward): 2.69.**

The tiny difference in decimals may seem insignificant to the layman's eye, so it should be clarified that, as per the scientific method, researchers make a very thorough analysis when they need to find out whether the difference between numerical values is relevant. In this study, the analysis showed a **statistically significant** difference from Group 1's grade to Groups 2 and 3. That is, the fact that the children in Group 1 knew beforehand that they would be **recognized** by their work **caused** a negative impact on their performance. Both Groups 2 and 3, which made the drawings under the same conditions (not knowing they would get a prize), had a higher performance.

If you thought these results were interesting, you'll be even more intrigued by the weeks following the experiment. When analyzing the children's behavior days after the study, researchers found that, when they were able to play again with the same materials of the experiment, Group 1 participants spent less time drawing than others. Moreover, it should be noted that children in Groups 2 and 3 had a slight **increase** in their interest in the materials used in the experiment, although not statistically significant.

If these weren't reliable scientific studies, it would be really hard for anyone to believe that recognition caused reduced performance, as well as a subsequent disinterest of participants in the activity—remember the children in this study were especially chosen for showing a natural motivation towards the task. We can assume that, when we do an activity **expecting** recognition, a strange phenomenon occurs to our motivation and, subsequently, our performance. Among the researcher's conclusions on the effect of extrinsic motivation rewards, we highlight:

> "[...] a central problem with our educational system is its inability to preserve the intrinsic interest in learning and exploration that the child seems to possess when he first enters school. Instead, [...] the schooling process seems almost to undermine children's spontaneous interest in the process of learning itself."

There are other scientific discoveries pertinent to this case. One research conducted by Rochester University found that, when external incentives are introduced for performing a task, people **lose intrinsic motivation** and, subsequently, devote **less** dedication to the task than when they had no incentives—which explains the children's lack of interest in drawing in the weeks following the experiment[6]. Therefore, if an individual works **expecting** recognition, they automatically **lose** pleasure in conducting a task, finishing a project, moving forward, achieving small accomplishments. They start to work **solely** to be praised.

If money and recognition can have disastrous consequences on your life, what else can you do to get motivated and be happy? If you decide to follow the teachings of self-help authors and motivational speakers, the only thing left to save you is **positive thinking**. After all, when you think positive, good things happen in your life, don't they? This belief is so strong in society that it's now common to hear that simply the strong desire for something makes "the universe conspire" in your favor. But does it?

POSITIVE THINKING, POSITIVE RESULTS? NOT SO MUCH...

Anyone who's ever been to a motivational talk knows that, at some point, the speaker will correlate reaching their goals with the ability to think positive enough. You can expect to hear something in the lines of "Look yourself in the mirror and make an affirmation that you'll reach your goal, you'll win, you'll beat that sales goal, you'll get that difficult client, that promotion you want so bad!" Some of these professionals even ask people to imagine themselves arriving to a party wearing that pair of jeans that no longer fits, with the weight and waistline they desire so much; or to imagine how their lives will be after getting that promotion, asking them to visualize themselves in a private office, driving an import car and being able to afford whatever they want; or to think about how their mood will improve when they can finally be with that one person they really love, but haven't had the courage to ask out yet.

Away from the spotlights, though, that same line of thinking is present somewhere else—bookstores. Just a stroll through the self-help isle gives you thousands of titles—all trying to teach lessons on how positive thinking, or simply desiring something with all your heart, can make "the universe conspire" in your favor, giving you what you want. But does repeating **to yourself** that you'll reach a goal, or **fantasizing** about how you'll feel in a future situation, or **frequently desiring something** really yields results? Science has been studying this topic for years, and the answers are very different from what lazy self-help advertises.

Researchers Yannis Theodorakis, Robert Weinberg, and three other colleagues studied the motivational effects on people caused by just talking to themselves positively before a task, and they made very interesting discoveries[7]. When analyzing the behavior of high-performing athletes, Theodorakis and his colleagues found that the athletes with the best results weren't those who said "I can do it!" before the game or event. In fact, there wasn't **one single** situation in which participants used a motivational phrase and did significantly better than their competitors.

Similar results were obtained by researchers Ibrahim Senay and Dolores Albarracín, from the University of Illinois, along with Kenji Noguchi, from South Mississippi University[8]. In a series of experiments, they asked participants to solve ten anagrams—an activity that consists of reordering the letters in a word (for example, RACE) to turn it into a different word (**CARE**). Anagrams are some of the best tools to evaluate people's performances in tasks involving rational thought and creativity. In this study, a group of individuals was instructed to make **affirmations** for one minute, saying they **would be able** to solve the anagrams. It turns out that this made participants solve **50% less** anagrams than those in the control study group. In a second experiment, participants were instructed to "think positive", writing affirmative words and phrases. They performed **100% worse** than those who wrote other kinds of words and phrases.

In the world of positive thinking, however, no one made more significant discoveries than Gabriele Oettingen, professor and researcher at New York University and the University of Hamburg. After over 20 years researching "the power of positive thinking", Oettingen made discoveries that disappointed the fans of *The Secret*. In one of her studies, Oettingen and her colleague Doris Mayer, from the University of Hamburg, asked senior university students to inform, on a daily basis, whether they had positive thoughts, images or fantasies about entering the job market, finishing college and looking for and finding work[9]. In the second stage of the study, students were instructed to write about these positive thoughts, images and fantasies. The third stage asked students to report the frequency with which they had these positive thoughts and images, on a scale of 10 points, ranging from "Very rarely" to "Very frequently".

Oettingen and Mayer, to their surprise, found that students which reported frequent positive fantasies about entering the job market received **less** job offers. Even more intriguing is the fact that, within this group of students who fantasized frequently, those already employed earned lower wages than the others, who fantasized less frequently. In addition, the researchers revealed that students who frequently imagined their success sent **less** resumes than their colleagues in the study. Similar results occurred when researchers evaluated the probability of students starting a romantic relationship, or profess their love to the person they were interested in—those who fantasized more had **less** chances of starting a relationship or professing their love. In this sense, students who fantasized about getting a good grade in a given discipline ultimately got **lower** grades and studied for **less** time. Finally, Oettingen and Mayer found that patients who fantasized positively about their recovery after a surgery showed **more** pain, **more** difficulty going up stairs, **less** movement in the operated body part, **less** muscle strength and **less** well-being. The conclusion was that thinking positive, in fact, generates **opposite** results to what people expect.

HOW IS THIS BOOK DIFFERENT?

This is also a book on motivation and happiness, but **based on scientific research**. I've been in contact with many works that promised to reveal the secrets of success, most having as a principle the **illusion** that, if people followed the author's formula for motivation and happiness, they would undoubtedly succeed. A success story is only **one** story. What one person does to reach the top may very well be the formula of **failure** to another. This book, **completely based on science**, can never have the luxury of analyzing just **one** case, or just the **most convenient** case to defend a point. To reach a reliable conclusion, science must analyze a large number of cases of a given phenomenon, as well as make several extremely robust statistical interpretations. If science were to defend its position using the same formula of these authors—illustrating only **one** case, the field of medicine could, for example, use the history of **one** person who smoked until age 95 and died of natural causes to conclude that **smoking is not bad for you**, or worse, that smoking is beneficial to your health, which, as we all know, does not correspond to reality.

Analyzing just **one** case, or using the **most convenient**, to defend a position is a behavior present in several other environments. Because **one** employee had an excellent performance following the company's current strategies, **all** others should perform the same. **One** company followed this strategy and was successful, so executives from other companies believe they'll succeed if they follow the same strategy. **One** person developed a certain habit and reached happiness, so we believe that, if we cultivate the same habit, we'll also be happy. **One** individual made certain decisions and became a millionaire, so we believe we'll also be rich if we make the same decisions. **One** successful businessman wakes up every day at 4:30, so we conclude that we'll be more successful if we wake up at the same time. **One** entrepreneur sold their startup for millions of dollars using a given method, so we think that using the same method, we can also sell our startup. **One** person lost weight by becoming a vegan, so we believe we'll also lose weight if we do the same.

> **As a professional that lives for science, I cannot write a book defending one single proposition, supported by one case that illustrates what people wished was true. That would be a book that defends exception.**

Science isn't perfect, but the scientific method is, without a doubt, the most trustworthy tool to help us make the right decisions.

A paper often takes years to be published in a well-respected scientific journal. Only impeccable papers with an enormous contribution to science can achieve such a feat. For an important scientific journal, the risks of publishing a discovery that presents a fault and could negatively impact society are taken very seriously.

To come up with this book, I selected papers published exclusively by the highest-raking scientific journals in the world, with studies by very renowned scientists, from the most prestigious universities in the planet. On this path, I've exchanged hundreds of emails with scientist from all over the world to dive deep into their methods and results. And I literally went further. In 2018, I traveled to over 10 cities in the United States to meet some of these scientists. I visited universities such as Harvard, Stanford, North Carolina University, New York University, and many others, in order to make sure that the content of this book really was faithful to the studies. These are some discoveries you'll find in this book:

- Why one of the secrets of happiness and motivation is the way you spend your money—not how much you earn

- Why the incessant search for money weakens your work performance, creates inappropriate behaviors and increases your dissatisfaction with life

- Why the meritocracy and financial incentives systems in companies lead to worse results, and what companies can do about it.

- Why recognizing others, instead of seeking recognition, is one of the quickest ways to succeed.

- How your life goals influence your happiness, motivation, health, longevity, creativity, relationships and other areas in your life.

- The surprising formula of personal and professional success.

- The reasons why Maslow was wrong, and what really motivates people.

- Why dreaming big or dreaming small is not the same work and does not yield the results you expect.

- The reasons why thinking positive reduces your chances of reaching your goals, and a tool to solve this problem.

- The risks in believing your success is determined by your gifts or your IQ, and what to do to become an expert in any field.

In addition to teaching you how to apply the findings of these studies to your daily life, one of the main objectives of this book is to make you change your understanding of the word **success**. It might be important for you to know, at this point, who I am and why this book's approach sought scientific references to demystify concepts around what can be considered success. I see myself as an extremely successful person, but I'm not a millionaire, top investor, franchise owner, startup founder, digital influencer, CEO or super-hero—I'm just a regular guy. Many books on success are written by individuals who reached material and financial success, but this is just **one** kind of success, and the **least** important to our happiness. Besides, being successful doesn't mean being happy! As you'll find out later on, financial aspects aside, many millionaires are not happy. Movie stars are no different. If we take a quick look at the tabloids, we'll find that they also suffer from depression, get divorced, gain weight, complain about not having any real friends, and even commit suicide.

It's easy to measure success by things we can **count**: money, investments, cars, clothes or real estate. For a long time, I also thought that was how you obtained success—especially while I was intoxicated by the corporate environment, in my time as an executive. That was until I found, through scientific literature, that success was in other things.

The Science of Choice

A paper published by researchers Sonja Lyubomirsky, Kennon Sheldon, and David Schkade showed that success is in our **daily choices**[10]. This discovery is of fundamental importance to those who want to know how to really build happiness and, consequently, success—as well as to get rid of life goals with negative effects on their happiness. The study found that **50%** of our happiness is **genetic**, that is, we can't change it. Another **10%** is connected to our current life **circumstances**. This means being married or single, earning more or less money, being a CEO or an analyst at a company, having children or not, driving a Mercedes or a Renault, living in São Paulo or Los Angeles, and living in a house or an apartment has much less impact on our happiness than we think. Finally, **40% of our happiness is in the activities we choose** to do on a daily basis. This is the best finding of this study, as it allows us to recognize that our happiness is largely under our control. The paper, published in the *Review of General Psychology* in 2005, reveals that this large share of happiness is in what researchers called ***intentional activities***, that is, actions in which people **choose** to engage, activities that **depend only on themselves**.

Upon understanding that happiness depends largely on our actions, we naturally feel an increase in what psychologists call ***internal locus of control***[11]. Someone with an internal locus of control takes responsibility for their life's destiny and is aware that this destiny came about because of the choices they made. This type of person understands that they are the ones in charge of their future, according to their daily choices. On the other hand, someone with an ***external locus of control*** attributes their destiny to factors that are out of their control, that is, they will blame external factors for past, current and future circumstances of their existence. As we can figure, people with an **external locus of control** have a **difficult time** in achieving their goals, as they put their happiness and motivation on **factors outside of their control**. Thus, they give up more easily on their life projects, because they believe there is nothing they can do to change their trajectory, they have no control over their future.

As clear as this process may seem to you now, understand that many **choose** to attribute a gigantic weight to external factors, in particular their current circumstances, those that correspond to **just 10% of their happiness**: how much they earn, what car they drive, where they live, their jobs, the clothes they wear, their family status, or their boss's mood.

Fortunately, having an internal or external locus of control is also a **choice**. A central problem in our personal and professional lives, however, is to base our decisions on what others are saying, tips from business magazines, tips from famous corporate "gurus" or "coaches", rules from motivational speakers and books, or our intuition on how things work, what leads us to **make choices that go against our own interests**, making decisions that undermine our happiness.

It's not due to a lack of work, money or dedication that we are failing to reach happiness, but to the choices that we're making.

The next chapters in this book will reveal:

- The right choices you should make.
- How to use your money to bring motivation and happiness.
- What material goods bring happiness and how to extract it from what you already have.
- The type of recognition you must seek to achieve the most intrinsic motivation.
- The alternative to positive thinking that makes you really accomplish what you want.

Science gives us the possibility to make decisions based on the results of millions of other people. This means that all you have to do is find out what paths were taken by those who had the best results, and then follow them. By using science to make decisions on our motivation and happiness, we can make the right choices, those that move us towards our interests. By using science as our greatest ally, we can finally make **happy choices**.

PART 1

MONEY

CHAPTER 1

Money, Motivation and Happiness

MORE MONEY ≠ MORE HAPPINESS

Gallup's research placing Paraguay as the world's happiest country for the last seven years is certainly a surprise, but several scientific studies support this information: **more money doesn't mean more happiness**. After decades of research, American economist Richard Easterlin, from the University of Southern California, found that during a given period in life—from 22 to 78—despite people's average income increase in certain periods and decrease in others, their happiness stays basically identical[1].

On the other hand, Hope College researcher David Myers revealed that, although the average income in the United States almost **tripled** from 1950 to 2010, overall happiness stayed the same—and this also happens in Europe, Australia, Japan and China, where despite the notable financial growth, people's happiness remains the same[2].

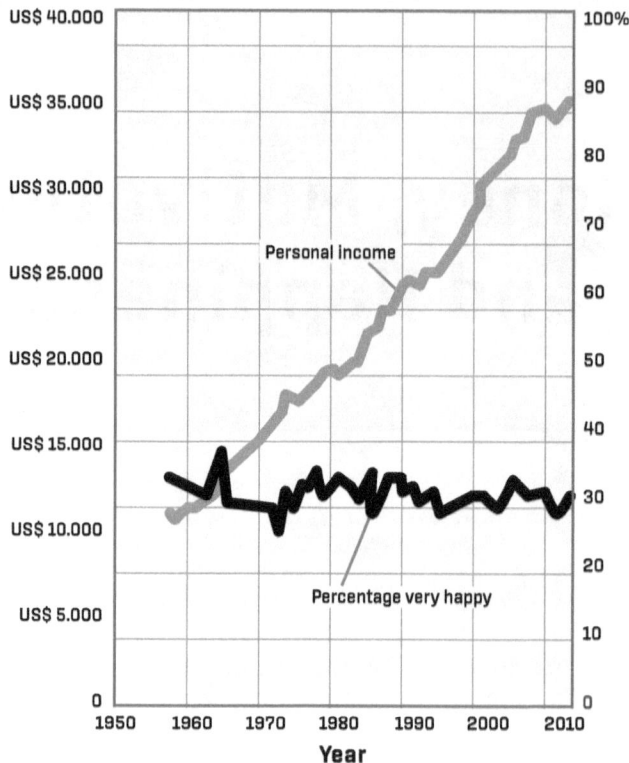

Average per-person after-tax income in 2009 dollars

A very conclusive study from the University of Illinois analyzed the life satisfaction level in 41 countries. Its finding was an extremely low correlation with wealth. It also showed that countries where people overvalue financial success have the lowest levels of life satisfaction[3].

If this whole wave of financial bonanza didn't bring positive results to people's happiness, it certainly must have promoted a significant growth in other areas, right? Yes, in the last 50 years, cases of depression increased tenfold[4], affecting over 322 million people—the Americas and Europe account for 27% of this figure. From 2005 to 2015 only, the number of global cases of depression increased nearly 20%, according to the World Health Organization[5]. Statistics show that money and technological evolution did not solve the main problems of individuals. In fact, they probably **caused** several other issues. University of Rochester's Richard Ryan and Knox College's

Tim Kasser concluded: the more central money is to people's lives, the more they suffer from depression and anxiety, and the more they show signs that their choices are led by what others expect of them[6].

This is an important point. What if our search for the **wrong** type of success is causing all this suffering?

Most scientists who studied this subject agree: after reaching a comfortable living standard, with a roof over our heads, clothing and food, having **more money doesn't bring more happiness**[7]. In a 2010 article published in the *Proceedings of the National Academy of Sciences*, Nobel Prize laureates Daniel Kahneman and Angus Deaton, from Princeton University, revealed that, from the moment an individual started earning US$ 75k a year in the USA, income increases **did not** cause increased levels of daily happiness[8]. They also report that only individuals who earned less than US$ 40k a year enjoyed a big increase in daily happiness when their income increased.

Of course, many countries will hardly reach a *per capita* income higher than US$ 75,000 a year, and, in many places, citizens can have an excellent life on much lower incomes. So the objective of the study was not to determine **how much** people should earn to be happy, but to show that money only brings happiness up to a certain **limit**. As the researchers concluded, "high incomes don't bring you happiness, but they do bring you a life you think is better".

The common saying "money can't buy happiness", therefore, is not always true. That depends on how much money you have! While a homeless person could experience an exponential increase in happiness from getting a job and a place to live, clothes to wear and the comfort of always knowing where the next meal is coming from, a billionaire who had a yearly increase of US$ 500,000 would remain with unaltered levels of happiness. It seems that if the motivation equation involves unknown variables, the happiness equation includes even less known ones. Actor and former governor of California Arnold Schwarzenegger brilliantly illustrated this fact: "Money doesn't make anyone happy. I now have US$ 50 million, but I was just as happy when I had US$ 48 million."[9]

THE UNKNOWN FACE OF MONEY

As contradictory as it may seem, earning a higher salary—one of people's most common aspirations in life—won't make you love your job more. An experiment made in the 1970s at the University of Rochester asked students to write headlines for the school paper: one group would work Tuesdays, and another would work Fridays[10]. While each group got together to debate the headlines, a "supervisor" was secretly timing how long it took each of them to produce each headline. A few weeks later, the Tuesdays group was informed that the paper would give them a budget of US$ 0.50 per headline (a motivating sum at the time), but they were not supposed to say anything to the Fridays group, as there was not enough money to pay everyone. In the beginning, when the work was unpaid, both groups took an average of 22 minutes to write a headline, but eventually the Fridays (unpaid) group started writing the headlines faster, reducing this time by half. Over the same period, the Tuesdays group showed no significant improvement, taking an average of 20 minutes to write each headline throughout the whole experiment. Besides, many members of this group **stopped attending meetings**, while members of the Fridays group continued to show up to work for free.

In this sense, a new experiment conducted by Belgian, Canadian and English universities shows that this connection between money and happiness is even more delicate than we think. In the study, participants of one group answered a survey that showed a photo of Canadian dollars next to it, supposedly used in "another study", while a second group was not exposed to the photo[11]. Then, researchers gave participants a piece of chocolate and instructed them to answer a new survey immediately after. As lucky as this study's participants may have been for getting a delicious chocolate, external observers unaware of the experiment's intent timed how long the members of each group took to eat the chocolate. Those exposed to the photo of the money ate **faster** when compared to the other group. In addition, these observers evaluated the facial expressions of members of both groups and reported that those exposed to the photo of the money seemed to enjoy the candy bar **less**.

In that same study, researchers found a correlation between the wealth of participants and their ability to enjoy daily activities: the richer they were, the less they reported enjoying life's little pleasures. According to other studies, this experiment also found a **modest** correlation between a person's wealth and their happiness[12], which leads to the conclusion that the slightly higher happiness of rich people is quickly taken away, as they enjoy daily experiences less..

FINANCIAL INSECURITY = LESS HAPPINESS

If having more than enough money doesn't bring happiness, we can assume that the consequences of having too little are devastating. In 1991, researcher Ralph Catalano from the University of California, Berkeley published an article about the existence of a strong correlation between economic insecurity and severe mental illness[13]. Another study, published by Case Western Reserve University, also alerts to a relation between income and self-reported negative emotions such as sadness, anxiety and hopelessness[14]. The more people suffer to pay the bills, the higher their number of self-reported negative emotions each day. Not by chance, several researchers reaffirm that the lack of money, or not agreeing on how to use it, is the main cause of divorce[15].

Renowned psychologist Elizabeth Dunn held a study that lead to a very special finding: although it doesn't increase happiness, money **reduces sadness**[16]. In this study, individuals with higher incomes reported not feeling more nor less happy compared to people with lower incomes, but they felt less sad than those with lower incomes—which once again shows that money is not an effective tool to increase happiness, but to **reduce sadness**. Another study affirmed that life's highly distressing moments were related to one factor: **financial insecurity**[17].

Considering these data, many companies should review their wage policies to ensure their employees could be free from the dangers of financial insecurity. This is exactly what Dan Price, CEO of Gravity Payments, did in 2015. Today, the lowest wage paid to a company's employee is US$ 70,000 a year, which guarantees their financial stability. With this change, Price saw Gravity's employee turnover rate drop and profits double[18]. Of course, this baseline sum can be lower or higher according to the reality of each country, and this is exactly why it should be taken more seriously. This change in pay is even more urgent in fields with a culture of paying low fixed wages and rewarding employees based on performance, like sales. The consequences of this practice can be disastrous, as suggested by Dan Ariely's experiments in

India, and Gneezy and Rustichini's in Israel. Science has long had evidence on how financial incentives for tasks involving **creativity**—like sales—can have adverse effects on people's performances[19]. Commissions increase the motivation of salespeople **beyond the ideal threshold**, causing them to pay too much attention to the task, in addition to constant financial insecurity. In fact, it's interesting to note that many sales professionals say they "love" money! But is this love natural or triggered by other factors unknown to them? Tim Kasser's studies show that people who frequently feel financially insecure—which is normal in the life of a commissioned salesperson—attribute a more important weight to money and material goods as signs of "making progress in life". Those that don't feel financially insecure rate material possessions and money as less important in their self-evaluations of how successful they are, which creates a big motivational advantage, in addition to more happiness[20].

A (VERY) OLD WAY OF THINKING

Our mistaken perception on financial incentives causing better performance comes from the post-Industrial Revolution period, when Ford and Taylor found that the workers in their factories produced more if their salaries were conditioned to their productivity. This means that the relation between money and performance was once true for companies, at a time when people performed exclusively **manual** labor—such as with Ford's and Taylor's employees. In the 21st Century, although many production industries still demand physical labor, the nature of the work in general is quite different. The challenges presented by companies require **cognitive** abilities, such as rational thinking and creativity. Despite this change, the "truths" found by industrial leaders of the 19**th** Century are to this day the basis of decision making for many CEOs and executives, which is unacceptable in the era of thriving scientific information that we live in. Companies love to sell themselves as innovative and "thinking outside the box", but the truth is that many still follow the same outdated strategies.

When we talk about pay in the sales field, most companies choose this industrial strategy, later spread by Michael Jensen and William Meckling as the **Agency Theory**[21]. This theory is based on the idea that companies need to share their responsibilities with their agents/employees so that, when the result is positive, part of the profits are distributed as benefits. If not, employees will feel no incentive to engage with the company's results.

The Agency Theory is based on the premise that humans are **naturally lazy** and will always **avoid work**, so people will only leave their comfort zone if they receive some sort of **incentive or punishment**. Thus, the company will pay its employees only when they bring results, a strategy that makes sense economically, but is otherwise gravely flawed. Unfortunately, traditional economy and many studies in strategic planning fail to account for something that's fundamental to people's performance: their **emotional state**. Humans are not robots that respond in a predictable way to financial stimuli, because the motivation equation carries many other variables.

In 2012, Ian Larkin, from the University of California, Los Angeles, along with renowned Harvard researcher Francesca Gino and Washington University in St. Louis' Lamar Pierce, published an article that explores every risk that the Agency Theory presents to companies, under both as economic and psychological perspectives[22]. Researchers showed that the predictions of the Agency Theory are flawed because performance pay is **less effective** than expected, as well as **more costly** than Jensen and Meckling considered. Some of the risks raised are the negative consequences on employee performance caused by the intensified **comparison** and **competition** amongst them, as well as increased **self-confidence**. As you continue reading this book, you'll understand how money creates a feeling of independence, making people act more confidently and not ask for others' opinions when making decisions, which is a big risk in the teamwork-reliant corporate world.

Larkin, Gino and Pierce noted that companies should seek fairer pay systems if they are not to suffer with reduced effort and skills, as well as employee sabotage. While companies feed the culture of rewarding their employees only if they bring results, science shows that the way this process works is **quite the opposite**:

> **Companies should first offer psychological conditions for employees to have good performance—guaranteeing fair wages and more autonomy, creating an environment that fosters good relationships, and developing individual strengths—and then ask for results**

All of these studies are in accordance with the findings of the world's most influential motivational researchers: Edward Deci and Richard Ryan, from the University of Rochester. Regarding the practice of offering financial incentives to motivate employees, Deci and Ryan, along with McGill University's Richard Koestner, held one of the most relevant studies in the history of motivation and reached a conclusion that challenges the motivational practices of many companies[23]. In a meta-analysis of 128 scientific papers, published in the *Psychological Bulletin*, researchers concluded:

"As predicted, engagement-contingent, completion-contingent, and performance-contingent rewards significantly undermined free-choice intrinsic motivation (d = 0.40, 0.36, and 0.28, respectively), as did all rewards, all tangible rewards, and all expected rewards. Engagement-contingent and completion- contingent rewards also significantly undermined self-reported interest (d = 0.15, and 0.17), as did all tangible rewards and all expected rewards."

The studies you've seen so far in this book show that the concept of the **Homo economicus**—meaning a human that makes decisions exclusively to maximize gains—is finally nearing extinction as science evolves. When are companies, governments and institutions going to be aware of this fact?

Many of the perceptions that people, companies and even scientists have about motivation are mistaken or out of date. Because of this, we'll explore in detail what motivation really means.

SO, WHAT IS MOTIVATION?

Simply put, **motivation is what makes us act**. But explaining what **causes** it is no simple feat. In fact, up until now science doesn't have a conclusion on which factors influence motivation—and I believe it never will. If at some point science reached a full understanding of how everything works, it would cease to exist. I think the main role of science is to analyze the knowledge we have available today and try to find whether there's anything **better** than that, something that **adds** to what we already know and can even prove us **wrong**. Motivation is one of these topics that gets constant, new contributions—new findings, destruction of previous convictions, and new knowledge being built.

Motivation is a trait that can't be directly observed in nature as can eye color, physical constitution or height. However, in such cases, science must observe and measure several variables at once. For hundreds of years scientists have been to understand this phenomenon that makes us act, live and work with more dedication and intent, being more productive and full of joy, fighting for a cause or goal, pursuing survival, among many other characteristics. At some point, researchers found that this phenomenon was linked to an individual's living conditions, health, salary, number of friends, marital relationship, personal and professional progress, goals, reputation, genetics, etc.

These scientists, then, decided to name this set of variables as **motivation**. In scientific language, motivation is a **construct** that can be partially explained when all of those variables, plus others, have been observed and measured. The variables observed in order to understand a construct like motivation are called **dimensions**. If we turned it into a formula, we'd have:

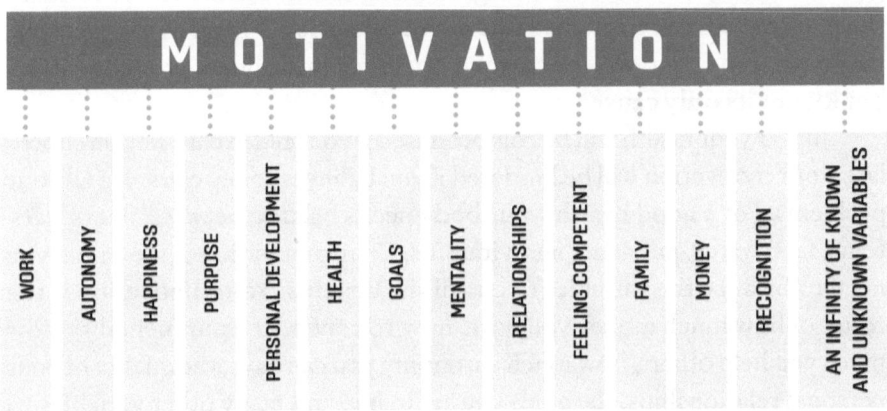

Although people intuitively know that motivation involves several variables, many still make the mistake of selecting **one** or **a few** of them to try to explain this huge phenomenon, reducing the complexity of this construct. In the business environment, many managers believe that their employees' motivation comes down to **financial interests**, so they use artifices to motivate them—commissions, bonuses, profit distribution and cash prizes, for example. In our personal lives, many of us also believe that the secret to motivation is to **accumulate as much money as possible**, as if this could solve any problem. These are pure examples of reductionism—human motivation is far more complex than a pile of cash.

Believing that just one variable will solve the entire motivation equation is a big mistake.

Of course, this equation has variables with **heavier weights than others**, but that doesn't mean they can explain the **whole** phenomenon alone.

On this subject, Boston University's researcher Nina Mazar told me that people tend to make use of reductionism to seem intelligent. For some reason, they feel superior when they affirm to have found **the reason** why a given phenomenon occurs. In the corporate world, for example, there's often someone trying to convince us that Apple is successful because of **one strategy** they followed, or that someone got rich because of **one decision**, but no phenomenon depends on **one single reason**. Many scientists like to chant the mantra **"correlation does not mean causation"**. Money, for example, may have some relation—or correlation, in scientific lingo—to motivation, but it's not its **only cause**.

Just as your health will be compromised if you feed exclusively on chocolate, your motivation will be hindered if you believe money can solve all your problems. For a good health, your body needs balance between fibers, proteins, fats, water, nutrients and vitamins. Your motivation is the same: you need to balance the variables to get all the benefits. Your motivation is the result of how much money you have, how you spend it, your mentality, how much you help others, how much autonomy you can have, the quality of your personal relationships, the goals you set in life, and many other variables.

WHY IT'S IMPORTANT TO BE MOTIVATED

Without action, you can't achieve your goals. What few people know, however, is how internal and external factors influence motivation. **Intrinsic motivation** comes down to following a goal to satisfy an **internal need**, like being better in what you do each day. It's often achieved with pleasurable activities not seen as work. On the other hand, the dangerous **extrinsic**

motivation encourages seeking a goal in order to receive an **external reward**, such as material goods, money and compliments. You should know that the motivational factors that you **choose** for yourself can cause positive or negative results in your life. **Your motivation is also a result of your choices**.

The problem with these choices is that you may believe something motivates you, while scientific studies prove that there's no correlation between motivation and external factors. Sometimes, a factor that you believe has an important weight on your motivation can influence you, but in general that will have a lot less weight than you imagine. So, in order to get every advantage of motivation, you must also choose the **right** factors, after all, people can change their motivational preferences throughout their lives. It's absolutely necessary to change opinions on the factors that motivate you, if your goal is to have a full, happy life.

The fact that you can change doesn't mean that people are entirely motivated by different factors, as a lot of our motivation comes from the **same** factors. Because there's a wave of "motivational gurus" telling us that we're all motivated by different things, some people may start nurturing the dangerous notion that they are unique, different from everyone else on this planet. This is not what science says. A series of studies done by Stanford University's researcher Chip Heath brought to light an important finding on this topic[24]. Participants of an MBA program were asked to rank, according to their personal opinion, the order of importance of eight motivational factors:

1. Themselves
2. Their classmates
3. Bank managers
4. Bank employees

The motivation items were:

1. Learning new things
2. Quality of fringe benefits
3. Amount of praise from your supervisor
4. Doing something that makes you feel good about yourself

5. Having job security

6. Accomplishing something worthwhile

7. Amount of pay

8. Developing skills and abilities

As you may have noticed, some of these items are intrinsic incentives (learning, feel good, worthwhile, skills), while others are extrinsic incentives (benefits, praise, security, pay). To make this activity even more interesting, Heath promised US$ 10 to every student if their predictions on what motivated their colleagues, bank employees and managers were correct in more than 30% of the cases.

Asked to rank the importance of the eight items to **themselves**, only 22% of the participants included an extrinsic incentive at the top of the list, but guessed that 32% of their colleagues, 54% of bank managers and 85% of bank employees would rank an extrinsic incentive as the **most important** of the list. But look at what happened: when asked to guess how **bank employees** would rank these items, participants guessed that the order of importance of the four main incentives for these professionals would be pay, security, benefits and praise—the four extrinsic incentives! On the other hand, the **bank employees** themselves said that, to them, the most relevant incentives were: skills, worthwhile, learning and benefits. Of the four main incentives, only **one** was extrinsic. The study showed that MBA students had a rather distorted view on what motivates others. Only 12% of the students correctly predicted more than 30% of what motivates other people.

The question is: don't most people make the same mistake about others and themselves? Repeated studies show that this tendency to believe that we act **differently**—and better—than most is common, due to the *uniqueness or exclusivity bias*[25]. This bias made Chip Heath's students make incorrect predictions, and the same pattern was repeated when the researcher made a similar analysis with the employees of a bank. People believe they are motivated by intrinsic incentives, but others, different from them, are motivated by **extrinsic** factors. You may have heard somebody say they work for **pleasure**, but their colleagues are only in it for the **money**! Coincidence? When he found that this trend was present in **all** four studies, Chip Heath called it *extrinsic incentives bias*.

Let's take a deeper look into the implications and consequences of the **extrinsic incentives bias** and the **exclusivity bias** in our daily lives and our workplace. If we have a **distorted** view of what motivates others, we can easily make wrong decisions about how to deal with the behavior of our children, spouses, employees, friends and family. In a company, a manager's mistaken view of what motivates their employees can cause financial incentives plans, profit distribution, awards, recognition ceremonies and other strategies that can undermine the desired results. Because this is exactly what happens in work environments, it's no surprise that a Gallup research showed that only 15% of people are highly engaged in their jobs[26].

It's because of these and other similar studies that I believe that one of the most important contributions of science to our lives is the notion that the "crystal ball" we all have in our heads is gravely flawed, and can change our behavior and take us on the wrong path to motivation. This is why it's important for the journey to the ideal motivation to be guided by science, as well as for our efforts to be concentrated on the **good variables of the equation**, those that increase intrinsic motivation.

The understanding of motivation also requires knowing one important piece of information: **motivation is not always good**. There are factors that motivate us instantly, while at the same time hindering our performance and reducing our long-term happiness. By rerouting our efforts to the good variables of the equation, in addition to increasing the probability of acting to reach our goals, we might receive the benefit of **more happiness**—emphasis on the *might*, as not all that motivates us makes us happier.

MOTIVATION AND PERFORMANCE: A TWO-SIDED RELATION

You need food to live, but excess food can also be harmful to your health. With motivation, it's the same. For you to super-perform a task, there's no need to be super-motivated. Just motivated **enough**. Although there's a popular belief that increased motivation **always** results in increased performance, this is not always true. And there are several studies on this topic.

Robert Yerkes and John Dodson made an experiment in which mice had to choose between two passage-ways within a cage[27]. The researchers randomly put a white box in one of the passages and a black box in the other. If the mouse entered the passage-way with the white box, it received a reward, but if it entered the one with the black box, it received an electric shock. The mice were divided into three groups: in one, the mice that chose the black box received weak shocks; in another, intermediate shocks; and in the last group, strong shocks. Yerkes and Dodson found that, surprisingly, the mice that received **intermediate** shocks learned to avoid the black box more quickly. Weak or strong electric shocks didn't motivate the mice to change their behavior so efficiently. In their famous paper, published in 1908, the researchers concluded:

"Contrary to our expectations, this set of experiments did not prove that the rate of habit-formation increases with increase in the strength of the electric stimulus [...] Instead, an intermediate range of intensity of stimulation proved to be most favorable to the acquisition of a habit [...]"

Thus, Yerkes and Dodson found that a person's performance was determined by their **level of excitement**: the higher it is, the better the performance. This study may seem no different from what we already know, after all, the concept that increased motivation causes increased performance is already widespread in companies and society. But there's a big problem here: this concept is incomplete!

Yerkes and Dodson concluded that there really is a **positive** relation between an individual's motivation and their performance, **but only to an extent**. When the motivation level crosses this optimal point, the relation to performance becomes **negative**: the higher the motivation, the lower the performance. An **underaroused** football player will never kick a field goal strong enough, while an **overaroused** player risks kicking the ball out of the field. For a precise field goal kick, the player must have the **optimal** motivation. This study originated the famous **Yerkes-Dodson curve**, illustrated below:

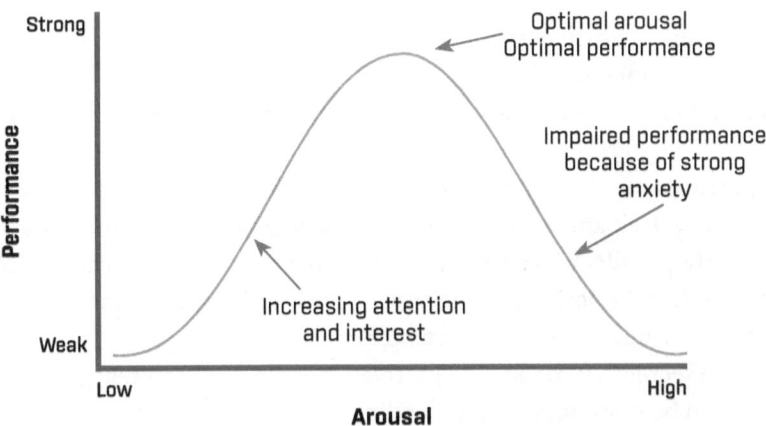

Although this finding is over a century old, very few people and executives are aware of it. Companies, governments and other institutions currently use financial rewards to increase employee motivation, failing to understand why this strategy doesn't result in the expected performance. Similarly, these institutions often use severe punishments in an attempt to improve behavior, which several studies have proven inefficient.

Uri Gneezy and Aldo Rustichini found that, in certain cases, fines and punishments make people **increase** their bad behavior[28]. It seems that paying a fine for an infraction releases people from guilt, acting as permission to act that way again. Scientific evidence of how money and motivation have a different—often contrary—relation than what people think are many, in the sense of making people both behave better and stop behaving badly.

Researcher Roy Baumeister, from the University of Queensland, Australia, found in a series of experiments that situations where people feel pressured to perform well—when they can win money, for example—make them give **more attention** to the task, which causes **decreased** performance[29]. When a group was asked to pay attention to their hand movements during a task that involved motor skills, Baumeister observed that participants had **worse** performance when compared to the group whose attention was not requested. The researcher also saw that, when inciting competition amongst participants, the increased pressure made them **pay more attention to the task**, which resulted in **poorer** performance. The same result is repeated when pressure is based on a possible financial gain, in case participants performed above average—which explains part of the results presented earlier, which used money as incentive[30].

From Oxford University, one noteworthy study in this sense analyzed Functional Magnetic Resonance Images (fMRI) to monitor the cerebral activity of participants during a given task. The conclusion was that, the more motivated participants were, the higher the attention of their brains to the **mistakes** they made. We can assume, then, that the more important an objective, the higher the activity in the area of the brain responsible for attention to mistakes, which can be **distracting**[31].

It's no secret that money can motivate people, but what few people know is that it can be **over**-motivating, leading to poorer performance. Increased attention is not the only result of a very high motivation level. Other studies show that it can make people think of the task involuntarily, trying to "control" movements that should be "automatic"[32]. In this sense, motivation blocks creativity, especially when financial incentives are involved, and makes people busy with thoughts of how great it would be to win the money, or how disappointed they'll be in themselves if they don't win, for example, factors that distract from the task[33]. In addition to these considerations, you'll find in this book one of the worst behaviors encouraged by financial incentives: cheating!

See why not all that motivates us makes us happier? Money increases motivation, but this excessive increase causes lower performance and inadequate behaviors, which in turn brings **less** happiness.

OVERACCUMULATION

Although the crystal ball in your head predicts that being materialistic will bring you happiness, several studies confirm that there's a robust **negative** relation between the constant acquisition of material goods, well-being and life satisfaction[34]. Many scientists reveal that one cause of this relation is the growing feeling of insecurity experienced by materialistic people[35]. This is because consumption is an escape valve for their anxiety, insecurity and lack of friends. In fact, a lack of friends is a factor **positively** related to materialism—studies show that materialistic people find it difficult to establish close relationships and evaluate their friendships as unfavorable, isolating themselves socially[36].

I have several friends who have worked for years for companies that indoctrinated their employees to think that accumulating money was the **only** sign of success. I remember two occasions from when I was an executive—at different times and companies—when I observed my coworkers at their desks, busy with calculations. When I asked what they were doing, I heard the **same** answer: "Calculating when I'll have my first million". Notice that these people never calculate how much **happiness** they'll have when they finally achieve that goal. Will they be happy forever? Or will they then condition their happiness to having two million?

One danger of linking your happiness to a future condition is that our goals are **constantly changing**. You sense you'll be happy once you reach a given salary, but when you do, you establish a new goal for an even higher salary. You sense you'll be happier when you buy a better home, but when you do, you start wishing for an even bigger home in a gated community. Not by chance, a 2018 study by Harvard researchers Grant Donnelly and Michael Norton, along with Tianyi Zheng, from the University of Mannheim, analyzed the happiness of four thousand millionaires and observed that, according to their statements, they believe they'll be perfectly happy only when their fortunes grow **expressively**[37]. Only 13% of the sample of millionaires said it was possible to be perfectly happy with the sum they already had, while 52% said they **needed a 500% to 1,000% increase** to consider themselves perfectly happy. These aren't stories you'll find in books that claim to teach you how to be a millionaire, are they?

Curious to learn more about this and other researchers in this field, I went to Harvard Business School to talk to Grant Donnelly, who warmly welcomed me at Frist Faculty Commons. Thinking about Donnelly, Norton and Zheng's findings, I asked him why people trust so much that money will make them happier. He explained that it's important for people to feel like they're always improving, constantly evolving. Money is a simple way to signal this climb, as it's easy to measure. But few are aware of the issues of measuring success with money, said Donnelly.

One of these issues is the human tendency to **compare** to others[38]. The moment you reach your goal of saving one million dollars, you realize a friend saved three million, then you condition your happiness to saving that amount[39]. When you get to three million, you make friends with people who have five million in the bank, and once again you condition your happiness to that goal. **It's a race you can't win!** Why do the millionaires from

45

Donnelly, Norton and Zheng's study don't consider themselves sufficiently rich? Probably because their friends have a few millions **more**. This is well illustrated in the movie Wall Street, where the greedy Gordon Geeko, played by Michael Douglas, is asked how much he wants to save until he's satisfied. His answer? **"More!"**

Looking at it from an evolutionary perspective, accumulating wealth makes a lot of sense for humans. For our ancestors, keeping stock of fruit, seeds, nuts, meats, fats and vegetables was essential to survival. In a time when individuals lived under the uncertainty of the next meal, the habit of accumulating as much "wealth" as possible certainly contributed to the prosperity of our species. However, today it makes no sense to accumulate wealth that **we'll never have the pleasure of enjoying**. We left behind a primitive reality of scarcity for a modern reality of abundance, and even though we can be immensely happy in a life with **sufficient** resources, our primitive roots are still in charge, leading us on a never-ending search for accumulation. This search, however, causes losses that we can't yet estimate.

The upward comparison we make when the core objective of our lives is to accumulate money and goods is not restricted only to those we know. In a series of studies, Joseph Sirgy, H. Lee Meadow and Don Rahtz concluded that people who watch TV frequently are less satisfied with their existence[40], as they start comparing themselves to characters in soap operas, TV series and movies, evaluating their own lives less favorably. And as the majority of spectators can't have the cars, clothes, bodies, dinners, jewels, travels, lovers and homes they see on TV, the feeling is that their lives aren't good enough, just because they're comparing themselves to realities that are the **exception**.

As a consultant, a few of my clients are companies in the luxury industry, and when I talk to their employees, it's common to hear them say they're not satisfied with their salaries. As you can imagine, employees in this business earn infinitely more than most people, wear branded clothes and drive fancy cars. Still, none of it is enough. Why? Probably because they interact daily with customers who drive Ferraris, wear even more expensive clothes, have homes in Aspen and spend millions in a single purchase. Their frequent contact with people who live an exception makes these employees base their financial perspectives on a distorted reality.

Social media has an even stronger role in reinforcing these comparisons, which makes consequences even more critical. Many people try to **compensate** this lifestyle inequalities by buying goods that give them status, in order to reduce the gap and prove their worth to themselves. This was the exact conclusion of a series of studies conducted by German researchers: inexperienced tennis players compensated their low performance using more expensive brands; law students with little experience compensated the low quality of their resumes by highlighting their prestigious vacation destinations[41]. When this happens, something even more critical hits these people: they spend amounts they don't have. And because they don't have enough credit to afford these expenses, the situation worsens exponentially: some acquire counterfeit items to try to gain and/or keep their status. By then, as if it wasn't enough, **infinitely** more troubling consequences occur—which I'll illustrate with a scientific experiment.

BUYING COUNTERFEITS

Humans have a curious relationship with luxury goods, so much so that those who can't afford them usually resort to buying replicas of designer watches, handbags and clothes. Every day, 400 thousand people visit the São Paulo popular shopping street 25 de Março looking for fake Louis Vuitton, Rolex and Diesel. Consumers of these products, influenced by soap operas, magazines and other media that support consumerism, usually believe that displaying a luxurious brand, even if not authentic, will bring them happiness, self-esteem and, more importantly, other people's recognition—a behavior that psychology calls *self-signaling*[42]. When someone wears a replica, their intention is to show their friends, family and coworkers that they're **doing well**, they're successful and have good taste. But what they ignore is the effect that these counterfeit items have on their behavior.

Harvard Business School's Francesca Gino and Michael Norton, along with Duke University's Dan Ariely, were impressed by their findings in an experiment conducted in 2010[43]. In this study, they bought several authentic sunglasses from French brand Chloé and asked university students to test them for a few days. Then, still wearing the sunglasses, the students were asked to perform a series of tests in which there would be an opportunity to cheat, obtaining financial advantage. The trick went like this: one group was told the sunglasses were authentic; another group was told that they were **counterfeit**; and the control group was given no information regarding the origin of the goods. It's worth noting an important detail about the data collection:

the researchers developed a means to find whether participants had cheated, giving them an imperceptible identification in each test.

Here are the results: 42% of the control group—the only one not informed about the origin of the sunglasses—and 30% of the people who were informed that the sunglasses were authentic cheated. Considering that this difference was not statistically significant, the hypothesis that the participants duly informed about the authentic sunglasses would behave **more ethically** was discarded. And how did the people with "counterfeit" sunglasses behave? More than 70% of them cheated! This means that a person who **feels counterfeit** for using counterfeit goods changes their behavior, and their chances of acting unethically increase. I'm sure neither you nor the people wearing these counterfeit products were aware of the consequences of this choice.

MONEY, INDIVIDUALISM AND DISHONESTY

In November 2006, the renowned journal *Science* published a very interesting paper. In it, researchers from the University of Minnesota, Florida State University and the University of British Columbia conducted nine experiments in which participants were stimulated with "money"—the quotes meaning that the money **wasn't real**[44]. In some experiments, participants ordered words into sequences that created phrases, whereas the groups stimulated with "money" received words **related to money**, while other groups should order neutral words. The conditions of the other experiments were similar: participants were stimulated with **board game money**; had to perform a task facing a wall that had a **picture of dollar bills**; were asked to perform a task in a computer with a screensaver of **animated dollar bills**; were asked to read out loud a composition about **growing up with abundant money**; and were even stimulated to imagine **a life with a lot of money**. The other groups in the experiments performed tasks **without** this "incentive", receiving stimuli that were considered moderate or neutral. What happened was alarming!

In different experiments, stimuli with "money" made participants take longer to ask for **help** on a difficult task, spend **less** time helping and explaining to a colleague, become **less** willing to help someone who suffered a minor incident, donate **less** money to scholarship students, sit **farther away** from their colleagues, choose individual experiences instead of fun group activities, and finally, choose to work **alone** in a task, avoiding group work.

In the corporate world, executives like to adopt speeches that emphasize how **teamwork** is valued in their companies, while paying commissions, bonuses, awards and profit distribution to their employees. In workplaces that were taken over by the fads of **performance pay** and **meritocracy**—in which individuals are paid, promoted or fired according to their **individual** performance—teamwork is basically impossible. The study authors, Kathleen Vohs, Nicole Mead and Miranda Goode, stated that money gives people a feeling of independence, like they can reach their goals without help—which clearly explains the negative consequences of individual meritocracy policies. Besides, the concept of meritocracy within a company, although admirable in theory, fails greatly in practice. In ever more complex work environments, an employee's performance hardly depends solely on their dedication and effort. Not that these factors aren't important, but an employee's performance today depends much more on **factors out of their control*** than on their **willpower**. Companies are long overdue in aligning their talk with their actions. Merit is achieved as a group, not individually.

If just **thinking** about money produces inadequate behaviors, **seeing** a large sum of it results in even more serious consequences. Harvard and Washington University researchers conducted a study in which, **before** performing a task, a group of participants viewed a stack of US$ 1 bills that totaled US$ 24, and another group viewed US$ 7,000 in several stacks. The result was that 85.2% of people in the group that viewed a large sum of money cheated on the task, compared to only 38.5% of the group that saw a small amount. Besides, the **magnitude** of the cheating was also different in both conditions: 80% of the group that saw the US$ 7,000 cheated **more**, while just 26% of the other group engaged in this behavior[45].

---

* State of the economy, quality of the company's products, payment conditions, logistics, credit policies, technological advances, efficiency of other sectors of the company, climate, price, competitor moves, leadership style, organizational environment, payment policy, goal definition, help from coworkers, among other factors.

A DANGEROUS GAME

In a yet unpublished study, Paul Piff, professor of the University of California, Irvine, created a situation similar to that of the previous experiment, leading two students to play a Monopoly game against each other[46]. After tossing heads or tails, one of them would win US$ 2,000 at the start, with an additional US$ 200 bonus at each round, while the other would win US$ 1,000 at the start, and a US$ 100 bonus at each round. The "rich" student could throw two dice at a time, going faster around the board, while the other could only throw one dice. To make it better, the "rich" student got a miniature Rolls-Royce as their car in the game. The results showed that, in several rounds, analyzing more than 200 people, the participants placed in the privileged position acted more aggressively than their opponents: they moved their pieces making more noise, used expansive and power postures, constantly affirmed to the other player that they had money, and became rude, ignoring the "poor" participants by avoiding eye contact.

This conclusion did not come from scientists only. A group of people without previous knowledge of the study also evaluated the "rich" players as aggressive, rude and competitive. Piff and his colleagues intentionally put a bowl of pretzels on the game table—and yes, the participants who ate the most pretzels were the "rich" ones. It's interesting to note that, even though they knew they were in a "rich" condition for pure luck, moments after the game started, these participants changed their behavior drastically—although their wealth was composed of **made up money**! Similarly, these players later reported to researchers that they believed they deserved their success in the game, showing pride in their strategies to win, completely disregarding the enormous advantage they had over the other player by pure luck at the toss of a coin.

Financial advantages create a false perception of **competence**, so much so as to make people forget relevant facts, like the game being clearly **manipulated** so that the players with the benefits could win. What about the company where you work? Doesn't paying financial incentives to employees produce in them the same feeling that they are extremely competent and **don't need others** to be successful? Doesn't paying financial incentives promote antisocial behaviors, instead of prosocial? What about parents that give their children financial incentives for good grades? Aren't they causing that same feeling in their children and taking away their intrinsic motivation, potentially turning them into individualist, antisocial adults, only capable of working for money?

These were some of the topics of my exciting talk with Paul Piff at the beautiful facilities of the University of California, Irvine.

> "Those that reach financial success become more autonomous, feel that they depend less on others and forget that their results were built with the help of many people. So they start to believe that their financial success depends on their individual effort only. This is why the rich begin to assume that those that have no money caused their own poverty by not working hard enough," Piff put it brilliantly. "Parents that reward their children for a good grade, or allow them to eat dessert only after they finished their veggies, send a clear message that studying or eating veggies must be very undesirable, since they need a prize to complete these tasks," he concluded.

This is the same message companies send their employees when they offer financial incentives for completing a task. "This job must be so bad that they have to pay me a bonus to do it," they must think.

In 2012, Piff had already shocked the academic community with his paper *Higher Social Class Predicts Increased Unethical Behavior*, which made the headlines of several media outlets[47]. In this paper, Piff and a group of researchers conducted seven studies to analyze the behavior changes caused by money, finding that individuals with luxury cars had a higher chance of cutting in front of other drivers at an intersection, and a lower chance of giving way to pedestrians on a crosswalk. Individuals from high social classes also had a higher tendency to make unethical decisions, a higher chance of taking candy from a jar reserved to children, and a higher chance of lying and showing greedy behaviors.

Another important finding was that, when individuals of a lower social class were encouraged to think of greed as something positive, their tendency to cheat was as high as that of richer people. This means **both** social classes can incur in unethical behaviors, but because Piff's study found that those in a higher social class are the ones with a higher tendency to be greedy, their chances of showing these behaviors increase significantly.

It's tempting to conclude, at this moment, that **all** rich people are dishonest and ill-behaved, especially because the situations you just read make you think **only** of times when you felt mistreated by someone richer, but that's not the absolute truth. "Not all millionaires act like idiots", Piff said during our talk in California. We've heard of extremely rich people with very positive behaviors, so the main takeaway of this study is that we should be on the lookout for how we're **led** to behave when we have a little more cash.

Piff's studies confirm yet another troubling behavior that other researchers had already reported a few years earlier: people in higher social classes are **worse** at reading other people's emotions[48]. The coauthors of this study, Dacher Keltner and Michael Kraus, from the University of California, Berkeley, found that, when in situations where they are led to see themselves as richer, people begin to feel **less empathy** for others. Researchers explain that, when someone lives in less favorable conditions, they **need others** to make decisions, which increases empathy and strengthens social bonds.

During our long talk, Piff told me that the rich start seeing only their own world as reality, which is why they have a hard time putting themselves in other people's shoes. This way, the rich behave poorly, which worsens their social interactions and pulls them away from their friends and family. The corporate world is no different. Jamil Zaki, director of the Stanford University Social Neuroscience Lab, told *Time* magazine that when a job depends on the employee's ability to read whether their boss is angry, they become **better** in reading their boss's feelings[49]. On the other hand, because of the feeling of independence caused by money and power, the boss gets **worse** at reading their employee's feelings—a very common situation in the workplace.

Dacher Keltner knows this relation between money and empathy at work very well. In one of his most famous studies, known as "the cookie experiment", Keltner separated participants into groups of three and randomly chose one person to be the "boss", who should assess how well the other two were working[50]. In the middle of the experiment, Keltner's team gave a plate with five delicious cookies to each trio. Which of the people in the group felt more comfortable grabbing **a second cookie**? Those who got the leadership role! In addition, the "boss" also showed behaviors related to lack of empathy, such as open-mouth chewing and leaving crumbs all over the table.

Unfortunately, only a small number of companies is willing to make strategic changes to the styles of incentives they offer their employees. And when those incentives don't yield the expected results, many blame the

employees, accusing them of being in their comfort zone. The truth is that many companies should start noticing that **they are the ones** in the comfort zone. After all, if every company follows the **same** strategy to offer financial incentives to their employees, are these organizations any different? Do they really "think outside the box"? Or are they in their **strategic comfort zone**? When they start thinking harder about the consequences caused by financial incentives and reduce them significantly, or eliminate them altogether, companies will start seeing more satisfaction, engagement, motivation, happiness and, of course, results.

In addition to all the hazards of life goals that prioritize financial and material success, the search for this type of success activates **our happiness's worst enemy**. And to present you to this enemy, I'd like to ask you a question: do you remember the second to last shirt you bought?

HEDONIC ADAPTATION

Was it hard to remember? Alright, I'll give you another chance. Do you remember the second to last pair of shoes you bought? I bet that one was hard too, but don't worry, you're not the exception! A lot of people have a hard time remembering their last few material acquisitions. This is due to a phenomenon called **hedonic adaptation**, a natural human capacity to adapt to both positive and negative situations[51]. Hedonic adaptation has been studied for decades by scientists all over the world, and the findings on this phenomenon have a huge value to us.

One 1978 finding was published in a rather intriguing paper by researchers Ronnie Janoff-Bulman, from the University of Massachusetts, and Phillip Brickman and Dan Coates, from Northwestern University, in the *Journal of Personality and Social Psychology*[52]. Aiming to evaluate the perspective of future happiness of a group of 22 lottery winners and 29 paralyzed accident victims, the scientists asked each participant to indicate, in a 0 to 5 scale, how happy they thought they would be in the future. Accident victims reported an average 4.32, whereas lottery winners reported an average 4.20. Researchers also asked participants to define, in the same scale, how much pleasure they obtained from daily activities: talking to a friend, watching TV, having breakfast, hearing a funny joke, receiving a compliment, reading a magazine, and shopping for clothes. Accident victims rated 3.48, while lottery winners rated

3.33. Both differences were **not statistically significant**, which led researchers to the surprising conclusion that **winning the lottery or becoming paralyzed has no impact whatsoever in future happiness**. It's curious to note that when researchers questioned participants about how happy they were in the present, paralyzed accident victims responded 2.96—still above average on a 0 to 5 scale.

On this same perspective, other researchers already found that, despite married people being significantly happier than singles, the couple's happiness goes back to normal after a few years of marriage[53]. Similarly, those that went through a cosmetic surgical procedure feel happier, but only for a short time[54]. Contrary to popular belief, people who live in warmer cities are just as happy as those who live in colder areas[55]. How is it possible that most people, right after a big change in their life circumstances, go back to their initial levels of happiness? Thanks to hedonic adaptation! It's because of this adaptation that you're happier for a few months after getting a pay raise, but as soon as you **adapt** to your new wage, your happiness goes back to normal. Because of it, you buy a new piece of clothing and automatically become happier, but after a few weeks you **get used** to the new buy and your happiness goes back to normal. It's because of hedonic adaption that, after you buy your dream car and enjoy immense pleasure in driving it for a few months, it soon becomes just your regular daily commute. This is why how wealthy someone is doesn't matter—they'll always adapt to what they have and seek **more**. In one episode of the TV show *Two and a Half Men*, after finding out that a beautiful woman was cheated on by her husband, character Alan Harper asks his brother Charlie why any man would do that. Charlie's answer was simple: "For every gorgeous woman out there's a guy tired of banging her." The bad news for Charlie is that hedonic adaptation happens to women too.

This phenomenon, as I explained, happens for both positive and negative events. Losing a job, moving to a smaller home or getting divorced, after a while, doesn't seem **so** bad. In more extreme cases, like a loved one or significant other passing away, it's common for people to evaluate these events positively after a given period—a phenomenon called *post-traumatic growth*, which also happens in near-death situations (surviving a heart attack, cancer, a serious car accident, a kidnapping, etc.)[56].

Negative experiences are inevitable to all of us, and this capacity to adapt is the certainty that, no matter how long it takes, at some point we will overcome most of them. It's not up for debate whether negative events impact us, but we should know that this impact **doesn't last as long as** we believe. Similarly, it's a mistake to believe that the impact of positive situations will last long—we also get **accustomed** to them

THE DOWNSIDE OF WEALTH

Now, let's see what happens to individuals that are very connected to consumerism and the accumulation of money when hedonic adaptation comes into play. Scientists found that people with these values report the highest levels of dissatisfaction with their lives, in addition to suffering from more depression, anxiety and stress[57]. This is because, by overvaluing money, clothes, cars or jewels, people adapt **even faster** to these goods, and consequently need more to achieve their normal levels of happiness—what psychologists call the **hedonic treadmill**[58]. If people that care too much about consumer goods get used to them increasingly faster, depending on increasingly **higher** doses of them to achieve the **same effect** on their happiness, we can conclude that the hedonic treadmill creates an effect similar to drugs! Over time, valuing money and material goods becomes an addiction that's hard to recover from, and in addition to extremely negative consequences to health, it can lead to debt—the exact opposite situation to what these people wish. Not by chance, a "hedonist" is defined as someone who only cares about their immediate pleasure, even if it leads to terrible future consequences.

Therefore, be aware of the kind of happiness you want to pursue in your life, because the more hedonistic we are, valuing money and material goods, the faster the hedonic treadmill starts to spin. You might even have the feeling of moving forward, but your happiness is in the same place.

Even though material goods and money generate only momentary happiness, the media and the corporate world insist on sending the message that you won't be happy until you're rich, have your own office, win awards, buy the newest smartphone, buy the newest car, use the same beauty products as Hollywood stars or wear that Italian designer outfit. This happens because the media is not in the business of happiness, but in the business of **selling ads**. Similarly, most of the corporate world is in the business of generating maximum revenue to stakeholders, achieved through the culture of sacrificing present happiness for financial success and power in the future.

As you can see, many have a mistaken view on what generates motivation. It's the same with happiness.

WHAT IS HAPPINESS?

If motivation makes us **act**, happiness is the **pleasure** we feel before, during and/or after acting. It's the satisfaction we experience when performing an activity, especially when it musters our strengths[59]. When we find ourselves intrinsically motivated and perform an activity that demands our strengths, we achieve a state of good mood, start to feel like life is worth it and understand that the work we're developing will bring some higher benefit than we can see in the moment. This is precisely the meaning of the word "happiness" in many languages: a combination of good mood, good life, and a sense of purpose.

Just like motivation is measured by a number of variables, happiness is a construct. Therefore, if we were to make happiness into a formula, we'd have:

HAPPINESS = MONEY + WORK + RELATIONSHIPS + KINDNESS + ACTS OF KINDNESS + PHYSICAL EXERCISE + GENETICS + BODY POSTURE + MENTALITY + POSITIVE EMOTIONS + NEGATIVE EMOTIONS + CURRENT LIFE CIRCUMSTANCES + LEISURE + AN INFINITY OF KNOWN AND UNKNOWN VARIABLES

One of the biggest mistakes in defining happiness is to believe it's only a **feeling** or the **result** of reaching a goal. Later on in this book, you'll find that happiness is a very different thing. Another mistake is to classify **sadness** as the opposite of happiness, when in reality, it's **apathy**. The feeling of sadness can be seen as beneficial in certain situations, as it can motivate us to make necessary changes. But **apathy**, on the contrary, paralyzes us and can stop us from acting—behaviors caused by the absence of happiness in our daily lives.

Our journey through the science of happiness will show that you often invest in activities that, although not pleasurable at the moment, are essential for building this feeling in the long term. We call this long-term happiness **eudaimonic**. Its opposite is **hedonic happiness**, achieved in the short term and capable of generating extremely negative consequences in your life. Hedonic happiness is achieved easily by eating a candy bar, gambling, consuming alcohol, and in extreme cases using illicit drugs. But what are the real consequences of these actions? This is why one goal of this book is to teach you how to achieve **eudaimonic happiness**.

WHY IT'S IMPORTANT TO BE HAPPY?

It's easy to understand the reasons why you should watch your daily motivation, but what is the point of being happy? Contrary to popular belief, happiness is not the **result** of success, but a **cause** of it. That's right: success happens **later** to people who are happy **now**.

This revelation comes from a study by Sonja Lyubomirsky, from the University of California, Riverside, Ed Diener from the University of Illinois, and Laura King, from the University of Missouri—extremely influential researchers on the science of happiness[60]. This wasn't any study. It was a **meta-analysis**. One single scientific study can have anomalous results, but when scientists conduct a meta-analysis, that is, "a study of studies", the reliability of their conclusions is much higher. And the conclusion reached by Lyubomirsky and her colleagues after exploring 225 studies that added to a sample of over 275 thousand people was:

> **Happy people have more chances of having great friendships, excellent marital relationships, higher salaries, higher performance at work, more creativity, health, optimism, energy and altruism than those that experience positive emotions less frequently.**

Just so you know how robust this relation between happiness and workplace performance is, this meta-analysis showed that **happy employees are, on average, 31% more productive, sell 37% more and are three times more creative**. Happy people also earn higher salaries in the future, according to a study that analyzed college freshmen and found that their happiness at the start of their academic lives had a positive correlation with their salaries **16 years later**[61].

Moreover, a surprising study conducted in 2015 analyzed the neural connections of 461 participants after answering different tests that measured their levels of satisfaction with life, income, education, memory and personality traits, and concluded that **people with more positive lifestyle and behaviors showed stronger connections between the areas of the brain related to memory, language, imagination and empathy, the ability to understand your feelings and those of other people**, which gave them great advantages[62].

Unfortunately, the popular belief is that, in order to be happy in the future, you must sacrifice your current happiness—which will actually cause you to not reach your main goal in life, simply because **your future success is the consequence of your present happiness**. It's because of this mistaken belief that the present involves sacrifices that you start dedicating **less** time to activities that would make you happier both today and in the future. Many spend most of the day in a job that brings no satisfaction, working late, handling ill-prepared bosses and toxic coworkers, just to correspond to the belief that, in order to be happy in the future, first they have to suffer. What actually happens, however, is that when you sacrifice your present happiness or condition it to a given achievement, you let go of the fuel that would make you reach your goals more easily.

Ask anyone you can find what is their main goal in life. With a few exceptions, the answer will be mostly the same: **"I want to be happy!"** Tal Ben-Shahar, a former lecturer at Harvard University, defines happiness as **the ultimate currency**[63]. You want to earn more money in order to be happier, you want to get married to be happier, be promoted to be happier, have children to be happier. But although happiness is the most important goal of our lives, every day we make decisions that **undermine** it.

In spite of this, in the past few years many gained awareness of our lack of knowledge of what happiness really is and how we should build it. The good news is that this search to better understand happiness is starting increasingly early in life, which we can observe from the fact that the science of happiness became the most popular Harvard course in 2006[64], and then the most popular in Yale in 2018, reaching almost 25% of undergraduate students[65]. These students feel that all their material possessions could not be enough to make them happy, that something in missing in their lives, that some direction is necessary. Strange? Not at all! Many of us, at some point, experience this same feeling that, despite everything we own, our lives are not complete. And the earlier you feel that, the less time you'll waste with goals that go against your well-being and, consequently, the more time you'll have to invest in your authentic happiness.

However, just like not all factors that motivate you make you happier, **not all that makes you happier can motivate you**. Knowing which factors increase your happiness without detriment to your motivation is crucial for success in your personal and professional life.

Although eudaimonic happiness and hedonic happiness are completely different, they are built very similarly.

DAILY HAPPINESS X LIFELONG HAPPINESS

Kahneman and Deaton's research on the relation between money and happiness analyzed levels of **daily happiness** for one simple reason. It so happens that, some time ago, in order to find out what brought people well-being, the research work had to be conducted over years of following up with participants. Currently, although it's been found that better health or a higher income create well-being, what was drawing the scientists' attention was the fact that good health or a good financial situation is built day after day. Taking into account that following up on the well-being of individuals for years is very expensive for institutions that invest in scientific studies, as opposed to following their **daily** well-being, which costs increasingly less, the conclusions about what really creates happiness and motivation in life change drastically when we stop analyzing a sequence of years and start analyzing daily experience—which can show important facts on the best decisions to make.

Kahneman and Deaton found that, although income increments over the years increased participants' well-being, that didn't improve their **daily** experience[66]. It's curious to note that, just like most people's concept of happiness is based on long-term achievements, they give up on their daily happiness for them. It's common to hear individuals say they'll be happy **when** they move to another neighborhood, **when** they win the lottery, **when** they can afford their dream car, **when** they're promoted, **when** they have children, **when** they get married, **when** they get a raise, **when** they lose weight, **when** they're recognized by their boss, etc.

The main issue with conditioning happiness to a future achievement is that we usually make inaccurate forecasts about how we'll feel after such achievement[67]. You believe that achieving a certain goal will bring you happiness until you get there and find yourself less happy than you thought. Another factor that undermines your happiness when it's conditioned to achieving a goal is that, like I've said before, what we want changes constantly. Remember, social comparison makes us always want more than we have. Happiness that is conditioned to reaching long-term goals, in addition to not being as great as we thought, is short-lived, due to hedonic adaptation. Moreover, you know that his approach is wrong especially because happiness actually comes **before** success.

This is why the real happiness we seek is that we achieve from our daily actions. Fortunately, these actions can in fact involve money and material goods. You'll be surprised to learn how!

CHAPTER 2

Ensuring the Best Profits

THE BEST INVESTMENT FOR YOUR MONEY

Warren Buffett is a happy and motivated person. You must be thinking this is a rather obvious statement, as it's common knowledge that Buffett owns a fortune of nearly US$ 90 billion, and is currently one of the richest men in the world. With over 70 years as an investor, Buffett has significant shares in companies like Apple, Coca-Cola, American Airlines, General Motors and Kraft Heinz. In 2016 alone, he made US$ 16 billion, which ensured him monthly gains of US$ 1.33 billion.

In the financial market, there are several professionals trying to teach investors Warren Buffett's tricks to **make** so much money in the stock market. But as Buffett said in an interview to CNBC in 2017, his happiness doesn't come from how much money he **makes**, but how he **spends** it[1]. In June 2017, Buffett donated US$ 3.17 billion to charity—in fact, he made the commitment to donate 99% of his fortune to social causes[2]. "My billions are useless to me, but they can be useful to other people", he said in an interview to PBS Newshour[3]. In that same interview, Buffett said that if he spent his money buying a giant yacht or 20 homes, he wouldn't be as happy as he is investing in **other people**. Despite his almost 90 years of age, Buffett goes to work at his company's office every day, and says that his secret to health is his **happiness**.

You must be thinking: "It's easy to be happy like that! Just 1% of this US$ 90 billion fortune is US$ 900 million!" But, is Buffett's secret to happiness and longevity the amount the has or the amount he donates? And does giving money to charity or spending it with others create happiness, even if the people doing the giving have a hard time paying their own bills? What if they really needed the money? This was the question that researchers from Canada, United States, Netherlands, South Africa and Uganda were looking to answer. Does investing in others always bring happiness?

Using data from the **Gallup World Poll**, that surveyed over 200 thousand people in 136 countries, scientists found a positive relation between happiness and donating money in 120 countries[4]. The increase in happiness when people spend their money with others is so significant that it corresponds to receiving a 100% raise in salary! This means that if you want to feel the same happiness you would if your salary doubled—except that a salary raise only causes **momentary** happiness—you should simply invest in other people—a behavior scientists call *prosocial spending*. This relation was shown to be positive regardless of the wealth of the country in which participants lived, teaching us what we may never forget: **humans were made to help each other**.

In a second study done with 820 people in Canada and Uganda, researchers separated participants into two groups: one in which people should remember a situation where they spent money on **themselves**; and another in which they should think of a situation where they spent money on **other people**. Shortly after, everyone was measured for their levels or happiness—or, in scientific terms, **subjective well-being**, meaning both positive emotions and life satisfaction. What happened? Those that remembered situations where they spent money on **other people** reported **higher** happiness compared to those that only spent money on themselves.

It's interesting to note that people's memories on how they spent money in Canada and Uganda were completely different. In Canada, participants more often remembered events where they bought, for instance, a piece of **clothing** for themselves or as a gift to others. In Uganda, people more often remembered situations where they bought a **medicine** for themselves or a friend. It's amazing to note that, despite the differences in how people spend money in both countries, the level of happiness reported was always higher when people remembered situations where they spent on **others** more than on themselves—even when spending on others compromised **their own well-being**, which was frequently reported by participants from Uganda. Other studies conducted by the same researchers with participants from India and South Africa had the same results: spending money on other people is more beneficial to your happiness than spending on yourself.

PROSOCIAL COMPASSION

In addition to the good feelings we have when we help others, when people see us helping others, their feelings also change! This is what Oregon State University researcher Sarina Saturn and her colleagues found by analyzing brain activity, heart rate and respiratory activity of 104 people that watched videos containing **compassionate** or **inspiring** situations[5]. Respiratory analysis is related to activation of the parasympathetic nervous system—which automatically calms us down—and heart rate is related to activation of the sympathetic nervous system—responsible for feelings of stress and arousal.

Researchers thought the participants selected to watch videos with **compassionate situations** would only experience parasympathetic activation, but, to their surprise, **both** systems were activated, which didn't happen to participants who watched videos with inspiring situations. Saturn explains that when we see people helping someone in need, first our sympathetic nervous system is activated—producing pain and stress—and only then is our parasympathetic nervous system activated—easing those feelings, calming us down and giving us pleasure when observing someone who is in pain be helped or soothed. This mechanism creates in us the motivation to help someone in the future.

Another revealing finding was from a group of researchers from Harvard and the University of California, Berkeley, in a series of three experiments[6]. In one, scientists separated study participants into two groups to watch a brief slide show. One group saw pictures that evoked **compassion**, while the photos shown to the second group evoked **pride**. After the slide show, participants were asked to fill out a survey reporting how much they identified with 23 different groups of people, including Stanford students, liberals, conservatives, celebrities, senior citizens, orphaned children, peace activists, homeless people, etc. In the paper, published in the *Journal of Personality and Social Psychology* in 2010, researchers concluded:

> "[...] the present three studies reveal that compassion and pride shift the sense of self-other similarity in opposite directions. [...] compassion was associated with an enhanced sense of similarity to others, in particular to those in need. In contrast, pride was associated with an enhanced sense of similarity to strong others, and a diminished sense of similarity to weak others."

One year earlier, Christopher Oveis, from Harvard, and Dacher Keltner, from the University of California, Berkeley, two authors of this study, had already found that the feeling of compassion activates the **vagus nerve**[7], considered the major nerve of the parasympathetic system—the one activated in Sarina Saturn's study participants. The vagus nerve is huge: it stretches from the head to the intestines, branching out to the brain, liver, kidneys, lungs, heart and other organs. When activated, it controls heartbeat, making it slower and promoting kinder and closer encounters between people.

The vagal system is also connected to a large network of **oxytocin** receptors, a hormone known for generating feelings of love and trust. In a similar experiment conducted by Oveis, Keltner and other four scientists, participants had electrodes installed that measured activation of the vagus nerve. According to data, exposure to people's suffering **increased** activation of the vagus nerve more intensely than exposure to images of pride. Because of this and other studies, the vagus nerve became known as the *compassion nerve*. Our own body **manufactures** stress when we witness suffering, which activates the vagal system and evokes feelings of **compassion, similarity, trust and love**, motivating us to help people in need. We really **were** made to help each other.

THE NEW GENIUS

At the end of the day, it seems that Warren Buffett is **even smarter** than we thought, isn't he? Another proof that Buffett understands that the most valuable investment is happiness is certainly the fact that he wishes to enjoy his wealth **while he is alive**. Many plan to give a destination to their material and financial fortunes only after death, which is a sad decision, as they'll never have the pleasure of enjoying what their money can provide to their family, friends or other people that don't have the necessary means for a decent life.

Unless your goal is to become **the richest skeleton in the graveyard**, spending your money on others **while living** is an investment that pays dividends never before seen by any stock exchange. This statement may seem subjective, as I understand that it's difficult to measure the happiness your money can bring other people. Therefore, I'd like to give you a new example. Let's see how donating your money can bring a personal return unmatched by any other investment.

Economist Arthur Brooks, who studied the annual income variation of 30 thousand American families, found a secret that few brokers know and would never divulge to their clients[8]. For every dollar **donated** to charity, a family earns **US$ 3.75 more** the following year. Yes, that's a return of 375% a year! This means that if you donate US$ 500 to social causes this year, your annual income might increase by US$ 1,875 next year, generating a profit of US$ 1,375. Brooks still found that people who dedicate their **time** to charity or who donate **blood** also increase their future income. Another interesting fact presented by his studies is that Americans donate more money compared to other nations because, naturally, they're richer, but also that they're richer **because they donate more money**. It's very important for the world that other nations follow these examples.

Looking at it this way, you might be thinking that:

Warren Buffett = (Leonardo da Vinci + Albert Einstein)[100]

And you're right! Every dollar Buffett donates can turn into an additional US$ 3.75 in his next year's income, which can be reinvested into even more people—consequently increasing his life satisfaction and his income for the next year. This cycle will only end if his children and relatives learned nothing from him.

The world would be so much better if, instead of measuring their own success and that of others by the amount of money accumulated, they start measuring it by the amount of money donated. Imagine if millionaires and other people competed to see who donates the most to charity? Wouldn't this social comparison model be the best for everyone? We could see science reveal that real success happens when, in addition to ensuring resources to yourself, you ensure resources to those less fortunate.

But can we achieve the same happiness as Warren Buffett and his billionaire buddies without fortunes like his to give away?

HAPPINESS IN AN ENVELOPE

Lara Aknin, professor at the Simon Fraser University, in Canada, decided to conduct an unusual study to analyze whether the way people spent money caused changes in their happiness[9]. In a Vancouver summer morning, Aknin went out on the street and gave away an envelope containing C$ 5 to several passersby. Some contained the instructions:

"Please spend this $5.00 today before 5pm on a gift for yourself or any of your expenses (e.g. rent, bills, or debt)."

Another group received an envelope with the same C$ 5, but different instructions:

"Please spend this $5.00 today before 5pm on a gift for someone else or a donation to charity."

To a third group, Aknin gave away an envelope with C$ 20 instead of C$ 5. Some had the instruction "Please spend this on yourself", and others had "Please spend this on others", in this case, ***prosocial spending***. The researcher registered each participant's phone number and asked them to fill out a short survey to know how happy each person was **before** spending the money in the envelope.

The way participants spent the money was very similar—many bought food or a Starbucks coffee, but with a slight difference: some bought it for **other** people. And how did this difference affect the happiness of participants? At the end of the day, the group that spent the money in the envelope on **someone else** seemed **happier** than the group that spent on themselves!

It's important to note that:

1. At the beginning of the day, the happiness levels of both groups had no significant difference.

2. There was no significant difference in happiness at the end of the study for those who received C$ 5 or C$ 20, despite one of the groups having the possibility to engage in prosocial spending **four times higher**. This means that the **way** people spent the money, and not the **quantity**, was what determined their happiness.

Now you know that, even if you spend a small amount of money on others, at the end of the day you can have as much happiness as Warren Buffett. In the paper, published in Science in 2008, Aknin and her colleagues Elizabeth Dunn and Michael Norton conclude the study by signaling that, in their research, people reported spending **10 times** more money **on themselves** than on others. Yet, their data proved that people have the mistaken perception that spending money on themselves creates more happiness than spending on others: another confirmation that humans insist on making decisions **contrary** to their own happiness, and that we absolutely need to use science to have a better life.

To achieve this goal, in addition to giving money to charity, your role is also to **convince other people to donate**. If we consider Brooks' findings, this will increase the number of donors, consequently increasing the future income of these families, and the country's income, generating jobs and moving the economy in a constant cycle.

PROSOCIAL SPENDING AND TEAM PERFORMANCE

Aknin, Dunn and Norton, still curious about the effects on happiness created by spending money on other people, decided to conduct a new study in 2008 to investigate whether prosocial spending could improve other motivational aspects[10]. This time, researchers had the company of two colleagues: Lalin Anik, from the University of Virginia, and Jordi Quoidbach, from Pompeu Fabra University, in Barcelona.

For the study, 88 salespeople from a Belgian pharmaceutical company were chosen to receive € 15 each. According to methodological standards, some of them were instructed to spend the money **on themselves**, and others, **on a teammate**. After a month, researchers revealed that the salespeople who bought something for their **teammates** had a **spectacular** increase in performance, while there was no improvement for those who spent the money **on themselves**. In fact, the salespeople that received the personal bonus brought the company a return of only € 4.50, leaving the company at a loss. On the other hand, those that engaged in prosocial spending brought a return of **€ 78** for each € 15 invested, generating a € 63 profit per employee.

Not yet satisfied, the scientists decided to try the effect of prosocial spending on 11 sports teams. Two weeks later, the teams whose players spent their money on teammates had a **higher percentage of wins** than those who spent the money on themselves. Every C$ 10 spent on teammates generated an **11% increase in wins**, while every C$ 10 spent personally resulted in a **2% reduction in wins**.

It seems that even in the most competitive environments, like sales and sports, encouraging people to spend their money on others results in interesting gains. These studies also show that money is not always an evil entity, as its effects on motivation and happiness are very significant if used to increase collaboration and improve relationships. Unfortunately, in our personal lives and the corporate world, we're encouraged to protect our own, as if life were a zero-sum game, where one wins at the expense of the other.

STRESS AND DONATING MONEY

According to science, the benefits of being generous with our money are so significant that sharing our wealth with other people can make us healthier.

In a study conducted by Canadian and Dutch researchers, some participants received US$ 10 and were told to share the money any way they liked with the other participant[11]. Those who received the money were informed that they'd never meet the other participant, who would have to accept any amount offered. They were assured that they could choose to offer nothing, if they so wished. As a result, on average, participants donated US$ 4.48—a little under half the amount. Researchers found that the lower the amount, the more ashamed they felt. This fact was proven when their levels of cortisol—the stress hormone—were measured in their saliva.

We can easily infer that **the more ashamed** participants felt for keeping most of the money, **the higher** the levels of cortisol in their saliva. This means that **donating** more money—instead of gaining more money—is one of the best weapons against stress. Yes, money can save your life, as long as you use it in the opposite way as what society, the media and the corporate world dictate. Later on, you'll get a better understanding of the relation between stress and your health and happiness.

It's interesting to note that Michael Norton and his colleagues found that donating money to others is not the only way to increase happiness—donating **time** to help someone also generates this return, which is in accordance with Arthur Brooks' findings[12]. But your happiness doesn't come only from investing your money and time on others. Adequately choosing how to spend it **on yourself** is fundamental.

BUYING HAPPINESS

Remember when I asked you to try to remember the second to last shirt you bought? And how difficult it was? Now, I'd like to ask a different question: do you remember the second to last vacation you took? I'm sure that remembering a trip was a lot easier, right? This happens because, fortunately, not all consumerism is negatively related to happiness. Several studies reiterate that the way you spend your money on yourself can also predict your life satisfaction.

A study by Ryan Howell and Paulina Pchelin, from San Francisco State University, revealed that when people are directed to think about their future happiness after buying a material good, in general their predictions are in accordance with reality. But when asked to predict how happy they'd be after investing their money in an **experience**, such as trip, two weeks after the investment they report being **106% happier than they had predicted**—another proof that the human crystal ball is flawed[13]. Researcher Sonja Lyubomirsky concluded that hedonic adaptation is slower when people consume **experiences** instead of material goods[14].

Another interesting discovery is that, since people usually have experiences **with others**, investing in these activities strengthens bonds of friendship, companionship and family[15]. Experiences increase the happiness of **several individuals** at once and sustain it for **longer periods**, while most material goods increase the happiness of just one person for only a **short time**. Experiences are also harder to compare, after all, how do you measure if your trip to Paris was better or worse than that of your coworker? Even if he stayed at a five-star hotel with his wife and dined at the fanciest restaurants, you could still say that your backpacking trip staying at hostels was **more rewarding** than his.

Another advantage of consuming experiences is that it facilitates **reinterpreting** moments in a more positive light, turning your memory of having lunch sitting on a bench in Central Park in New York into one of the most rewarding experiences of your life. Positively reinterpreting events can even make you laugh when you remember that you were stung by a bee that day.

Although hedonic adaptation studies show that we have less pleasure from material goods over time, Sonja Lyubomirsky found a way we can derive pleasure from material goods for longer. We must make a **conscious effort**. Lyubomirsky emphasizes that the owner of a Porsche, for example, will continue to have pleasure using it for longer if they use it to seek experiences—like a road trip to an unknown destination—or strengthening family bonds—using the car on trips with the kids, lending it to a family member, etc.—or remembering how lucky they are for having this luxurious means of transportation.

More recently, researchers Sandra Matz, Joe Gladstone and David Stillwell, from Cambridge University, found that material goods can bring long-lasting happiness if combined with people's personalities[16]. Analyzing over 70 thousand financial transactions in the United Kingdom, they concluded that a technology professional, for example, can achieve long-term happiness by purchasing the latest MacBook or Bose headphones; a poetry lover will find satisfaction for months from buying dozens of books; and an avid surfer will have motivation and happiness for a long time after purchasing a new board.

Another investment with huge returns to your happiness is spending money buying **time**[17]. That's right, investing money to have **more time** to do activities you love and make you happy brings huge profits. Hiring someone to clean the house and do the laundry, buying ready-made meals so you don't have to cook, or hiring a bike messenger to make errands for you is a fundamental investment that allows you to dedicate yourself more to activities that muster your strengths and increase your positive emotions.

This discovery was made by researchers from British Columbia University in a series of six studies with over 4.6 thousand participants. Their conclusion was that "having more free time is probably more important to happiness than having more money". People who chose to pay more to fill up the tank at gas stations closer to home reported being happier than those who preferred to drive longer distances to save money. Participants that preferred winning a US$ 120 voucher for home cleaning were reportedly happier than those who chose a cash prize of US$ 50. The popular saying goes that "time is money". This is true if you take into account that the ultimate currency is your **happiness**.

Therefore, when you spend your money on yourself, make sure to prioritize experiences such as trips, dinners, theater plays, movies, visits to museums, outings, theme parks. Invest in items that are strongly related to your personality and, whenever possible, buy time. Don't forget to invite other people to enjoy your investment in experiences to the max. Several studies prove that those who attach more value to experiences with other people are also happier than those who invest in experiences alone.

Your money must be used to maximize your happiness, not your wealth.

One of the most fantastic findings on the impact of experiences is that people feel more pleasure **anticipating** and **remembering** an experience than living it[18]. Think of your last vacation, for example. After defining your destination and planning what to see, where to stay and where to eat, didn't it feel for a moment that you were already there? Didn't it give you pleasure? Even after years have passed, every time you see a souvenir you brought from your trip, enjoy a meal that makes you remember a restaurant from that trip, watch a movie set on that city or see a photo of a sight you visited, for a moment it seems like you're there again, and so your happiness levels increase.

Experiences cause happiness and motivation **before, during** and **after** you consume them, which is rare for material goods or money. When you choose to invest your resources on material goods, you experience positive emotions for a short time, as you soon get used to what you bought, and it stops giving you pleasure. On the other hand, every time you choose to invest in experiences, you feel positive emotions with **anticipation**, **consumption** and **memories**, which last **forever**. In a few pages, you'll understand why frequently living positive experiences is extremely important to your well-being.

If you have a leadership role and is responsible for the happiness of those under your command, it's important that **you** choose how to reward them. An employee you lead will hardly remember the time he paid his electric bill thanks to the cash bonus he received, but he'll **never** forget the weekend on the beach he won for his good performance at work.

If a company's employees had the power to choose between **money** and **experiences**, which do you think they'd choose? Would they make the decision that maximizes their happiness? I believe this time your crystal ball may have made the right prediction!

STOP ACCUMULATING, START APPRECIATING

As we've seen, humans have a primitive tendency to believe that happiness lies in accumulating wealth. However, in the historical moment of abundance in which we live—at least for good part of the population—this trend is proving to be one of the greatest enemies of happiness, due to hedonic adaptation. By increasingly accumulating money and material goods, we feel **more and more dissatisfied** with life for never thinking we have enough; so the hedonic treadmill only goes faster and faster. Luckily, there are several scientific studies that teach us how to **slow down the hedonic treadmill** so that our happiness, life satisfaction and health will increase—in addition to helping others with our money, choosing to invest in experiments, donate and buy time, another big secret is **to stop wanting more and start being thankful for what we have!**

Since the early 2000s, researchers Robert Emmons and Michael McCullough have tried to discover the real effects that **gratitude** causes on humans[19]. In one of their most important researches, they conducted three studies for nine weeks. In one group, participants were encouraged to write five events from the previous week for which they were **grateful**; in a second group, they were encouraged to write about five **annoying** situations that they faced in the previous week; and a third group, the control, was conditioned to write about five circumstances of the previous week that **affected** their lives. Later, researchers asked participants to report with what intensity they felt **more than 30 negative and positive emotions**—including interest, disinterest, irritation, sadness, stress, joy, determination, hope and enthusiasm—as well as with what **intensity** they experienced feelings related to **gratitude**. Emmons and McCullough also measured the amount of physical symptoms reported by participants (headache, tiredness, stomachache, skin irritations, congested nose, coughing, among others), their reactions after helping friends or family, the time they spent exercising, how they assessed their lives during the previous week and what were their expectations for the following week. Who would have thought that a study about gratitude could involve so many variables?

These scientists found that the simple fact that **participants remembered and wrote once a week about five things for which they were grateful** made them assess the previous week more positively, have **more positive** expectations about their next week, report **less physical symptoms**, spend **more time** exercising and express **more positive than negative emotions** when they had the opportunity to help someone. Who would have thought that this simple exercise could **improve** so many variables?

In a second study, the control group was replaced by another, called **social comparison**. Its participants were encouraged to write about things they had, but other people **didn't**. Because us humans naturally compare ourselves to each other, when we devote ourselves to seeing our similarities and differences with those who have **less**, we somehow feel better and more grateful. It's common to teach our children that they should be thankful for their food, toys, home, clothes and other things, **because many people don't have any of that**. That way, we believe our children will learn to value what they have. Unfortunately, science reached a conclusion that will disappoint many parents: this comparison has no effect on our well-being, and doesn't even change our behavior!

In this study, the second group had to write about five events from the week before for which they were **grateful**, and the last group, about five things that **upset** them the previous week. Therefore, one group expressed **gratitude**, the other, **irritation**, and the third made a **lower social comparison**. An important differential in this second study was that instead of writing **once a week** about their gratitude, irritation or social comparison, participants should do so **every day**. The result: when analyzing variables, compared to the first study, scientists found that there was a significant and **even greater** difference in the relation between positive and negative emotions reported by participants in the gratitude and irritation conditions. We can understand that the fact that group participants were conditioned to remember and write **every day** about things for which they were grateful **increased the intensity** of the positive emotions they felt.

Remembering and writing daily about the things you're grateful for makes your happiness grow!

Researchers also found that those conditioned to gratitude presented a higher prosocial behavior compared to **the other groups, reporting to helping others more frequently**. Although these last two studies didn't find benefits to the health of people in the condition of gratitude, as in the first study, an article published in 2017 by Emmons and other scientists revealed that this feeling is linked to **a lower amount of A1c hemoglobin** in the blood stream, an indicator of the amount of sugar in the body directly related to people's health[20].

If writing about the positive emotions experienced during the day helps us be happier, what can we do when we experience a **negative** emotion? Swear? Vent? Write! James Pennebaker, a researcher from the University of Texas, shows that writing about your deepest feelings for 20 minutes, four **nights** in a row (yes, the end of the day is the best time for this activity), helps **minimize the impacts of trauma**, reduces **negativity** and makes you **move on with your life**[21]. Pennebaker also reveals that **hiding** your problems can lead you to the doctor 40% more often than people who **deal** with them.

One tool people believe to be effective for dealing with traumatic moments or anger—**venting**—was shown to be extremely **dangerous** in a study conducted by the Eindhoven University of Technology and the University of Colorado[22]. In this study, scientists found that those who unloaded their anger—for **example, complaining** in the workplace—reported subsequent **bad mood**, and **less satisfaction and pride** with how they performed that day. The worst part is that this effect was also present the **day following** the study. It's because of scientific conclusions like these that you **should always** avoid following tips based on popular beliefs.

Considering what we've seen, one of the best exercises is to have a **gratitude journal**, in which **every night**, before sleep, you'll write five facts of your day for which you're grateful. This exercise will make you **pay more attention to the small moments of your life**—such a delicious meal, a hug from your child, a beautiful sunset, a conversation with your best friend—**and enjoy them again**. That way, you reprogram your brain to have pleasure even with worldly events which no longer had an effect on your happiness. And for those who believe that happiness is the result of reaching a goal, gratitude becomes even more positive for leading us to be happy in **the present**.

The secret to happiness is not in reaching your destination, but in making the most out of every step of the way.

In a scene of the fun *Kung Fu Panda* animated movie, the character Master Oogway tells Po, the panda: "**Yesterday** is history, **tomorrow** is a mystery, but **today** is a gift: that **is why it is called the present!**" Are you valuing this gift or are you conditioning your happiness to what can happen tomorrow and what has happened in the past?

It's worth thinking, however: isn't the secret to success to have a commitment to long-term goals and **resist** today's pleasures? According to the popular "Marshmallow Experiment", carried out by Walter Mischel, children who managed to resist the temptation to eat one marshmallow immediately in order to eat **two** marshmallows a few minutes later had more successful lives[23]. The problem is that most people's interpretation of this study is **incomplete**! People don't usually remember the tool developed by the children to resist immediate temptation: **doing something pleasurable while they waited**. Contrary to what you might think, the children who succeeded in waiting to eat two marshmallows were not those who were **suffering** while waiting, but those who started **singing a song or distracting themselves with imaginary games**. In order to achieve their long-term goals, these children first invented healthy ways to **enjoy the present**. Dreaming of how happy you'll be when you can wear your teenage pants again, despite generating an initial motivation, sustains your motivation to lose weight **less** than being **aware** that you can start to lose weight **today, eating as much as you want**, if you just choose not to eat wheat flour, grains, sugars and starch-filled food—the real bad guys of obesity[24].

> **To achieve your goals and be happy in the future, you should first find ways to self-gratify today.**

Remember that the happiness you seek is eudaimonic, not hedonic. Therefore, just like the children in Mischel's experiment found ways to **enjoy the present without eating *the* marshmallow**, you must also find strategies so that **the present** is your ally in the search for your long-term goals.

This was exactly what researchers Ayelet Fishbach and Kaitlin Wooley, from the University of Chicago, found in 2017, when they published a paper demonstrating that people with alternative (and healthy) ways to get immediate gratification are those who have **the greatest persistence** in seeking long-term goals[25]. Finding a friend whose company you enjoy to be your gym partner, understanding how your brain works better every day when you don't eat wheat flour and listening to music while working to deliver that report to your boss are simple ways to **enjoy the present** during your journey to achieve longer goals.

Being grateful is also important to raise your awareness of the good things you **already have**. When your focus is to accumulate goods and money, you naturally forget what you already have, becoming eternally dissatisfied and using consumerism an escape valve to your frustration. Gratitude **slows down the hedonic treadmill**, because it makes you **remember** the things you've already conquered and derive happiness from them again. So, make an effort to write varied facts in your gratitude journal, because if you write the same thing every day, your arsenal of positive emotions will be small. It's natural that sometimes you'll write repeated facts, but in that exercise, it's important to be guided by the saying "variety is the spice of life".

WHAT PEOPLE "THINK" ISN'T WHAT WORKS

When you start absorbing and practicing the findings you read thus far, I'm sure many of your friends, family and especially coworkers will tell you that you're thinking like a **loser** that doesn't care about money or success. They'll tell you **money does increase happiness** and that you should care, first, about yourself. They'll also tell you that this way of thinking is to **justify** your current lack of money.

I remember a situation in which I presented the numerous studies I did for my previous book, *The Incredible Science of Sales*, to the vice-president of a large bank. When I shared studies similar to the ones you just saw, about the negative relation between money and work performance, this executive told me that my suggestion of replacing employees' commissions for higher fixed salaries was a "pact of mediocrity". This opinion is nothing out of the ordinary, now that you know that most of the time, what people "think" happens after an intervention—like cutting financial incentives for sales—is not always what **really happens**. Julia Galef, president of the Center for Applied Rationality, warns us that one bias we should worry about when making decisions is **motivated cognition**[26]. Say you're in doubt about whether commissions work, and need to decide on it at your company. Because you spent **years** believing that financial incentives work after developing and implementing performance pay systems several times and because **your own salary is based on commission**, you'll probably **refute** any argument that financial incentives aren't efficient. Because people are not aware of this bias, they'll leave it intact, influencing opinions and decisions **without even realizing**. I can show every scientific paper in the world about the downsides of financial incentives, and you'll **always** find a way to justify why **your world should remain the same**. And they say humans are rational...

Galef explains that most people's definition of the term "rational" is similar to "whatever I happen to believe", so we judge as "irrational" whatever **disagrees** with me. Motivated cognition is also explained by the fact that your brain can **more quickly** process information that **confirms** your opinion, according to a 2018 study by researchers from the Hebrew University of Jerusalem[27].

In science, one of the most explored behaviors is *confirmation bias*, which shows how people assess information more favorably when it **confirms** their own points of view, and unfavorably when it is **contrary** to their beliefs[28]. One main function of the brain is to spare energy wherever possible so it can be used in decision-making moments when our life is at risk, which were common to our ancestors. That's why evolution molded our neural system so that it makes the most effort to confirm our beliefs and find quick explanations that discard opposing facts. This is because our brain considers that thinking **again** about something you **already have** an opinion on is a waste of energy[29]. Our brains are constantly fighting to keep **the world as we know it exactly as it is**, which keeps us from forming new opinions that could even improve our lives.

Unfortunately, not even scientific evidence is spared from people's judgment. In the era of information abundance in which we live, we can just as easily find papers stating that eggs are good for you and papers that state the opposite. Depending on your initial belief, you'll choose one side or another. Even the online search engine we use to find these articles is already customized according to our navigation history, and will preferably deliver those articles that **confirm** our opinion.

Do you believe money brings happiness? Type in that question on your preferred search engine and it'll return an avalanche of studies that confirm that. Do you think a left-wing government is better than a right-wing one? Search online and you'll be "surprised" to see that all your beliefs are actually true!

This way, it's easy to notice that motivated cognition and confirmation bias **distance** us from rational thought. Now that you're aware of these phenomena, start paying attention to the judgements you make: are they really rational or are there other unconscious reasons influencing them? It's also interesting to note how these biases drive the decisions of your social circle. Start observing and I'm sure you'll be more and more aware of how common this phenomenon is and how important it is to avoid it.

It's because of these flaws in our crystal ball that new fields in science have been drawing the attention of researchers, because they also consider human emotions in the decision-making process. One example is ***behavioral economics***[30], whose contributions have been so significant to humankind that the 2017 Nobel Prize in Economic Sciences was given to Richard Thaler, from the University of Chicago, a pioneer in this field of study[31]. Other scientists in the field have also been awarded a Nobel, such as the famous Daniel Kahneman, from Princeton University.

One curious fact: a few years after my meeting with that vice-president, the bank where he worked sold their operations in Brazil to another institution, due to the low profits of "non-mediocre" strategies that reduce human motivation to money. In a nothing short of fantastic article—*Why the Assholes are Winning*—renowned Stanford University researcher Jeffrey Pfeffer explains how our vision of **success** became distorted lately[32]. He emphasizes that, in 2015, only four institutions were listed **at the same time** in *Fortune's* both Most Admired Companies list and Best Companies to Work For list, hinting that public **admiration** for a company and the **reality** of their employees are **completely opposite**. The article is a warning about the excessive value placed on the "results over people" culture that's been spreading around workplaces. In it, Pfeffer notes:

> "It seemingly doesn't matter what an individual or a company does, to human beings or the environment, as long as they are sufficiently rich and successful. Money, indeed, trumps all. Moreover, because money can serve as a signal of competence and worth, no amount of money is ever enough. Much like a drug, money and status become addictive."

One of your greatest challenges, if you wish to be happy and motivated, is precisely to not listen to the terrible advice people will give you, often **contrary** to the numerous studies done by scientists over a lifetime. Studies that have the power to change our perspective on what is the right path to follow.

Surprised to find how money can have good or bad effects on your motivation and happiness? As important as it may be, money is not everything. Science shows that there are other simple ways to achieve true motivation and happiness without using money.

CHAPTER 3

Far Beyond Maslow

MOTIVATION IS WORTH A LOT MORE THAN MONEY

In this book's Introduction, I've shown the results of Uri Gneezy and Aldo Rustichini's experiment with Israeli students, in which the group who was only given a talk on the importance of their work raised more money than the other groups, who were given the same talk but with the promise of gaining a percentage of the money raised during Giving Day. If motivation was explained solely for the financial variable, the group with the possibility to gain 10% of the amount raised would be the winner, but as we've seen, motivation can't be reduced to a pile of cash. From what you saw in this experiment, there are other variables to motivation with a heavier weight than money, and one of them had a crucial role in the highest performing group. Receiving as incentive only a brief talk on the importance of their work, the winning group was shown the purpose of their activity.

Purpose is a variable that boasts people's intrinsic motivation. So that you understand the importance of purpose for motivation, nothing better than presenting a study by renowned researchers Jane Dutton, from the University of Michigan, and Amy Wrzesniewski, from Yale University, the biggest references in this field[1].

Research shows that people approach their work in three ways: as a job, as a career, or as a calling[2]. Those who work merely in exchange for financial gain have a job. Those who work with the main objective of growing and climbing the hierarchy of a company have a career. On the other hand, those who seek pleasure and accomplishment have a calling. Dutton and Wrzesniewski were impressed to realize that people with the same role see their work in completely different lights, finding equally different levels of motivation and happiness.

A team of hospital cleaners, for example, was clearly separated into those who saw their work as a job and those who found purpose in it. The first group, with a limited view of their role, performed tasks with as little effort as possible and avoided interactions with coworkers and patients. These individuals didn't enjoy doing cleaning work, considered it as having a low level of specialization and were not willing to put in extra effort to perform tasks that were out of their scope, engage with others or change processes. But another group of cleaners acted differently, frequently performing tasks that were out of their scope and making extra effort in their interactions with coworkers, visitors, patients and other members in their unit.

Amy Wrzesniewski says that, in an interview conducted for this study, she asked one of the cleaners: "What do you do here at the hospital?" He said, "I cure patients." Wrzesniewski asked him to tell her more about his work, and he said he did everything he could to help patients get better, and a part of that was ensuring his work gave them clean and sterile rooms so they could be cured. This is an example of someone that sees a calling, instead of a job or career. This kind of professional can feel that their work reaches far beyond what they can see at the moment, that it carries a meaning.

The cleaners that had a job, on the other hand, saw their work as limited to cleaning, and couldn't see the impact of their service to patients, doctors, visitors and coworkers. These professionals, when asked about what they did at the hospital, replied with the exact job description of their roles given by HR.

Cleaners in the **calling** group, on the other hand, enjoyed their work, considered that it required a high level of specialization and did all they could so that people in their unit (nurses, doctors, servers, etc.) worked as smoothly as possible. These professionals understand that they're capable of making the world a better place with their acts, which is simple and doable for anyone willing to act. All professionals studied by Dutton and Wrzesniewski had "**Janitor**" written on their nametags, but some understood that their role was far greater than cleaning. They could see beyond that label. **What about you? What do you do at work?**

YOUR DREAM JOB

Wrzesniewski and Dutton taught us that we can all turn the job we **have** into our **dream job**. It all starts with **effort** to see how we impact our customers' lives, the economy and the divisions of the company we work for. **Every work has a purpose**, but few can see it. One proof of this is Gallup's finding that only 12% of interviewees believe that their lives are better because of the company where they work—that means that 88% of people believe that their companies make their lives **worse**[3]. Gallup also publishes the report *State of the Global Workplace*, which measures the engagement of workers all over the world. In its last edition, the number of workers that reported feeling highly involved and enthusiastic about their work was only 15%[4].

Have you ever wondered why your job in the company exists? Is it to make a client happy, help another team in the company be successful, make a process faster, help the company save money or earn more money, increase your city's GDP? In addition, every work allows you to develop skills, become better at what you do and become able to deal with situations outside of the workplace more easily. This process is called *Job Crafting*: with a conscious effort, you define your work to find purpose, achieving the motivation you need to wake up happy every day and increase your engagement, because you know that your work contributes to your well-being and that of many others. The **choice** between seeing what you do as a job, a career or a calling is completely yours!

That was exactly the choice that Adam Grant, from the Wharton School, led community college call center employees to make[5]. Anyone that's ever worked at a call center knows that the workplace and the work itself aren't the most enjoyable. The pressure is huge, autonomy is almost non-existent, and rejection from potential clients during calls is very high. In this call center, employees were tasked with calling potential donors soliciting contributions that would be converted into student scholarships.

Adam Grant put a group of these employees to talk in person with students who received scholarships, while a second group didn't experience this contact. One month after the interventions, employees that had a personal encounter with students **increased their time on the phone by 143.67% per work week, in addition to raising 170.63% more money per week**. The group that didn't meet with the students showed no significant improvements in any of these variables. Increasing call time from 107.55 to 260.73 minutes per week (2.42 times more), as well increasing the amount raised weekly from US$ 185.94 to US$ 503.22 (2.71 times more) was only possible because the employees who met with scholarship students learned the real purpose of their work—they understood how it positively impacted people's well-being. One surprising factor of this study is that the talk between scholarship students and employees lasted approximately **five minutes**, showing that people can get that understanding on the importance of their work without too much effort or time.

Similarly, researchers from Harvard and University College London found that when cooks at a restaurant could **see the patrons**, they made **tastier** dishes[6]. In addition, this small intervention brought a 22.2% increase in client satisfaction and reduced the wait time by 19.2%. Ryan Buell, one of the paper's authors, says that when employees see the client, they feel more appreciated, understand that their work carries meaning, get more satisfied with their work and increase their willingness to make an effort. This means that talking to the people impacted by their job, or simply observing them, even if not for long, will provide motivation and performance hardly achieved by external incentives.

Back to the Israeli students that we met in this book's introduction, it's easier to see that those who saw their work as an **opportunity to help others** had an excellent performance[7]. On the other hand, the students who saw their work as an **opportunity to make the most money** had lower performance. This difference in motivation was so clear in the study that Gneezy and Rustichini noted:

"If a person is rewarded for performing an interesting activity, his intrinsic motivation decreases."

The work required from students on Giving Day was very interesting, because they could feel that their effort would result in other people's well-being. The short talk reminding students of the importance of their work **increased** this feeling of intrinsic motivation, as you can see in the first group's performance. But the moment the second and third groups received an **extrinsic incentive**—money—right after the talk, their intrinsic motivation decreased, and with it, their results. Moreover, when intrinsic and extrinsic stimuli happen **at the same time**, we can note that the extrinsic incentive has more weight and undermines performance. George Loewenstein explains that, in cases like this, from the moment an individual receives financial incentives to perform a purposeful work, the possible financial gain makes them **not to see themselves as virtuous individuals**, causing worsened performance[8].

In Lepper, Greene and Nisbett's experiment, we saw that the children who were informed that they could get a prize for their drawings had their work's quality rated lower than those by children who didn't know about the prize[9]. Also, in the days following the experiment, children who had the possibility of a reward dedicated less time to their drawings. The offer of an **extrinsic reward** for work that **was** interesting to the children made them **lose their intrinsic motivation to draw** in just a few days.

The motivational consequences of intrinsic variables, like purpose, and external variables, like money or recognition, are clear. Other interesting researches on these topics come from a series of studies by Belgian and American universities, where participants were chosen to get involved in learning, exercising or healthy eating activities, and were informed that the process would help them reach a certain goal[10]. For some participants, the goals were **having financial success, becoming more physically attractive and gaining higher status. For others, the goals were personal growth, getting involved with a group of people, and improving health.**

In these studies, results revealed that when tasks are related to **extrinsic** motivators, people's performance and persistence are worse. These scientists found that connecting their work to extrinsic motivators made people process the necessary information to complete tasks more **superficially**, showing difficulty seeing what they do as whole. So they are **less flexible** and have **difficulty concentrating** on the task.

This is why you must always concentrate on increasing the weight of the good variables of your motivation. Having **intrinsic motivators** driving your choices is essential to perform well at work and lead a happy life. One of the easiest ways to find this intrinsic motivation in what you do—especially if you're just starting to change the way you think—is to involve your **family** in giving meaning to your work. You can, for example, determine that your purpose is to **ensure financial safety to your spouse, a good school for your children, good health in old age to your mother, a good example for your grandchildren, and financial help to your siblings when they need it**. If you're in a leadership position at your company, it's important to make it clear to your team that their work gives each other **personal and professional growth, a better society, positive connection with coworkers and clients, as well as well-being to each other's families**.

PURPOSE AND YOUR HEALTH

Having a purpose in life and work isn't beneficial only to your motivation and happiness. Dr. Patricia Boyle and her colleagues from the Rush University Medical Center found that **having a purpose** substantially reduces the chances of **Alzheimer**[11]. This study involved 246 senior citizens and showed that, despite the disease's damage to the brain, those who reported having purpose in life showed better cognitive function than the others. If that wasn't enough for you to understand the importance of having and understanding purpose, a study that lasted 14 years and followed 6 thousand people concluded that **people with purpose live longer**[12]. This pattern was found among young people, adults and the elderly, which surprised scientists. Patrick Hill from Carleton University, one of the paper's authors, reports that having a direction in life may help us live longer, regardless of **when** we find this direction.

But perhaps the most significant finding on the effects of having more direction in life is that **having a purpose changes the expression of your genes**. A study conducted by renowned researcher Barbara Fredrickson, whom you'll meet in more detail later on, showed that the genes of people who reported a deep sense of purpose in life showed **less expression** for inflammation and **higher levels** of antivirus and antibodies[13]. It's impressive that even the way you face your work has consequences, activating or deactivating certain genes, increasing or reducing your chances of getting sick. Steven Cole, Fredrickson's co-author, mentioned that every participant had surprisingly similar levels of positive emotions—feeling equally well. But although the emotional state of both groups was similar, their genomes responded very differently. In an interview for the UCLA website, Cole said that **feeling good** and **doing good** are interpreted differently by our genome[14].

This sense of life purpose creates the desired *eudaimonic happiness*, which is long-lasting but not always enjoyable right away. For example, when you're a part of a big project at school that will bring large benefits to your life and others, although you're very tired and the work isn't exactly pleasurable, you can work all night and still find it in you to wake up at 6 a.m. the next day—your purpose keeps you **motivated** and feeling a **different** kind of happiness.

It's of utmost importance that you seek your purpose in life and work today: your motivation, happiness and health will thank you!

CORPORATE PURPOSE

Just because people can find purpose **by themselves**, it doesn't mean that companies are exempt of their responsibility of motivating employees—quite the opposite. Researchers from Southampton University, in England, found that working in **a place with purpose** makes people 13% more productive[15]. Today, for many companies, having a purpose is no longer just marketing, it's become a **mission**.

Swedish toothbrush manufacturer The Humble Co. and American manufacturer Smile Squared, for example, give one of their products to a child in need for every purchase. Figs, a surgical apparel manufacturer, donates one hospital kit to less fortunate countries for every kit they sell. The founders of Warby Parker, after finding that high quality glasses are extremely expensive because **one single** company owns or licenses most brands we know, decided to sell their products for a fair price, donating one pair of glasses for each pair sold. Donating soccer balls to children in need for every sale is the business of One World Play Project. Bixbee donates backpacks to children in need for every unit sold. Better World Books has donated over 24 million books using the same system. Gloves, scarves and hats are sold by Twice as Warm, with the intention of making donations to people in need for every sale. Every bar of soap sold by Pacha Soap Co. is another donated to someone in need. Besides, the company also builds water wells in communities without access to the most basic human necessity. "Giving poverty the boot" is the slogan of Roma Boots, founded by Romanian Samuel Bistrian. The company sells rainboots and donates them to orphaned and needy children in the same "one for one" model, with a mission to donate one million boots by 2020. Building water wells in impoverished communities is what moves Jonas Umbrellas, an umbrella retail company. The company chose water as their donation because one child dies every 21 seconds from problems related to the lack of sewage systems, and because over 748 million people in the world don't have access to clean, treated water. American bank Aspiration not only charges lower fees and offers more profitable investments compared to other large banks, it also donates 10% of their revenue to charity. It's not only people who benefit from companies with purpose, but animals as well. Bogo Bowl, for example, has the mission to provide food for sheltered dogs, donating one bag of dog food for every bag sold. And if you wish to purchase products like these and many others that create a more sustainable world, e-commerce platform Earth Hero has the purpose of only selling products by companies who are seriously committed to our planet.

The business model of many of these companies, known as "one for one", was pioneered by Toms—a shoe manufacturer that donates one pair for each pair sold. Toms later started looking for new problems in the world that could be solved by their business. So, it started selling sunglasses to help people in need who couldn't afford them, even helping those who needed ophthalmological testing and surgery. Today, Toms also sells backpacks, bags and coffee, respectively converted into educator counseling to prevent school bullying, midwife training for the safe delivery of babies in places with little medical attention, and drinking water to impoverished communities.

Many of these companies were **born** with a different purpose than most. But we must ask: are they profitable? After all, a company is supposed to be profitable, right? This is true **in part**, because just like people **die** if they don't produce antibodies, companies **die** if they don't profit. This doesn't mean that **people's life purpose is to produce antibodies, just as we can't say that a company's purpose is to be profitable**.

Companies exist, first and foremost, to fulfill a need of society.

Some go even further, fulfilling a need and helping those less fortunate have opportunities. After all, pairs of shoes, toothbrushes and bars of soap are not just products, but **platforms** that give people conditions to study, not miss school days, have higher self-esteem and better hygiene and health. For companies that fulfill their role in society brilliantly, **profit is but a consequence**, a result that makes them fight for their purpose even harder.

As we've seen, money motivates people to act, but those that come to work for the money also leave their jobs because of it. Now, those that come to work for the **impact** generated in society are faithful to the cause and are extremely dedicated to their tasks. I see a similar reality in the work I do with startups. Many founders are obsessed with the goal of turning their companies into **unicorns**, so they replace the intrinsic motivation of building a company that could make a big impact in society for financial motivation. A successful startup isn't necessarily a unicorn—one that's worth over US$ 1 bi—but one that **delivers to society the value it set out to build**, one that **solves the problem that inspired its creation**.

Having a purpose larger than money is a choice that both people and companies should make.

But the benefits of choosing purpose in life and work don't end here. They offer an even bigger advantage, because they reach another **crucial** factor for motivation.

AUTONOMY AND THE HUMAN BEING

Dutton and Wrzesniewski emphasize in their article that motivation caused by Job Crafting originates in the necessity of feeling some sort of control over an individual's own tasks. From the moment cleaners saw purpose in what they did—helping patients get cured—it brought new meaning to their work, making them feel like they had more **autonomy**. After all, if the role of a cleaner is to help people get cured, it's **completely under their control to do their best for that to happen.** When you change your way of thinking about the purpose of your work, your feeling of freedom automatically changes, creating very positive results for your motivation. For years, scientist from all over the world have been finding evidence that **autonomy** is one of the pillars of human motivation. It's the feeling of being **in control** of your life, of having options, of knowing you have **freedom of choice.** This factor is so important to our motivation that the lack of it can create catastrophic consequences.

In a scientific experiment that illustrates this issue, researchers Ellen Langer, from Harvard University, and Judith Rodin, from Yale University, separated residents of a nursing home into two groups[16]. Every study participant received new potted plants: the first group was told to **personally** take care of their plants, while the second group was told the nursing home team would take care of them. After a few months personally caring for their plants, members of the first group reported feeling happier, were assessed as more active by the team of nurses, and dedicated more time to entertaining activities such as watching movies, participating in contests and talking to others. But these weren't the only consequences: months after the experiment, researchers were surprised to find that 30% of members of the second group had **died**, against only 15% of members of the group that had the **autonomy** to take care of their plants. This example, as tragic as it is, illustrates that the feeling of autonomy is crucial for human beings.

One study that made a lot of noise in the scientific community is another proof of that. New York University and Stony Brook University researchers put students to perform tasks that required high concentration, then, all of a sudden, a loud and uncomfortable noise could be heard in the classroom[17]. Having difficulty concentrating, students began to make mistakes, their heartrate and blood pressure blew up, and many started sweating. However, some participants were given access to **a button** they could **press** to stop the noise. These participants were calmer and made less mistakes. The curious thing, however, is that **none of them pressed the button**! This shows that the simple **feeling** of having **some control** over the noise made them automatically perform better. Autonomy trumps stress!

Renowned scientist Martin Seligman, from the University of Pennsylvania, spent most of his life studying the phenomenon of *learned helplessness*, and, along with colleague Steven Maier, made some of the most significant findings in the history of positive psychology[18]. Let's say the goal you were given at work is too high, and even dedicating enormous effort the entire month, you're not able to achieve it. The second month, you dedicate **even more** in the hopes of reaching that goal, working even longer than usual, but you fail again. The third month, you put in **extreme dedication**, sacrificing time with your family, working late at night and weekends, but can't reach your goal once again. The fourth month, you fall into learned helplessness: **you understand you have no control over your goal**. From then on, you start assuming that no matter how much effort you put in, it'll never be enough to reach your goal. You give up on it and start making less effort, as you lost hope of a positive future. One danger of learned helplessness is that, because you've been conditioned to give up on your goals due to a sequence of failures, you have no motivation to even dedicate to more realistic goals that could be reached.

From 1967 to the early 2000s, Seligman and Maier believed that learned helplessness was built after an individual went through a prolonged period of difficulty. But in the early 2000s, Maier and other scientists began making new discoveries on that phenomenon and analyzing learned helplessness from a different angle. A series of new studies were conducted until, in 2016, Maier and Seligman published all of their revised findings in *Psychological Review*, surprisingly revealing that they were wrong about the causes of learned helplessness[19]. The scientists said that helplessness is a part of the **original configuration** of human beings after being through long periods of hardships; so it wasn't **learned**, but **inherited** from our species' evolution. If you feel like it's impossible to reach a certain goal after a given time trying, the original configuration of your brain makes you **stop trying**, aiming to not spend your body's energy unnecessarily.

Maier and Seligman revealed that, in fact, people **learn** to feel **out of control**, leading them to feel helpless and give up on efforts. Along with other scientists, they even found the exact brain circuit activated by helplessness, which Seligman lovingly named *the hope circuit*. Besides the numerous possibilities brought forth by these data, such as the development of more efficient medication and treatment to deal with depressive episodes, the best part is the finding that **it's not suffering that leads to helplessness**, but the feeling that **you don't have control over your fate**.

It's interesting to note that, in this experiment, students that felt like they could control the noise kept calm and performed better than those who learned that they had no control—despite working conditions for both groups being the same: under the influence of a terrible noise. This is just another consequence of the feeling of lacking autonomy: loss of hope in a better future.

Early on in life, we experience the need to be in control of our decisions, to have autonomy over what we do. After learning to eat by herself, a child will feel irritated if her parents try to feed her or take away her cutlery. Similarly, many people prefer to have control of the steering wheel instead of letting other people drive. Many insist on being present for every meeting at work, in their communities or at school, so they feel like they control their fate. Situations are common where people want others to perform tasks the way they would do it, in addition to the numerous cases of professionals that condescendingly state that if they weren't there, their workplace wouldn't function, because they're living the illusion that they control their team's fate. Having control over our fate is a tremendous motivational force. We are born, we grow, and we die wanting to control the several aspects of our existence.

A lack of autonomy can cause sometimes irreparable damage to human beings. However, as you can imagine, feeling in control generates extremely positive results for people and companies. A group of Chinese, American and Canadian researchers showed, in a study, that employees with feelings of autonomy over their lunch break were less tired at the end of the day compared to those who didn't have such feelings[20]. In an article published in 2017, researcher Daniel Wheatly from Birmingham University analyzed over 20 thousand people and concluded that employees with autonomy reported more well-being and satisfaction at work[21].

"High levels of control over tasks and schedules have the potential to generate significant benefits for the employee, which was evident from the reported levels of well-being.", said Wheatley.

The data for this research showed, yet, that women value more autonomy of their working hours and working from home, while men are more impacted by tasks, work pace and order. In this same perspective, Peter Warr, organizational psychologist and professor at Sheffield Univeristy, said in his research that there are six main factors to creating a workplace capable of inspiring employees[22]. Among these factors is the **opportunity to have**

personal control, in the sense that employees need freedom to solve the company's problems as they see fit, as well as to use their skills and predict the results of their actions.

Finding purpose in work and life are ways to **increase the feeling of autonomy**. And the best part is that this search depends on your own efforts only. But it's up to companies to find ways to not only awaken the feeling of purpose in employees, making changes to their corporate values, but also to give them more autonomy. Employees feel a sense of autonomy when the company gives them the freedom to choose to arrive at the office between 8 and 10 a.m., to have lunch when they judge best, to choose where to eat, to make as many breaks as they want, to present their opinions on strategic issues without fear, to inform which flights and hotels they prefer for a business trip, to choose their own teams in projects, to dress the way they want (as long as it's appropriate for that industry), to choose their own desks, to work at home a few days of the week or to choose their vacation time. Small interventions within a company can generate big results.

If you're still not convinced of the benefits of autonomy in the workplace, allow me to present a final study, conducted in 2006 by Cornell University and Babson College researchers[23].

Christopher Collins and Matthew Allen studied 323 small businesses varying in size from 8 to 600 employees, and found that when an environment of autonomy was created, there were **higher revenues** and **lower turnover rates** compared to controlling environments. Another finding was that companies aiming to grow benefited even more when they created a workplace with more autonomy, and showed revenues 12% higher and turnover rates 14% lower than companies that exerted control over employees. But here is the best part: companies with more than 50 employees were especially benefitted by autonomy, reaching a revenue growth almost **three times higher** than that of controlling companies and a 13% lower turnover rate.

Collins and Allen define that companies with environments of autonomy are those that offer employees a big share of freedom to monitor their own performance, trusting from day one that they will finish their tasks without the need for direct supervision. On the opposite side, controlling companies are those that closely monitor daily activities, give managers—not employees—the responsibility of controlling the execution of tasks and the work schedule, and use several explicit rules and procedures to control the actions of employees. These brief definitions help us understand why some people love their jobs, while others hate them.

WHAT MASLOW NEVER PROVED

After more than 45 years of scientific research, Richard Ryan and Edward Deci, from the University of Rochester, are known in the scientific community as the **biggest authorities** in the motivational field. Their research changed the course of this field, but unfortunately not all professionals—including professors—know about their findings. The result of this situation is notable in companies and universities that still apply dated concepts to determine how human motivation works, such as *Maslow's hierarchy of needs*[24].

Surprisingly to many, Maslow's theory has **no scientific validity**, because the psychologist never collected enough data to prove his observations on the mechanics of motivation. In 1976, more than 30 years after Maslow's theory came out, Lawrence Bridwell and Mahmoud Wahba reviewed every article by every scientist who tested it until then, finding **no evidence** of a hierarchy of needs, much less of the five motivational levels proposed by Maslow[25]. Testing Maslow's theory failed mainly because his vague and incomplete ideas are difficult (or impossible) to measure[26].

In 2016, Ken Sheldon from the University of Missouri and two of his colleagues published a paper that analyzed work satisfaction, commitment, financial safety, well-being and other characteristics of over 15 thousand Russian workers, evaluating Maslow's view that, in order to activate and achieve higher motivational levels, people should first have their basic needs met[27]. The study found no evidence of this, but found a weak and statistically significant correlation between meeting basic needs and expressing high motivational needs. In sum, the paper shows that high motivational needs **are not dependent** on basic needs, but they can really be **more expressive** when those have been met.

What drew the researchers' attention, however, was finding that an **inverse** order of needs could be more important: when **high** motivational needs were met, they could **provide the resources** people need to face and solve their **most basic** motivational needs, such as safety and money. This conclusion was only possible, however, because Sheldon and his colleagues' study replaced the high motivational needs proposed by Maslow with the **psychological** needs proven by Richard Ryan and Edward Deci's research. If correlations to support Maslow's theory were lacking or statistically weak, that was not the case for Ryan and Deci's theory, proven to be highly important for the motivation of the workers studied

SELF-DETERMINATION THEORY

The biggest contribution of Ryan and Deci to science was **Self-Determination Theory**, which appeared when the researchers started testing the effects of extrinsic rewards on intrinsic motivation[28]. In 1971, Deci published the article that originated a series of other researches he conducted along with Ryan[29]. In this study, Deci selected two groups of students to solve extremely simple puzzles for three days, under the following conditions::

	DAY 1	DAY 2	DAY 3
EXPERIMENTAL	NO REWARD	WITH REWARD	NO REWARD
CONTROL	NO REWARD	NO REWARD	NO REWARD

See the difference? While the control group would perform the task receiving no reward during the three days, the experimental group would not receive a reward on Days 1 and 3, but would receive US$ 1 for each puzzle solved on Day 2.

Deci timed the groups while they worked on the tasks. He considered that the **longer** each group worked, the **higher** their motivation.

On Day 1, both groups showed a lot of dedication to the task. On Day 2, however, the experimental group showed **higher** dedication than the control group, because of the financial reward they could receive. On Day 3, the groups acted as Deci expected: knowing they would work without a reward, the experimental group **dedicated a lot less time to the task**, while the control group **kept working with the same motivation**.

In a new experiment, Deci found a similar behavior when the number of students who participated in the third session of the study (unpaid) fell expressively compared to the second session (paid), while the number of students participating in the control group **increased** from the second to the third session[30]. A few more years of research led Deci and Ryan to conclude that humans are:

1. Naturally dedicated;
2. Intrinsically motivated;
3. Mastery-oriented.

Besides, Ryan and Deci still showed that these traits are inherent to human nature, that is, **they don't need to be learned**[31].

Right now, it can occur to you that **you** have these traits, but **other people** that you know don't, so let me remind you of the extrinsic incentives bias—**what you assume about yourself is true for other people as well**! It's a mistake to think you have good behaviors while other people don't.

Notice that, in these experiments, the control groups didn't need **any** incentive to work, or even to work **more**: they did so **naturally**. This proves our naturally dedicated, intrinsically motivated and improvement-oriented traits. But what happened when an **extrinsic** incentive came into play? After being influence by a reward, the students **lost** those traits!

On the cold afternoon I spent at Meliora Hall talking to Ryan and Deci at the University of Rochester, they both explained to me that financial incentives undermine intrinsic motivation because they change the way people explain their motives for performing a given task. When people are initially engaged in pleasurable work, they're motivated by a sense of **choice and autonomy**. In that case, if asked why they're working hard, they'll say something like "because it's fun" or "because I like it". But once they're paid to work in the same task, when asked why, they'll respond "for money" or "to show others how good I am". This is because incentives encourage people to **alternate their motivational circuits from intrinsic to extrinsic**. This way, those who are motivated by rewards or recognition will hardly have a sense of **full satisfaction** with the task they're performing, because such extrinsic motivators distract them from the fun, interesting, and challenging aspects of it.

Notice that motivation is **highly influenced by environment**. That's why it's increasingly important for executives, parents and leaders in general to take care of their motivational strategies in order to preserve people's natural—and amazing—traits. From the moment companies understand that their employees care only for themselves, avoid work, are lazy, do nothing more than what's necessary, want to stay in the comfort zone and hate their workplace, managers begin to use strategies to increase control, usually through extrinsic motivators such as incentives and punishments. With this, managers end up **creating**—instead of solving—these problems. Strategies based on incentives and punishments end up directing employees to change their motivational circuits, which forces them to focus only on the tasks for which they'll receive these incentives and not be punished. Thus, they begin to see their work as a **job** and perform worse, resist change, cause conflict with their colleagues, not work harder than absolutely necessary, seek to "save their own" instead of collaborating with the team and enter the comfort zone.

This process leads managers to believe that their perceptions about employee motivation are correct, which increases their control in the workplace even more, causing them to increasingly believe that incentives and punishments are the only way to mobilize employees. In the long term, insisting on this strategy leads to a high turnover rate, low engagement, increased labor lawsuits and certainly worse financial results for the company. "It's a self-fulfilling prophecy," Ryan explained during our conversation. "People may have the intelligence and skills they need to show excellent performance at work, but if the environment doesn't allow them to use these traits, they lose motivation," added Deci when mentioning the importance of creating an appropriate motivational environment within companies.

Ryan and Deci use two models of motivation as the basis of their Self-Determination Theory: **autonomous** and **controlled**. **Autonomous motivation** awakens feelings of **interest**, **pleasure** and **value**. It's fueled by the feeling of being engaged in an activity out of **free choice**, so that it's done with immense **self-will**. On the other hand, **controlled motivation** causes an individual to perform an activity in order to receive a **reward** or avoid **punishment**, that is, this model of motivation is generated by feelings of **obligation and pressure**, in which one works **with no freedom or self-will**. Ryan and Deci have found that, when an individual performs a task **autonomously**, their performance, well-being and engagement are higher than when the task is performed with the feeling of control.

This theory also takes into account that the human being has **three basic and universal psychological needs:**

1. Competence
2. Relationships
3. Autonomy

In the absence of these factors, people are never able to achieve optimal well-being and performance, and suffer future psychological consequences. "In order to be happy, a person needs, first and foremost, to have their psychological needs met," said Ryan. Finally, the theory presents two sets of autonomous motivation—the intrinsic and the extrinsic. Intrinsic motivation is that achieved through a task considered interesting and pleasurable. On the other hand, extrinsic motivation happens when the individual performs a task for another type of interest. The scientists demonstrate, however, that there's a powerful way to turn extrinsic motivation into intrinsic motivation, although it requires a lot of effort. For this, they must think about the value that the activity produces, and integrate that value as part of themselves[32]. In this sense, we can't help but think about how Job Crafting helps transform extrinsic motivation into intrinsic, that is, turning a job into a calling. It's interesting how autonomy and purpose are closely linked, isn't it?

I asked Ryan and Deci why, like other scientists, they were so discreet and didn't go to great lengths to spread their findings to the corporate world, consulting with companies, producing social media videos or giving lectures. They replied that, although they knew that such actions would bring them a large and immediate financial return, their role was to **conduct scientific research**, which is slow and not profitable, but which in the long run leave a **legacy**. Here's a great example of purpose at work.

TWO CONFLICTING FORCES

One of the biggest difficulties I have faced since the launch of my first book, *The Incredible Science of Sales*, is convincing business professionals that **commissions generate worse results**. And this is easily explained by **autonomy**. The commission system creates the illusion that a salesperson has full autonomy in the construction of their salary, that their results depend on effort only. In line with that belief is that of sales managers—the first to speak about "the salesperson's salary only depends on themselves". At the same time, salespeople's preference for variable wages will generate less happiness in their lives because, as you found from some studies mentioned before, the relation between money and motivation tends to lead to worse performance, which will certainly create a feeling of **incompetence**— that basic motivational need discovered by Ryan and Deci. And because not even salespeople know why, despite the possibility of earning a high salary, they can't perform well, they'll continue to act according to the belief that they can build their own salary, until they can no longer suffer from their failures and enter into a negative spiral of thoughts.

Martin Seligman reveals that, in situations where we experience negative emotions frequently, our inability to deal with and overcome these difficulties can be explained by the three P's: **personalization, penetration** and **permanence**[33]. **Personalization** is when an individual attributes the negative event to themselves, saying that they are to blame for what happened, when the cause is often something external. **Penetration** is the individual's perception that this negative event will impact **all areas of their lives**: financial, personal, professional, family, etc. But **permanence** is the feeling that this negative situation **will never change**. It's because of this last P that it's so difficult to deal with depression, because the mind of someone in this condition is not capable of visualizing a future different from the moment experienced, causing the feeling that things will **never** improve and draining the forces needed to get out of this state.

It's not just salespeople who suffer from these conflicting forces. Every time we put money first in our lives, because of the sense of freedom it brings us, we leave our families and friends in the background, resources that would **truly** bring us closer to the happiness and motivation we need to succeed. We want the sense of autonomy we get from money, but we don't know the negative consequences that this feeling produces in us.

In our daily choices, we also believe that the more choices of restaurants, books, clothes, cosmetics, cell phones, cars, or fruits we have, the happier we'll be because of the sense of **autonomy** that having choices provides. However, researchers like Sheena Iyengar and Barry Schwartz argue that quite the opposite is true: the **fewer** options we have, the more satisfied—and happy—we are with what we choose[34]. You have certainly been to a restaurant with a very extensive menu, which made you take 30 minutes to choose a meal, and when the dish was served, you certainly though: "Why did I choose this? That one must be a lot better!" Iyengar explains in her research that the greater the variety of products we are exposed to, the greater the chance that we'll immediately **regret** what we've chosen, which causes a feeling of sadness. Too much autonomy can **be good for our motivation in the short term, but bad for our overall happiness**.

In cases like commissioned sales, we should put aside our sense of autonomy in the short term to think of the **long-term** benefits our choices bring us. A salesperson with a high fixed salary may even lose their sense of autonomy in the construction of their own salary, but they'll **gain** a sense of autonomy for being able to **plan** the purchase of property, for example, without the uncertainty of not knowing whether they'll be able to pay their mortgage due to the ups and downs of commissions. This pay model allows the salesperson to know that, regardless of their short-term result, they'll earn a good salary, capable of motivating them in the long run. Earning a high fixed salary also makes them happier because, as you may remember, having financial security reduces the number of negative emotions people experience.

Ryan and Deci's researches are invaluable to society, especially as they reveal that, in order to achieve good performance and experience a sense of competence, the **type** of motivation is more important than the **quantity**. The evidence is clear that autonomy is a basic motivational necessity in human beings, and that one way to achieve it is to seek a **purpose** in what we do. But to fully understand motivation, we still need to explore the importance of competence and relationships.

PART 2

RECOGNITION

CHAPTER 4

Negative, Stressed, Sick and with Fear of Missing Out

NATURALLY NEGATIVE

Imagine you're in the jungle. You haven't eaten in three days—you're starving. During one of your morning walks, you find an apple tree, with only **one** apple remaining. The anticipation of a positive experience makes your mouth water, imagining the pleasure of eating that fruit. So you jump and pick that priceless apple. When you're about to take the first bite, a sound coming from a nearby tree interrupts you. What should you do? To make a decision, you must consider your positive emotion—"This apple looks delicious and I'm starving!"—and your negative emotion—"That noise must be a tiger wanting to eat me!" Which would you choose?

This was a very common situation in the lives of our ancestors, after all, we lived in the jungle competing with all the other animals for food. So, making **quick** decisions was crucial for survival and the continuation of our species.

In a moment like that, due to the feeling of **threat** presented by the situation, you'd have a spike of the hormone cortisol in your body. Cortisol activates a response mechanism called **fight or flight**[1]. When a large amount of this hormone enters the bloodstream and fills it with glucose, your blood goes straight to your **muscles**[2], providing immediate energy for your body to face a threat or stressful situation—**fight or flight**. Under the possibility that the noise from the tree came from a tiger, your immediate reaction will certainly be to run to escape[3]. Your brain would hardly act **rationally** to face this new challenge[4]. If it did, by the time you pondered whether the noise came from a rodent or a bird, **the tiger would have already caught you**!

One of the effects of cortisol is precisely this: it helps us make a quick decision that increases our chances of survival[5]. This is why an elevation in blood cortisol levels can partially shut down a part of the brain called pre-frontal cortex[6]—responsible for planning, projecting the future, language and rational thinking—and activate a neural primitive part called the **amygdala**, whose function is to make decisions to ensure you stay alive: **take the apple and run**[7]! This hormone can also increase your heartbeat, directing more blood to your larger muscles (in preparation for fight or flight) and making you breathe faster. Consequently, oxygen in the brain is reduced so it can be supplied to other organs and muscles, reducing the brain's performance.

You have certainly felt the effects of cortisol during an argument. When tension starts to rise, people start yelling at each other, often saying things they didn't mean. When a couple fights, for example, it's common for them to not speak for hours after a conflict. If you've been in that situation, you know that in the end, it's always the same: some time later, after calming down, both parties remember what they **should** have said at the moment of a fight to win it. But why didn't they think of that during the fight? Because their cortisol levels were high, and the "rational" part of their brains—their pre-frontal cortex—was partially shut down, so **they couldn't find good arguments or be creative**.

Negative emotions can partially shut down a part of the brain responsible for creativity, narrowing the possibilities we can see. Negative emotions diminish our world view.

At first, this mechanism may not seem beneficial to humans, but it's quite the opposite: if our species was capable of making the decisions that made us be in the top of the food chain today, it was because of this mechanism, that releases cortisol in situations where we need quick energy. Today, cases are rare of people living in the same conditions as our ancestors, but we suffer from different threats, like losing our job and not being able to pay our bills, or having our car stolen. Despite the huge difference in the severity and number of threats felt by cavemen and modern humans, our primitive defense mechanism still works as if we lived in the wild. Because millions of years ago we had to stay 100% alert to what could go **wrong**—stepping on a snake, being attacked by a panther on a tree, hearing a strange noise in the proximities—we're **naturally negative**.

To this day, we continue to stay more alert to negative things in our environment than positive ones, a phenomenon science calls ***negativity bias***[8]. Some studies reiterate this by showing that the number of emotions considered negative outweighs that of positive emotions by, on average, three or four to one[9]. When you get your child's grade report, for example, what grades get your attention, good or bad? When you visit a news site, what headlines stand out to you, positive or negative? In companies, it's no different: there's plan A, but also plans B, C and D, in the case the first course of action doesn't go well. Generally in cases like this, companies know how to execute plans B, C and D, but have no idea what to do next if plan A is actually successful

A VIRUS IN YOUR BRAIN SOFTWARE

The human brain was **programmed** by evolution to **look for** the negative more frequently than the positive. That's why that aunt of yours that won't stop complaining—every family has one—is not **bad** person: she's simply **a person**, with a negative bias like all others. I remember when I was preparing to give a speech to over five hundred people and the venue's projector stopped working, significantly delaying the event. A young man started talking to me, and in less than five minutes told me about a friend who crashed his car against a truck and died, a crime wave in a small town nearby, corrupt politicians and, obviously, how bad the event infrastructure was. I could **choose** to stand there and talk to him longer, but at the first opportunity, I turned to another participant. This man was also **a person**. I'm sure you've been through similar situations and, in many cases, you face them every day! Yes, the world is full of humans, negative by nature.

One big problem of the cortisol hormone is how long it takes to metabolize in the body: it's **slow**[10]. That's why, when we have a negative moment with our spouse, or when we read bad news on a site, we remember these events **all day**. Negative emotions enter our body and cause long-lasting effects. Remember cortisol partially shuts down the part of the brain responsible for creativity and argumentation? That's why you only remember things you should have said in a conflict **long after** it happened. Small loads of cortisol don't cause major health problems, and can in fact make you act! In the morning, for example, your levels of cortisol are higher precisely to give you the energy to get out of bed and start your day. The problem is when these loads of the stress hormone increase in frequency and intensity—we can say stress is related to several conditions that cause premature death[11].

In a study that analyzed the impact of stress on 1,552 twin sisters, for example, it was found that when one sister feels more stress, her telomeres—the DNA "caps" that protect the extremities of our chromosomes—appear to be **seven years older**[12]. As we grow old, our old cells die and give place to new ones. Each time they divide to form new cells, we lose a portion of our telomeres, so they get shorter over the years. Telomere shortening is associated with premature death and a higher change of heart attack. Besides, this reduction in telomeres causes our new cells to form without complete genetic information, which makes them get older and die faster. Without telomeres, we lose the capacity of producing healthy cells. Stress, therefore, reduces the survival time of our cells, consequently shortening our telomeres **faster** than normal. Let's take Harvard's Michael Norton's study, where people were asked to share their money with a stranger. The researcher found that those dedicated to sharing more equally had lower levels of cortisol. I hope that makes it clear just how important is generosity.

As other studies have also shown, knowing that there really is a relation between stress levels and accelerated aging is crucial for you to make the best **choices** in life[13]. These choices can even program your brain differently, ridding it of the negativity virus that comes with our factory settings.

FIGHTING THE FEAR TO LOSE

The dangers of the ***negativity bias*** are evident not only when we talk to our family and coworkers, but also when we turn on the TV, listen to the news on the radio and visit news portals online. This evolutionary desire to **look for** negative things, however, has a price. In 2015, researchers Michelle Gielan, from the University of Pennsylvania, and Shawn Achor, from Harvard University, partnered up with American newspaper *Huffington Post* to study the impact that negative news have on people's lives[14]. Researchers observed that watching only **three minutes** of negative news in the morning makes participants increase their chances of saying they had a bad day by 27%.

In addition to making people feel bad, as opposed to what the media "thinks", negative news aren't enjoyable to spectators or readers. A research done by one of the world's biggest authorities in viral marketing, Wharton School's Jonah Berger, in partnership with colleague Katherine Milkman, reached the conclusion that negative news were **shared less** than other types of articles online[15]. Another research revealed, yet, that products announced along with negative news had a very reduced chance of being purchased[16].

Michelle Gielan leads a movement called ***transformative journalism***, that fights for the reduction of sensationalist and negative news, precisely for the terrible impact they have on people's lives. I believe every country should be proud to have a movement like that, as we're all flooded with TV shows that focus on the negative. Gielan states that it appears that journalism is in its teenage years, desperately asking for attention in any way it can.

With all the technological advances in the past few years, which facilitated the way we consume content, many people simply can't stop craving news every few minutes. This sort of addiction has been concerning researchers all over the world, and it's been called **FOMO** (Fear Of Missing Out)[17]. Fear of missing out on important news is a big villain to well-being, not to mention work productivity. The good news is that there are strategies to fight it, you just have to make the right choices. One of them is to keep your phone away from the workplace, ideally in a different room, in order to reduce the impulse of checking it every instant. There are even numerous apps in the market that can be used to block internet access for as long as you want, in order to fight the temptation of checking news sites. You can also turn off all of those automatic notifications that make your phone blink like a Christmas tree. In the beginning, as with any other change, this habit will be hard to form, but with time, not using your phone or not browsing aimlessly online will become natural.

> **Don't worry: if something really important happens in the world, you'll know! In fact, unless you're a journalist, you definitely don't have to be the *first* to know!**

However, you should know that the biggest downside to this mechanism of staying tuned for every negative event is a dangerous **imbalance** between positive and negative emotions. In fact, most of us experience **positive** emotions much **less** than what's necessary in order to have a **good life**. Shall we find out how important that is?

CHAPTER 5

The Advantages of Positive Emotions

THE CONSTRUCTION OF A POSITIVE BRAIN, THE FORMULA OF HAPPINESS, SOCIAL CONTAGION AND THE EMPATHY NEURONS

As opposed to negative emotions, which release cortisol, **positive emotions** have a different effect on your body. Many types of positive emotions release **oxytocin**, known for being the happiness hormone. Oxytocin slows down our heartbeat and allows more oxygen into the brain, increasing our capacity to **trust**, **collaborate** and **relate** to others[1]. The happiness hormone also lowers the impact of negative emotions on our well-being, as it reduces the amygdala's reaction and helps regulate emotions, making it more difficult for us to lose control of them[2]. Besides, oxytocin **increases our attention to positive facts** that occur in our daily lives.

This hormone, however, has a slight flaw: it's metabolized in a very **short** time[3]. As opposed to cortisol, which is metabolized slowly, oxytocin is metabolized very quickly in the body, which amusingly confirms the saying "a poor man's joy is short-lived"—which is only partially true, as a rich man's oxytocin behaves exactly the same.

Now that you know how cortisol and oxytocin act differently in your body, what's your conclusion? Yes, that to be **happy** you must experience positive emotions **much more frequently** than negative ones. However, if negative emotions were important for the survival of our species, what was the role of positive ones? What did they provide other than hormonal changes?

This was the question that renowned researcher Barbara Fredrickson, from the University of North Carolina, wanted to answer. And after decades of research, she made some of the most significant discoveries in the history of positive psychology until then, one of them in partnership with Christine Branigan, in an experiment with 104 people[4]. In it, a few participants were led to feel **serenity** or **admiration** (positive emotions), while others were led to feel **anger** or **fear** (negative emotions). The control group was led to neutral emotions. Next, researchers **proposed** an activity: **according to what you're feeling, organize a list of what you want to do now**. Results: the group that experienced **positive emotions** made a longer list compared to others—positivity increased their capacity to see possibilities. Experiencing positive emotions **increased the motivation** of these participants, since they felt the desire to act more than the others.

In this same study, Fredrickson and Branigan presented a few images and asked participants to inform which of the two images in the bottom row were more similar to the one on the top.

You see, the lower-right image is also formed by squares. However, the lower-left image resembles the top image **as a whole**—a set of shapes forming a triangle. Will all participants arrive to this same conclusion—that the top image is a triangle formed by squares? Are all people capable of seeing the images as a whole and connecting them?

Scientists found that this vision of the big picture depended on the emotional state of an individual at the time of the experiment. When presenting several images similar to the triangle of squares, and asking participants to point out their similarities with other figures, those that were injected with positivity **before** the task demonstrated a higher probability of making associations using figures as a whole—their field of vision had **broadened**. Those injected with neutrality or negativity could not see the relationship between the figures as a whole—their field of vision had **narrowed**.

In a new study, Fredrickson put facial sensors on participants to monitor the electrical signals of two muscles: the **zygomatic** muscle, responsible for raising the corners of our mouths when we smile, and the **eye orbicular**, which forms the famous "crow's feet" in the corner of our eyes when the smile is **real**[5]. Sensors were able to monitor even extremely light electric signals, captured long before these muscles gained strength to create any facial expression. Fredrickson and colleagues found that the **joint activation of these muscles predicts higher attention of participants in subsequent tests**. Something amazing happens when you're smiling—you get more motivated, notice more possibilities, can see things as a whole and stay more alert afterwards.

These studies gained fame, and other scientists tried to replicate them in their labs. At Brandeis University, for example, a group of researchers made the participants of a study look at groups of images in a computer while a very sophisticated camera captured their eye movements sixty times per second[6]. Before the experiment began, a group of participants received a small bag of chocolates—a way to evoke **a positive emotion**—while the other group wasn't so lucky. Obviously, researchers told the lucky group to only eat their chocolate at the end of the study, which all of them did. The set to which participants were exposed always consisted of one central image and two peripheral images. By monitoring the eye movements of both groups, scientists confirmed that the eyes of the participants that received chocolates **moved more** than the other group. Besides, participants influenced by positivity fixed their eyes for **longer** on the peripheral images. **Positive emotions expand our world view**, make us **see more detail**, **reveal more possibilities**.

Scientists from the University of Toronto conducted a similar study in which, in addition to monitoring the peripherical vision of participants, they applied a test to measure their creativity[7]. After learning the results of previous studies, you won't be surprised to know that the group led to feel positive emotions before the tasks showed **broader peripheral vision, as well as more creativity**.

In the 1990s, researchers from Cornell University found that doctors who received a bag of candy **before** an appointment reached a **more accurate diagnosis**, with a **lower** chance of remaining fixated on their initial ideas—remember that on your next visit to a doctor or dentist[8].

Want more examples? A group of scientists from the University of California, Berkeley, reached the conclusion that **managers who were positive** made more accurate and careful decisions, in addition to being more effective in their relationship with their subordinates[9]. Another study, made by researchers from California State University, the University of Michigan and the University of Toronto signaled that positive managers spread their positivity to their teams, resulting in **higher collaboration** between team members, as well as a reduction in the efforts necessary to complete their work[10].

Another fantastic discovery by Barbara Fredrickson happened when a group was made to experience positive emotions for five weeks in a row. As the weeks went by, the positivity of participants **increased**; they became **even** more open and saw even more possibilities[11]. And why is this relevant? The importance of this study is clear when these people go through **difficulties**. Taken by positivity, they reach **more solutions** to solve their problems, and their minds are **more open**, which helps deal with difficulties and face them more easily. Also, other studies by Fredrickson found that positive individuals **recover from trauma faster**[12]. On the other hand, someone infected by negative emotions can't find solutions for their problems, which makes the situation even worse.

Remember the three Ps found by Martin Seligman[13]? The last P is for **permanence**, that is, someone that faces frequent negative emotions starts feeling that the negative situation will **never get better**. Is it clear now why this feeling of permanence happens? **An individual, when flooded by negativity, sees fewer possibilities**, and if they don't have positive emotions "in stock", they won't have the strength needed to get out of a bad moment. Often, in cases like this, the **only** option the depressed person can see is suicide. Notice how negativity feeds **more** negativity into your life. But fortunately, positivity also feeds itself. **Which will you choose to feed yourself?**

These are not all of the benefits of positivity. Several other scientific studies prove that, by frequently experiencing positive emotions, people are **more satisfied with life**[14], **have better friendships and romantic relationships**[15], **enjoy the present more**[16], **love themselves more**[17], **have lower signs of depression, are more optimistic, understand their life purpose better, build better mental habits, have higher quality social interactions**[18], **show more resilience**[19], **have lower levels of stress-related hormones**[20], **have better immune systems**[21], **suffer less from high blood pressure**[24], **sleep better**[25], **have a lower chance of hypertension, diabetes**[26], **heart attack**[27] and, unsurprisingly, **live longer**. Not by chance, in a famous study that analyzed the contents of the diaries of 180 catholic nuns, researchers for the University of Kentucky found that those who expressed **high numbers of positive emotions** in their diaries lived, on average, **10.7 years longer** than the others, living to be an average of **93.5** years old[28].

BROADEN AND BUILD

After collecting so many scientific evidence on the benefits of positive emotions, Fredrickson named her findings the **Broaden-and-Build Theory**[29]. Positive emotions have a more important role than just keeping us happy, as they **broaden** our minds, make us more alert, uncover new possibilities, increase creativity and openness to new ideas. Over time, this frequent load of positive emotions helps us **build** physical, intellectual, social and psychological skills, increasing our resilience, reducing the impact of negative moments, improving our relationships and giving us better health. In addition to all these findings, the studies of Barbara Fredrickson have shown, also, that positive emotions had a fundamental evolutionary role for our species, since the skills built from them **increased our chances of survival** and helped us get where we are today.

> **Positive emotions are like a "workout" for the brain, making it stronger each day.**

Every time you spend your money on others, remember or write things for which you're grateful, or show recognition to someone who helped you, what you're doing is simply **increasing your load of positive emotions in life**, which allows for a series of interesting changes in building the person you'll be in the future. Remember the study by Jane Dutton and Amy Wrzesniewski with the cleaning team at a hospital[30]? The cleaners that saw their work as a **calling**, taking care with their interactions with the hospital team, patients and visitors, consequently increased their load of positive emotions and, therefore, were able to **see the impact of their work as a whole**. On the other hand, those who avoided interacting with others and didn't recognize purpose in their work saw their tasks as **limited** to just cleaning.

Many people believe that happiness is a state reached by big positive emotions, but that's not true. As we've seen from Barbara Fredrickson studies, **small** positive emotions are enough to increase and sustain happiness. Obviously, a **single** positive moment can't change your life, but the slow and steady buildup of positive emotions makes a big difference. And what are the positive emotions that bring all of those benefits? Barbara Fredrickson's evidence points to **joy, gratitude, serenity, interest, hope, pride, fun, inspiration, fascination** and **love**.

After learning bout Fredrickson's studies, many people come to the conclusion that one secret to happiness is to **increase** positive emotions and have **zero** negative emotions, but this perception, apart from being wrong, is dangerous. You may not **choose** to experience negative emotions, but they'll certainly **choose you** at some point. Remember that negative emotions are **inevitable**—no one is safe from arguing with their spouse, being mistreated by a client or coworker, being unnecessarily scolded by their boss, being yelled at by an angry driver, or being mugged. Negative emotions often help us make decisions that generate **positive** consequences on our lives, such as divorce in an abusive relationship. Negative emotions are necessary not only for our happiness, but also for our motivation, as they make us act! Later on, in Part 3, you'll see in more detail how important **negativity** is in reaching your goals. Therefore, the **combination** of **positive and negative** emotions is paramount to building happiness.

A few pages back, I mentioned that most people don't have the proper balance between their positive and negative emotions, which causes them to lead **less** happy lives. But what is the proper balance between these emotions? Is there a magic formula? The big news is that yes, there is something even **better** than that: **a mathematical formula that works like magic!** This formula is probably the most significant finding of Barbara Fredrickson's career—and certainly one of the most important in the history of positive psychology

THE HAPPINESS RATIO

In early 2003, Barbara Fredrickson received an email from Chilean consultant Marcial Losada, in which he said to have developed a mathematical model based on the Broaden-and-Build Theory. At that time, after a long career in manufacturing, Losada was retired and didn't have much experience as a scientific researcher, which intrigued Fredrickson and made her take longer than normal to respond to his email. Persisting, Losada sent Fredrickson an article he had been writing, which drew her attention immediately and a first meeting between them became inevitable. After a few hours explaining the dynamics of his mathematical models, Losada guaranteed Fredrickson that he could find the **exact** ratio between positive and negative moments that could distinguish the **corporate teams** capable of **thriving** from those that would **fail**. Sensing that such a finding could bring huge benefits to society, Fredrickson went on academic leave to dive deep into the world of dynamic systems, introduced to her by Losada. What they both found together was nothing short of **amazing**.

Losada's work during his time in manufacturing consisted in studying the traits that differentiated successful teams from low-performance teams. For that, Losada had to obtain data about how these teams behaved in different everyday decision-making moments. Thus, Losada built a special lab room where **60** corporate teams got together to develop their strategic plans. For executives, this room was nothing special, but behind mirrored glass, Losada's trained team coded the contents of **every** phrase stated by each participant of these long talks[31]. Three models of phrases were coded:

- Positivity/negativity
- Other/self
- Inquiry/advocacy

What's the tone of conversations in these three dimensions? Positive or negative? Later analyzing data on profitability, client satisfaction and evaluations from superiors, coworkers and subordinates, Losada's team was able to identify which of these 60 teams could be considered **high performance**, which could be considered **low performance**, and which had high performance in some indicators, but low in others, resulting in **medium performance**. It was at this time that the beauty of Losada's complex mathematical system appeared. Teams considered high performance showed a ratio between positive and negative moments of approximately **6:1**, while low performance teams showed ratios lower than **1:1**. Medium teams had ratios close to **2:1**.

Interactions between high performance teams had a higher frequency of **encouraging and positive phrases**; **conversations focused on the team**, on the person who had the word or the company; and **questions** to explore and investigate everyone's arguments. On the other hand, low performance groups had interactions with a high frequency of **negative, sarcastic and cynical phrases**; conversations about people **outside the group**, showing a **lack** of harmony between members; and **advocating for points of view** during arguments. In his consulting work, Losada saw that simply encouraging people to build better interactions and instructing leaders to give more positive feedback to their subordinates made team performance grow by **more than 40%**—a spectacular result in a time when companies were already satisfied with much lower increases in employee productivity[32].

Complex mathematical models as the one developed by Losada—in this case, a non-linear dynamic system—have an interesting point in common: when time data are plotted into a graph, the image of a **butterfly** appears, revealing all the complexity of the variables—a process scientist call **chaos of the system**. This chaos continues until a given point, when variables finally come together and bring balance and predictability to the chaotic system. One thing that's specific to this model of system is that small changes to **one** of the variables can have huge effects in the **fate** of the system over time. It's because of these studies that the term *butterfly effect* was coined. *Does the Flap of a Butterfly's Wing in Brazil Set off a Tornado in Texas*? was the title of the famous article published by Edward Lorenz, professor at the Massachusetts Institute of Technology (MIT) when he found the dynamics of non-linear systems studying climate conditions[33].

Using the system developed by Lorenz, Marcial Losada saw in his study that the balance between positive and negative moments during meetings would determine if this team would have high, medium or low performance. The size of the butterfly in the graph is directly conditioned to performance: high performance created tall and wide butterflies; medium created shorter and narrower butterflies; but for low performance, the data didn't form the image of a butterfly, but a sort of circle that shrunk in size over time, showing a "dead" system.

HIGH PERFORMANCE TEAMS

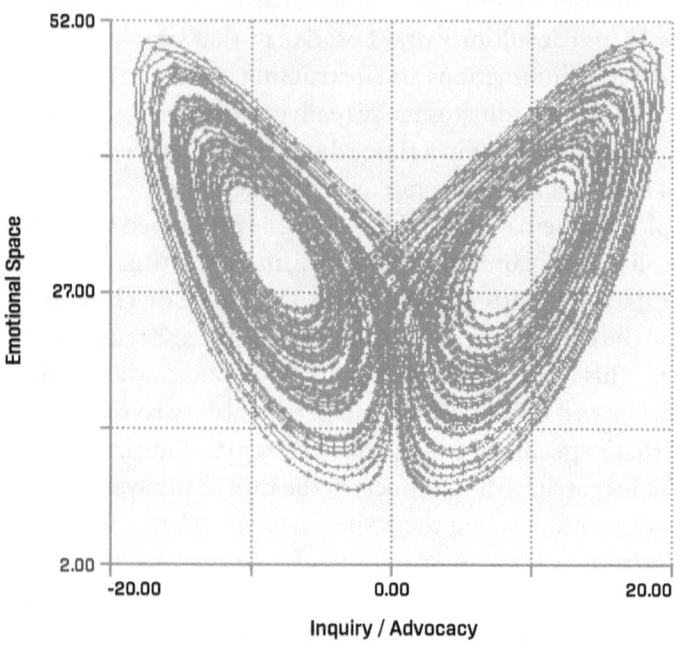

MEDIUM PERFORMANCE TEAMS

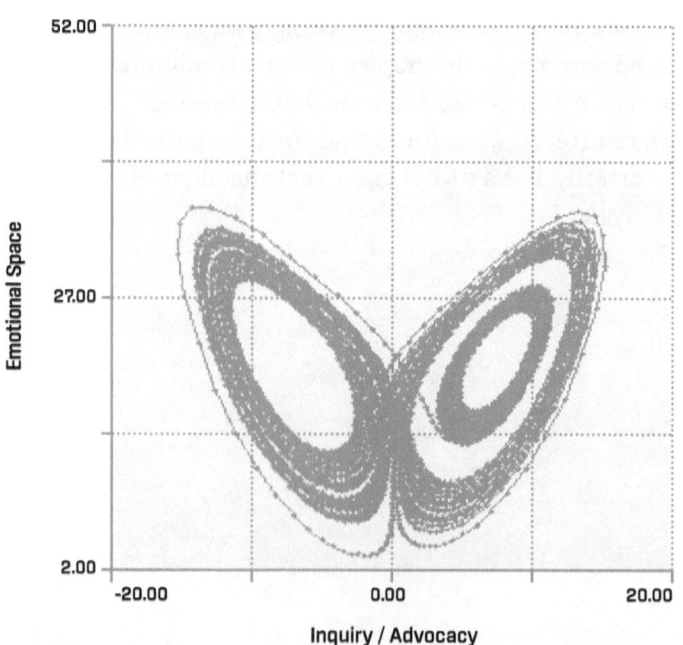

LOW PERFORMANCE TEAMS

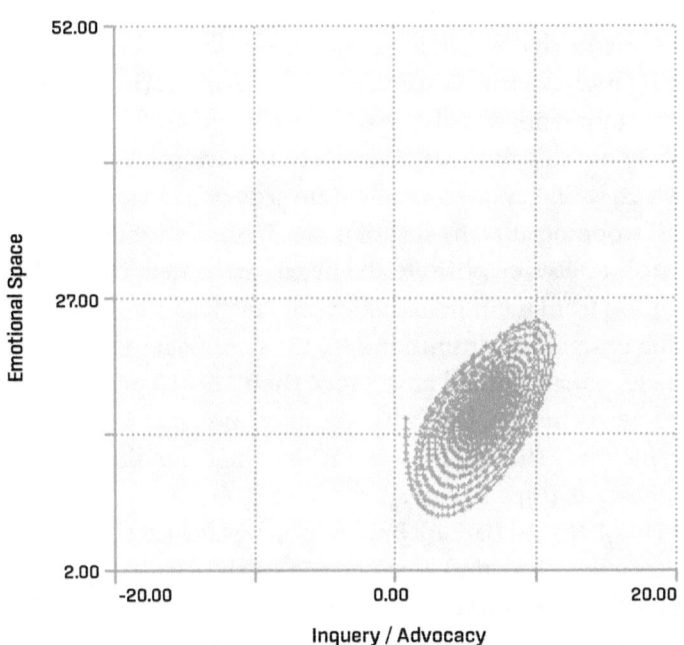

OVERLAPPING OF HIGH, MEDIUM AND LOW PERFORMANCE TEAMS

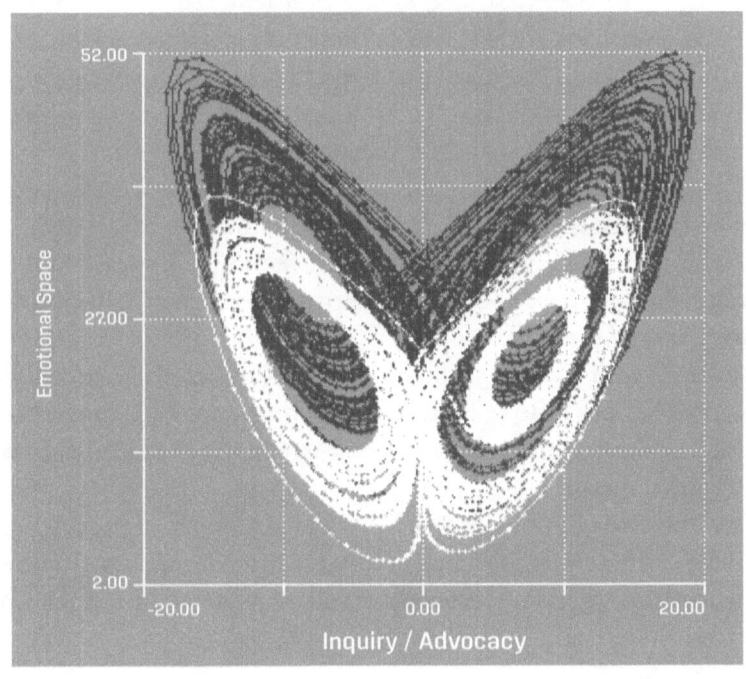

What Losada wanted to find was the **exact** ratio between positive and negative moments that would form the image of a butterfly such as the one representing high performance teams. If a team's ratio between positive and negative moments was **above** this number, it would indicate high performance. Below this number, teams would have medium or low performances, which would create a smaller butterfly or a circle that would shrink in size until stopping at some sort of point. In sum, Losada wanted to know the **exact point** between positive and negative moments that would make a team transition from medium to high performance.

Losada reached the number 2.9013. This means that, for **every** negative moment, a team should have **more than 2.9013** positive moments to reach good performance. This ratio became known as **Losada's Line**. Not by chance, his study showed that the ratios of high, medium and low performance teams were, respectively, approximately 6:1 (above 2.9013:1), 2:1 and 1:1 (both below 2.9013). Barbara Fredrickson was delighted with these results and, with this figure in mind, decided to test this **positivity ratio**. Losada found the ideal ratio of success by testing **teams**, but Fredrickson wondered if this formula would work to study the success of **individuals**.

Fredrickson used two groups of individuals to test her hypothesis[34]. First, each member of these groups had to answer a survey that attested to *flourishing mental health*, a **rare** condition achieved by only 20% of people[35]. Then, every participant had to report their daily emotional experiences for four weeks. How many positive and negative experiences did each person have during the day? As I mentioned previously, negative emotions are stronger than positive—as per the **negativity bias**[36]—but despite this difference and the fact that humans are naturally negative, most of us have more positive than negative emotions in a lifetime[37]. With the exception of people who suffer from poor mental health, **feeling bad is rare in humans**. This trait of having more positive than negative moments in life is known as *positivity imbalance*.

Back to Fredrickson's test, after a month collecting data, she could finally analyze whether the ratio of positivity in both groups had some relation to the mental health state of each individual. Would the Losada Line be consistent with individuals?

The universe obeys to certain laws, and as complex as it may be, these laws can be extremely simple. One of them is: two hydrogen molecules combined with one oxygen molecule (H_2O) suffer an alteration in their physical state according to temperature. A tiny change in temperature can turn H$_2$O into **water or ice**. It wouldn't be too bold to say that **success** also obeys a similar and extremely simple law. In one of the groups analyzed by Fredrickson, people with **good mental health** showed a ratio between positive and negative emotions of **3.2:1**, while others showed **2.3:1**. In the other group, however, people with good mental health had a balance of **3.4:1**, while others reached on average **2.1:1**. When I said that most don't experience positive emotions **enough** to reach success, I was citing this study—in both of Fredrickson's samples, the **vast majority of people showed an approximate balance of 2:1**[38].

Fredrickson and Losada were not the only researchers to find an ideal ratio for the success of groups and individuals. Award-winning researcher John Gottman, who has been studying romantic relationships for over 40 years, found that the way that a couple interacts daily can predict the longevity of the relationship[39]. Gottman's studies show that **successful marital relationships** have positivity ratios close to **5:1**, and unsatisfactory marriages, in turn, had ratios **lower than 1:1**. This ratio in interactions is so important that Gottman found that it can predict with 94% accuracy whether newlyweds will stay together or divorce in the next ten years.

In turn, psychologist Robert Schwartz, from the University of Pittsburgh, when treating 66 patients with depression, found that those who presented **excellent** signs of improvement reached a positivity ratio of **4.3:1**[40]. Those who showed **average** signs of improvement hat a ratio of **2.3:1**. And those who showed **no signs** of improvement in their depressive states had ratios close to **0.7:1**—a number that is in accordance with other studies showing that, in general, the levels of positivity of depressed people are **lower** than 1:1. Does the finding that happiness is the **cause** of success make sense now?

One interesting phenomenon that happen to us, for example, is that when we close a deal, we usually start closing many other deals right after that. "When it rains, it pours," as the saying goes. You may even believe that this is some kind of *force majeure*, but it's simply a reflection of positive emotions. When closing a deal, you get a charge of positive emotions that allow you to be more creative, interact better, see things as a whole, see more possibilities, be more motivated, be more resilient, and negotiate more calmly in future opportunities. It's because of this initial charge of positivity that you begin to have a better performance and end up closing other deals or making other achievements within a short period. This "good phase" can go on until your ratio between positive and negative moments falls to below 2.9013:1. So, how about making an effort to keep your ratio always above that?

Despite the great consistency of positivity ratios that may work like laws of nature, whether in teams, couples or individuals, Barbara Fredrickson **never defended a magical number**. "Science is never finished", she said during the talk we had at the nice town of Chapel Hill. In any case, Fredrickson says that her and other scientists' most important discovery is that, in order to be successful in the many areas of our lives, **we need to experience positive moments much more frequently than negative moments.**

CHOOSING POSITIVE EMOTIONS

The benefits of having frequent positive emotions are many; still, many people **choose** to feel negative emotions, or can't see the opportunities to increase their positivity charge throughout the day. I hope you're not one of them! When do you **make an effort** to have positive moments in your day?

> Do you listen to the funny stories your children tell you during breakfast or do you prefer to keep your head inside your phone reading the latest tragedy that happened in the world while you were sleeping? When you drive to work, do you listen to negative news or happy songs? When you arrive at the office, do you choose to stay in the clique that does nothing but complain about the company all day long, or do you prefer to talk to a colleague who always lifts up your spirits? Do you choose to say "hi" to every coworker that passes you by in the halls, or do you lower your head and pretend to do important business on your phone? When you sit down at your desk, do you visit exploitative news sites or watch a funny video to start your day right? Do you remember to thank the efforts your spouse makes around the house, or do you only see your own efforts? Do you spend your money on experiences and helping others, or do you prefer to buy that piece of clothing that's in fashion? Do you surprise your friends and family with small gifts, or do you think that's a waste of money? Do

you personally thank the coworker who sent you the information you needed to deliver a report, or do you think he was just doing his job? Do you think you should always be doing something, or do you make time in your day for a moment of stillness and "doing nothing"? Are you always challenging yourself to learn new things, or do you think you know it all for having a leadership role at the company? Do you think about how much you evolved over the years to get to where you are now, or do you worry about the future and ruminate about the past? Do you believe your individual effort can make your country better, or do you think things are never going to change? Do you meet with your childhood friends from time to time to reminisce about the good old times, or do you consider that each hour spent with them is an hour lost at work? Do you make an effort to have family over on weekends, or do you think this only leaves your house messy? Do you make an effort to see how many good people there are in the world, or do you only pay attention to those who steal, lie and cheat? Do you watch movies that inspire you to change things in your life, or do you watch violent movies with the message that you can't trust anyone in this world? Do you visit places that fascinate you with their beauty, or do you prefer to be locked in watching TV? Do you try to strengthen your marriage every day, or has the routine made you even stop saying "good morning" to your spouse? Do you choose to be close to your spouse when you're together, or do you prefer to sit on the other side of the house "doing your thing"? Do you kiss and hug your children and tell them you love them before leaving the house, or do you think these moments will just make you late for work?

These are just **some** of the positive choices you can make to increase your level of positivity during the day. They're simple, but require **effort**. And this effort is not only impacting **your** life—your responsibility to choose positive emotions is than you think.

SPREADING YOUR EMOTIONS AND BEHAVIORS

One day, at a birthday party, I noticed something peculiar. Sitting at one table were only blonde women, at another, only brunettes. Sitting at yet another table were several obese people. Some tables gathered groups of smiling people, others, angry people. I know this sounds like the beginning of a joke, but it's in fact the result of a phenomenon called *social contagion*.

In the 1990s, physician Nicholas Christakis helped patients nearing death, and could feel first-hand how much the passing of a loved one impacted their family. This impact led him to research a phenomenon called the ***widowhood effect***, something we've all seen: it's when someone **recently widowed passes away** shortly after their spouse has died[41]. One day, Christakis received a call that changed the course of his research forever. Right after leaving the home of an elderly woman in a terminal stage, **the best friend of that lady's son-in-law** (it's complicated, I know) called Christakis with a concern. That lady's **daughter**, exhausted from looking after her mother, **transmitted** that exhaustion to her **husband**, who got sick, and consequently worried his **best friend**. That was when Christakis found that the effect of losing—or being close to losing—a loved one went beyond the family, following a path that impacted **other people** who often **weren't even acquainted with the deceased person**. Christakis named this phenomenon **social contagion**[42].

After a few years and millions of dollars invested in research, Nicholas Christakis, now a professor at Yale University, was surprised to learn that you and I are **directly influenced** by the behavior of people we don't even know or have yet to know. The researcher found that, when a person becomes obese, there's a high chance that not only their **friends** will become obese, but also their **friends' friends**. Christakis' studies in partnership with James Fowler showed that people gain or lose weight, get happy or sad, earn more or less money, pick up or stop smoking, **all together**, in synchronized movement. This means not only that the behavior of other people influences your own, but also that **your behavior influences that of other people**.

Humans have a false notion of control of their own fate, but the truth is that we are a **reflection** of the people closest to us, and also of the people closest to our friends and family, and so on. In fact, a study published in 2010 in the prestigious journal *Science* had evidence that groups have a **collective intelligence**. This collective intelligence has no relation to the individual IQ of each person, but does have a correlation to the **social sensibility** of its members. Groups in which each person's IQ is average, but **collective intelligence** is high, score higher than groups of people with high IQs in which the collective intelligence is lower[43].

The social contagion phenomenon is so strong in our lives that, if **a friend of yours** smokes, your probability to start smoking increases by a whopping 61%. Even if the smoker is **a friend of a friend**, your probability to start smoking increases by 29%. And, to make things worse, if **a friend of a friend of a friend** smokes, there's an 11% chance that you'll pick up the same habit[44]. We're all **strongly** influenced by up to three degrees of separation in our social circles. Scary, isn't it? Not so much. The bright side of social contagion is that **you can use it for the good.** Your **behavior** is more important than you think.

Fowler and Christakis noticed that when people were close to someone who was happy, their happiness increased[45]. In fact, the closer they lived to a happy person, the happier they were themselves. Researchers said that this increase in people's happiness from living with a happy person is more significant than a US$ 10,000 raise in annual income. Yes, happiness pays higher dividends than what you can see at the moment. If you have doubts on the type of capital to invest to increase your happiness, science shows that one of the safest investments is your social capital. Another similar study, published by a London University researcher in 2007, found that improving your relationships can increase your happiness similarly to a £ 85,000 annual income[46]. The study still points to something you already know: real increases in income can't buy much happiness.

Many people mistakenly believe that happiness related to interactions is built through deep conversations, while science shows that it is actually developed with frequency. Ed Diener—one of the founders of positive psychology—and some of his colleagues noted that, over time, we get happier when we have several positive interactions during our day instead of a few deep interactions[47]. Spending an entire day talking to your best friend will bring you less happiness than if you had thirty positive interactions, even if small, that day.

You must remember the study by Jane Dutton and Amy Wrzesniewski with hospital cleaners, where one of the choices of those who wanted to increase their sense of purpose at work was to **make an effort to have good interactions** with patients, visitors and coworkers so that these interactions could **brighten their day**[48]. Extracting more satisfaction from work is another benefit of interactions to your motivation and happiness, as well as an additional proof that **frequency** is more important than **intensity**. Previously, I presented a study made by Canadian, American and Chinese researchers about the employees of a company that felt less tired at the end of the day when they had autonomy over their lunch break. Guess what was one of the activities they did during their break to obtain this benefit? **Social interactions** with coworkers[49]! John Trougakos, one of the study authors, revealed that using their lunch break for **lonesome** activities, like **relaxing**, made employees feel **more tired** at the end of the day, as contradictory as it seems

INTERACTIONS WORTH THEIR WEIGHT IN GOLD

One of your main roles in social contagion is to guarantee that **every** person you interact with leaves with **a smile**. You need to be aware that **your behavior is extremely important to your happiness**, as well as to other people in the world. Your interactions are one of the most effective tools for you to **experience, accumulate and spread positive emotions**. Speaking of that, how are your interactions today? Do you make an effort for **every** interaction, **every** day, or just the ones that are important to you? Do you take the interaction opportunities that arise, or do you prefer to dive into your phone, signaling to others that they **don't exist**?

Recognizing people is also recognizing that they exist.

Many become "invisible" to us in our busy lives, and with that we miss valuable chances each minute. How are your interactions with the gas station clerk, the cashier at the supermarket, your child's teacher, the restaurant server, the gardener, your subordinate at work, the intern, the cleaning team at your office? Do these people **exist** to you? The attitude of investing a few **seconds** to be nice to them, recognizing that they **exist**, can generate an unimaginable transformation. Those "invisible" people may be suffering with a sick child, being unnecessarily scolded by their boss, being mistreated by a client, having problems with their spouse, having debt they can't pay off or going through a difficult time with the recent passing of a loved one. For many, having **one** nice interaction in a day is something rare. A brief cordial interaction can immensely brighten someone's day, and even make them **find solutions** to solve their problems after accumulating a **positive emotion**.

In my intense routine of traveling to give speeches, workshops and consulting, it's common to see in airports people that **let slide** numerous opportunities that would increase their positive emotional charge and would make their day happier and more productive. Inside the plane, many prefer to dive into their phones instead of interacting with the passenger next to them. People prefer to handle their own luggage instead of helping other passengers place or remove their bags from the overhead compartments. They prefer to get out of the plane as fast as possible instead of being nice and letting others pass in front of them. These small acts of kindness, **micro-moments of happiness** that you can create, can later be the **fuel** to give you a **great idea** for a new project at work, to find the solution to a difficult negotiation that's been dragging on for months, or to **overcome** a delicate personal moment.

These advantages don't only benefit you—each person touched by your kindness can also obtain similar results. It's a win-win behavior! Remember, experiencing positive emotions can help broaden and build your brain. Moreover, according to the findings on the effects of social contagion, every interaction can provide enormous happiness, which will be **transmitted** to people you'll never even meet. When you make **every interaction count**, you get happier, the person who interacted with you gets happier, the next person they interact with also gets happier, and so the contagion spreads, possibly even getting back to you! Remember that an interaction is not only a **conversation**, the simple act of passing by someone and greeting them with a **look** or **head movement** already counts as an interaction.

INTERACTION'S WORST ENEMY

It's everywhere: in your pocket, on your desk, on your car seat, in the hands of your child. It grows in numbers by the day, and is found more and more often anywhere. It can't reproduce, but proliferates with impressive speed, and you may even be using it to read this book. Yes, I'm talking about the worst enemy of the modern world: the smartphone. How many times have you seen people gathered around a meal and **not talking to each other** because they're interacting with **other people** on their phone? And how many times have you realized that **you're the one doing that**? How many times have you realized how many **opportunities you're missing** of increasing your positive emotions and transmitting happiness by interacting **personally** with your friends, family and coworkers, because you **choose** to exchange messages with **others** while you're with them?

If you want to be happy and motivated, one precious tip is to use your phone **the least you can**. Be **really** present with the person you're talking to! Is there anything more annoying than talking to someone who won't put the phone down? What is the message that they're giving you? "I might get a **text** with a **meme** that's **more important** than our conversation." Don't forget that this is also the message **you** send others when your phone is visible during a conversation. The study *The iPhone Effect*, conducted by Virginia Tech, shows that the mere **presence** of a phone ruins the quality of an interaction[50].

Don't get me wrong: I also think smartphones are an incredible invention. But what science proves is that they're even more incredible when we use them when we're **alone**!

THE INDUSTRIAL CULTURE OF UNHAPPINESS

When you believe that the secret to success is to work without rest to accumulate as much money as you can, this choice keeps you away from your friends and family, and it reduces the time you spend socializing. This causes you to have **fewer interactions** during the day, your happiness decreases and, with it, your probability of being successful. "Wealth increases the distance between people," said Paul Piff during our talk. "When they start earning more, they buy bigger houses in bigger lots and distance themselves from their neighbors. In this house, rooms are bigger, everyone has their own room, everyone has their own car. These factors reduce social interactions and make people more and more individualistic," he concluded.

The longer you spend running after goals **alone**, the **further** you are from reaching them. This is why, if you ask any positive psychology scientist what's the main predictor of happiness, they'll say it's **relationships**. Remember how Edward Deci and Richard Ryan found that **relationships** are one of the basic universal motivational needs of human beings—without the feeling that we love or are loved by others, that we care for people and they care for us, or that we belong to a group, we **lose** big part of our motivation. The problem is that, in the race for money, we always think we can leave relationships **for later**.

Many companies have a culture of staying late, as people believe this will increase productivity. This culture, however, keeps employees away from their friends and family, resulting in the **opposite** result. This type of organizational culture, incorporated into the lives of many executives, assumes people are machines performing heavy manual labor. In a production line there's a **direct** relation between the **number of hours** worked and **productivity**, but in an office, this relation simply doesn't exist for most employees. Office work is **creative** by nature, so someone who worked **eight hours** can deliver the same results at the end of the day as someone who worked **three**. In a factory, where work is manual, an employee with a three-hour workload will hardly be as productive as one with an eight-hour workload. Even though we're in the 21st Century, many companies still develop 19th Century workplaces.

Another example of this industrial culture in offices is that many companies create environments that **don't encourage** interaction between employees—people are forbidden to talk among themselves, and during shifts where some are having lunch, others are **working**. Once again, the goal of increasing productivity won't be met because of the **lack of interaction** and **positive emotions** in the workplace.

Another unfortunate decision many companies make: noting that two people that sit next to each other are becoming friends, they **separate** them; after all, work is work, right? What these companies and leaders don't know is that friendships have a **very important** role in productivity. Researchers from Western University, Ontario, Canada, revealed that when we're close to people we get along well with, we're in a better mood and are more creative[51]. Tom Rath, Gallup researcher, after analyzing more than 15 million interviews, found that the importance of friendships in the workplace is far greater than we imagine[52]. Rath and his team revealed that having best friends at work increases **engagement seven-fold**.

Psychologist James Pennebaker, a researcher at the University of Texas, explains that **relationships create efficiency and accelerate goal achievement**[53]. Explaining something to someone we barely know takes a long time—and they take longer to understand, too. But when we explain the same thing to a **friend**, it takes us **less** time—and they understand much faster. The closer we are to someone, the higher the probability of understanding and communicating **faster**, generating **efficiency**. And a new study proves this without question.

In a paper published in 2018 in the renowned journal *Nature*, UCLA's Carolyn Parkinson and researchers Adam Kleinbaum and Thalia Wheatley, from Dartmouth College, revealed that the brains of people who are friends function in incredibly **similar** ways[54]. Using data obtained by functional magnetic resonance images (fMRI) to observe the cerebral activity of participants while they watched a series of videos, they found that the stronger the friendship bond between them, **the more similar their neural reactions** to the videos. Many other studies show that we have a natural preference to choose friends according to our similarities (age, race, gender, hobbies, names, etc.)[55], but this finding shows for the first time that we also choose friends for another factor, until then invisible—**the way we interpret and react to daily events**.

A study conducted by Australian researchers that analyzed 1,477 senior citizens shows an extra benefit of friendships: **longevity**[56]. Those with a large number of friends lived 22% more compared to those with few relationships. Surprisingly to many, the group of scientists also found that the relationships with family members and children had a **very low impact** on longevity—having **many friends** was more relevant than every other dimension related to the participants' longevity. A meta-analysis of 150 studies conducted by scientists of Brigham Young University and the University of North Carolina analyzed data on the chances of mortality of 308,849 people and confirms this data: those with good friendships **increase** their chances of survival by 50%[57]. According to researchers, having **few** friendships has the same impact on people's longevity as **smoking 15 cigarettes a day**, and it's more harmful to health than being **obese** or **sedentary**.

In our talk, Richard Ryan told me that relationships are one of the most effective tools to develop awareness and stay alert to our choices in life. Honesty in a friend's opinion makes us less gullible to external forces and values that can negatively shape motivation and happiness. Friends help us escape the traps of life and bring us back to reality.

This is why companies should **encourage workplace friendships**, changing the layout of their offices, implementing short breaks during the day so people can **talk**, promoting **parties**, **reunions** and other events that allow employees to **interact** more. The more initiatives a company makes to increase interactions and friendships between employees, the better the results.

Kim Cameron, professor at the University of Michigan, conducted a groundbreaking research in the field of interaction. She and her colleagues mapped the employees of a company according to their ***relational energy***, that is, **how much** each employee energized, motivated and revigorated others with their interactions, instead of leaving them exhausted or feeling drained after conversations[58]. What they saw was highly surprising: the level of relational energy **predicted** the team's performance **four times more** accurately than networks based on influence or information. This makes it clear that providing a positive impact on your coworkers' lives through your interactions puts your team on a more accurate path to reach goals than trying to **influence them to do what you want using your authority or other means**. At the end of the day, it seems that those water cooler talks are really important, aren't they? Besides, this group of scientists found that employees have better performance, are more engaged, more satisfied with their work and have more well-being in their homes when **led** by someone with a **positive energy**.

The consequences of social contagion and interactions to your happiness and motivation show how really fantastic nature is. Humans express more incredible powers than we think. What few people know is that, a few years ago, a group of Italian scientists found a **superpower** we all have—and it will convince you even more of how important your behavior is.

MIRROR NEURONS

On a beautiful summer day in 1991, at the lab in the University of Parma, a monkey with a series of threads connected to the F5 region—an area of the brain related to planning and some body movements—sitting on a special chair, waited for a group of scientists to return from lunch. Every time the monkey held, manipulated or moved an object, some neurons in his brain became active, and a monitor emitted a sound: **beep, beep, beep**. A certain university student came back from his lunch break holding a masterpiece of Italian cuisine: a *gelato*. The young man was preparing to start the work, enjoying his *gelato*, when he heard a sound: **beep, beep, beep**. He quickly looked at the monkey, but the animal wasn't moving. Not thinking much about it, he moved on with his tasks and, when he licked the *gelato* again,

again he heard the sound: **beep, beep, beep**. Baffled, looking straight at the monkey, the assistant once again licked the *gelato*: **beep, beep, beep** went the monitor. But the monkey didn't move.

What the assistant witnessed was one of the greatest findings in the history of neurology: there's a set of cells in our brain called **mirror neurons**[59]. Mirror neurons make our brains "train" certain actions by simply **observing** other people perform them, as if **we were the ones** performing these actions. When watching a football game, for example, you're not only using your vision to follow what happens on the field: the areas of your brain related to running and kicking are **all activated**, as if **you** were right there on the field. This is why the mirror neurons of the monkey at the University of Parma were activated by simply **observing** the assistant eat the *gelato*, making the areas of his brain responsible for this movement to become active and "train" the same movement.

Our ancestors obtained great benefits because of mirror neurons, especially because **learning** to perform a movement by simply **observing** it facilitated a series of daily actions, such as using tools, picking fruit and hunting animals. These neurons also had an important role in developing communication, because at that time there was no language: we communicated through gestures[60]. Mirror neurons still carry a fundamental function in sharing emotions: if one of our ancestors saw an expression of fear in one of his mates, for example, his mirror neurons would become active and help him prepare for a possible threat, since this could signal the presence of a predator that was outside his line of vision[61].

Recently, scientists in this field revealed that mirror neurons have broadened their function, becoming responsible also for **empathy** in humans[62]. When we see someone happy, our mirror neurons become active and make us want to **feel** what that person is feeling. When we notice that someone is annoyed, our neurons make it so that we feel the same emotion. It's because of mirror neurons that in a classroom, for example, when one student sneezes, others automatically start sneezing. Or when someone yawns, others feel the need to yawn as well. It's because of mirror neurons that, when you see the expression of fear of a character in a scary movie, without realizing it, you make the **same** facial expression and start feeling **fear**, even though you're not **experiencing** the same situation and you're **aware** that **nothing** in that screen is **real**.

Mirror neurons have the role of putting you in someone else's shoes, even if just for a moment, making our relationships better. Remember Sarina Saturn's study, in which the sympathetic nervous system, responsible for feelings of **pain** and **stress**, was activated in people who witnessed situations of suffering[63]? And what about Dacher Keltner and Christopher Oveis, who found that the exposure to images of suffering activated the vagus nerve, evoking a feeling of **compassion**[64]? Coincidence?

One experiment conducted by New York University researchers shows that our emotions don't spread only when we interact face to face, but also when we're exposed to words that carry certain emotions[65]. In this study, participants received a sequence of words and had to reorder them to form a phrase that made grammatical sense. One of the groups received **rude** words (aggressively, bother, intrude, interrupt), while others received **polite** words (respect, honor, patiently, cordially) or **neutral** words (exercising, occasionally, rapidly, normally). Upon receiving a sequence of words such as **THEY HER BOTHER SEE USUALLY**, the participant should reorder them, for example, into the phrase: **THEY USUALLY SEE HER BOTHER**. When instructed to deliver their tasks to the researcher in the other room, things started getting interesting.

When entering this other room, every participant was faced with the same situation: the researcher was talking to another student, who seemed to have trouble understanding the task. In fact, this "other student" was part of the group of researchers, starting the interaction when noticing the arrival of one of the participants. The intention was to time how long it would take for the participant to **interrupt** the conversation. Would the tone of the ordered words have any effect on how long the participant would wait before interrupting? As you can imagine, 65% of students primed on rudeness interrupted the conversation, and did so after an average of 326 seconds. The participants of the group primed with neutral words interrupted the conversation after an average of 519 seconds, and only 48% of them interrupted at all. Participants of the group primed on politeness interrupted after an average of 558 seconds, and only 17% of them showed this behavior. Notice how the tone of the words you write in emails and other messages directly influences the behavior of people that read them? But that's not all. The types of words you're **exposing yourself to** also influence your future behavior. Have you been reading the news in the morning? What about accessing sites with negative news? Watch out!

Speaking of interactions, we must be aware that **our feelings are contagious to other people**. When you make an effort to smile, you're nice in your interactions and start a conversation by saying something positive to someone else, their mirror neurons become active and there's a great chance that they will **smile, be nice and respond with something equally positive**. Remember: they want to **feel** what **you're** feeling.

In the same article that presented the scrambled words, the New York University scientists concluded that we can change the behavior of other people simply **expressing what we want them to copy**. This finding, aligned with the activation of mirror neurons, proves that if the initial tone of your talk was positive, there's a very high chance that the other person will copy your behavior. Similarly, if you interact showing signs of **irritation or sadness**, realizing what you're feeling, this person can copy the **same expression** and, although they might not feel irritated **immediately**, it might not take long for them to start feeling like that, as incredible as it seems.

However, because humans are negative by nature, many people believe that it doesn't matter whether a conversation starts on a positive note, the other person will probably express something negative during that interaction. However, in an interaction between a positive person and a negative person, who do you think will win? We're led to believe that the negative human nature will prevail, but two researchers from the University of California found that whoever wins the battle in an interaction is **the party that most expresses their emotions**[66]. The more positivity you show, the more you activate the other party's mirror neurons, increasing their chances of expressing something positive. Remember that the **opposite** is also true. So, every time you're interacting with a negative person, try to express positive things frequently, making them see the other side of the situation. So, there's a great possibility that this individual will change their behavior and start expressing in a more positive way..

One change in your behavior has the power to make other people's behavior change as well.

Just don't forget that being positive **doesn't mean being a dreamer**, or a **Pollyanna** that insists on an annoying optimism disconnected from reality. Being positive is to be optimistic about an excellent future, but keeping it **real**.

The effects of social contagion and the system of mirror neurons are fascinating. And the implications of these phenomena in our daily lives can also be felt when we activate one of human's basic motivational needs: recognition

CHAPTER 6

Unrecognizable Recognition

REVERSE RECOGNITION

In the beginning of this book, you learned about the study conducted by Mark Lepper and colleagues, in which children that could receive great **recognition** for their work ended up making drawings that were **rated poorly** by a group of judges and, later, **lost interest** in drawing altogether[1]. You also learned about the experiments of Dan Ariely with other researchers, in which a group that could receive the equivalent of **five months**' salary had **worse** performance compared to other groups who didn't have such a generous incentive[2]. Numerous other studies showed that, when working with the possibility of obtaining material recognition, the consequences on our performance are **catastrophic**. So, does that mean recognition doesn't motivate people? Quite the opposite.

In a 2009 paper published in the *Journal of Personality and Social Psychology*, brilliant researchers Adam Grant and Francesca Gino found that simply **thanking** someone for helping you has incredible effects on future behavior[3]. In this research, participants were induced to believe that they'd participate in a study to evaluate their writing and feedback skills. For that, they were supposed to write feedback on the cover letter of a fictitious student, Eric Sorenson. After receiving feedback from every student, scientists responded to the feedback (in the name of Eric Sorenson) individually, in two ways:

> **Group 1 –** "Dear [name], I just wanted to let you know that I received your feedback on my cover letter. I was wondering if you could help with a second cover letter I prepared and give me feedback on it. The cover letter is attached. Can you send me some comments in the next 3 days?"
>
> **Group 2 –** "Dear [name], I just wanted to let you know that I received your feedback on my cover letter. Thank you so much! I am really grateful. I was wondering if you could help with a second cover letter I prepared and give me feedback on it. The cover letter is attached. Can you send me some comments in the next 3 days?"

See the difference? Participants in Group 2 received a **small recognition** with the phrases "**Thank you so much! I am really grateful**." When scientists want to investigate something, they obviously can't tell the study participants what is actually being investigated, in order to not contaminate the data. In this case, Grant and Gino's goal wasn't to analyze the writing or feedback skills of participants, but discover what happens when we're shown gratitude for helping someone. Do we display different behaviors whether our work is recognized with gratitude or not? The answer is a huge **yes**! What happened was impressive: 66% of participants in the second group helped Eric again, while only 32% of the first group did.

In a second experiment, researchers tested whether the same effect would occur if, instead of receiving another feedback request from the same student, they received a feedback request from a different student—in this case, the fictitious Steven Rogoff. Does receiving recognition from one person increase the probability of helping another? The answer, again, is a **clear yes**. Of the participants who received Eric's email expressing gratitude, 55% helped Steven. Only 25% of those who received Eric's email with no expression of gratitude helped Steven. We notice, then, that a positive interaction also makes gratitude **spread** through social contagion.

In a new experiment, researchers tested the influence of expressing gratitude **in person**. This time, each participant evaluated Eric's cover letter individually in a room. At the end of the activity, an actor came in to deliver a few papers to the researchers. The actor identified as Eric and thanked some participants for evaluating his cover letter, but not others. Next, the researcher delivered a second model of Eric's cover letter for feedback. Compared to people who didn't receive recognition, those who did spent **more** time working on the second cover letter.

Finally, Grant and Gino conducted a test at the donation center of an American university, where employees were tasked with calling potential donors to raise funds for the university. One group of employees was visited by the department head, who thanked their hard work and contribution to the university. A second group was not visited. Simply being thanked **in person** made members of the first group **expressively increase** the number of calls made to potential donors compared to the period before the experiment, in addition to feeling an increase in their efficiency and value, measured through surveys. Gino and Grant clearly concluded in this study that the increase in number of calls was caused by the **recognition speech** of the department head, since every one of those employees had a **fixed salary** and, therefore, had no commissions or other financial incentives to increase the number of donations.

These experiments show that recognition and gratitude—expressed in person or not, through **words and gestures** instead of trophies, awards, diplomas, money and plaques—really motivate people. Edward Deci found similar results in a study in which a group of students **maintained** their motivational level for a task right after receiving positive feedback[4]. It's worth noting that the positive effects were obtained in these experiments because the recognition received by participants was a **surprise**. Just like the children in Lepper and Greene's study had a better performance when they **weren't expecting** a reward, the participants of Grant and Gino's study helped the fictitious student after they received an **unexpected** thank you note.

Maybe **recognizing** your work is not a strength of your boss, spouse, parents or friends precisely because our understanding of the power of recognition for motivation is **wrong**! What few people realize is that, in order to get the **maximum benefit** of recognition, the path to follow is **opposite** to what most people choose.

In order to be happier and more motivated, you must recognize others instead of waiting for recognition.

Yes, the way recognition powers our motivation is the **opposite** of what we would expect. When **you** take the initiative and change your behavior, other people you come in contact with change their own behavior as well, because of our system of mirror neurons and social contagion. That's exactly what happened in Grant and Gino's experiment. When fictitious student Eric had the **initiative** to thank people for their work, **more than double** these people helped him a second time, compared to those that didn't receive this recognition. When those who received Eric's recognition were asked to help **another** student, Steven, **more than double** helped him as well, which proves the power of mirror neurons and the contagion effect.

Notice that your recognition activates people's motivation, making them more willing to act and help you in the future. Remember that your **behavior** influences the behavior of your social circle and vice-versa. **Who do you want leading this circle: you or other people? Do you want to follow or be followed?**

Unfortunately, many people in leadership roles have a policy of not complimenting their employees, because they believe the illusion that this gesture will make them feel like they don't need to be better. With this behavior, leaders miss the opportunity to give their subordinates the motivating feeling of **competence**, and they also undermine **teamwork**, as the effects of a single compliment to a single person—when sincere—can go a long way.

When you recognize someone, you get happier, and they get happier—both parties experience **positive emotions**. Because of mirror neurons, you pass this happiness on to the next person you interact with, just like the person who was recognized will also pass their happiness on to their next interaction—that's social contagion in action. And so on, reaching people you'll never even meet. Who caused this? **You!**

Many of the studies presented so far have the purpose of increasing your **individual** happiness, but what you must understand is that happiness is at its maximum potential when it's **collective**. Recognizing others and making an effort in **every** one of your daily interactions are tasks you can easily practice to increase the happiness of **many people**.

Making other people happy is what allows each of us to be happy individually.

Also, remember to recognize that people **exist**, and don't miss out on the opportunity to experience and spread positive emotions in your daily interactions. Paul Piff told me that one of the most effective tools to get a more realistic world view and achieve more empathy for others is to have **interactions outside the comfort zone**, making an effort in conversations with individuals from lower social levels.

As you've seen, one of the biggest allies in our motivation is the feeling of **autonomy**, of having control over what happens in our life. When you understand that the benefits of recognition are reaped when you **take control of it**—instead of having a passive behavior and waiting for recognition—what you're doing is **increasing your feeling of autonomy**. Thus, you begin to understand and feel that it's your own behavior that brings you more control over your fate.

In the corporate environment, one of the most positive forms of using recognition and evoking the feeling of autonomy in employees is to make them decide for themselves who should be **promoted** within their teams. In addition to the benefits already mentioned, giving employees autonomy to promote one another also increases **collaboration** at work, as people start to understand that their fates no longer depend on individual results or the boss' mood, but on how much they collaborate for the success of the **team**.

Having a **passive** behavior regarding gratitude, or desperately trying to **get recognition** from others, can be very dangerous. When you condition your motivation and happiness to **other people's** applause, you automatically **give up control** of your own happiness.

DESPERATE FOR RECOGNITION

Nowadays, it's not hard to see that many people are desperate for recognition, not just in the workplace but also in their personal lives and social networks. They make posts trying to show how dedicated they are at work, to expose their brilliant political views, to advertise that they're traveling to an exotic destination or going to a fancy restaurant, in sum, everyone is bending over backwards to **get the most likes**. And when they don't get the return they expected, they feel sad—and decide to **post** about that, too. The ultimate honor goes to those who post photos of events where they were recognized by their companies, expecting **even more recognition** from their social networks.

One of these days, I was playing with my son at a nearby park, and next to us was another dad playing with his two kids in a soccer field. I was amazed by how, instead of **interacting** with his boys, this dad was recording a video of himself "running in the park". He'd go to the track next to the field, film himself running for ten seconds, stop and come back. The man did that many times until he was satisfied with the video he wanted to show, and then spent several minutes posting it to social media and interacting with those who commented on his post. Meanwhile, his two boys were playing **alone**. That day, I really witnessed how addictive the search for recognition is, making us **miss out** on the moments that are really important in life.

Away from social media, other resources like plastic surgery, extravagant outfits, exaggerated muscles, famous designer-branded clothes, cars, jewels, watches, fashionable hairstyles, bags and luxury accessories are widely used by many to obtain recognition. In addition to the feeling of lack of control, these people also begin to suffer from the effects of a phenomenon you know well. When you receive recognition from others, you get happier, but your happiness soon goes back to normal. Because being happy is a good feeling, your natural behavior will be to seek to **increase** the frequency of these "happy" moments, therefore, you'll do all you can to receive **more** recognition from others. When this happens, you get happier, but your happiness goes back to normal even faster. And what happens with the daily repetition of this habit? Over time, you start needing higher and higher doses of recognition to get the **same** happiness. You get hooked by **hedonic adaptation** and the amount of recognition you get no longer matters: you'll **always** feel like it's not enough.

This doesn't mean that receiving recognition from others is a bad thing, as we know compliments are very nice. In fact, getting recognition evokes the feeling of **competence**, one of the basic needs studied by Richard Ryan and Edward Deci. When **you start** the recognition cycle, other people will naturally recognize you too, which makes this strategy even better. What studies show is that you shouldn't give too much importance to other people's recognition in your motivation and happiness. The problem, in this case, is the frequency with which we hear that recognition is motivating, leading us to believe that **we also need recognition** to be happy—but as you've found, what we commonly believe that motivates us is not what really creates personal satisfaction.

A research conducted by a Harvard scientist signaled that leaders put recognition at the **top of the list** of factors they believed motivated employees, while employees reported that **other** factors motivated them much more[5]. When you believe you need other people's compliments to be happier, your motivation starts to be guided by **external** recognition, a huge risk to your happiness.

THE REAL RECOGNITION

To keep hedonic adaptation away, you must take advantage of the power of recognition to **express your gratitude** to people who have helped you or are helping you. There's a large body of scientific evidence about gratitude being one of the **most powerful** ways to recognize others. One group of researchers from three American universities asked a group of people with poor mental health to write a weekly **gratitude letter** to someone, for three weeks. As a result, they presented improvements in their mental health shortly after the experiment[6]. But this health improvement takes time—the signs started to appear only on the **fourth week** after the experiment was over, and increased expressively for the **next 12 weeks**. Moreover, this was only possible for the participants who wrote letters with more positive than negative expressions.

The consistency of the power of gratitude and the Broaden-and-Build Theory is amazing. One interesting finding of this study is that, in order to obtain better mental health, people **didn't even need to send the gratitude letters**, revealing that just the exercise of writing them brings huge benefits.

However, as you'll see in a while, studies show that the greatest benefits of a gratitude letter come from delivering it **in person.** In any case, it's interesting to know that just **writing** a letter has benefits.

To wrap up this study, researchers Joel Wong and Joshua Brown wanted to know if there were any brain alterations on those who expressed gratitude. So, they selected a sample of these participants to measure their levels of brain activity three months after the first experiment. Compared to the people who didn't write gratitude letters, this group showed more intense cerebral activity in the medial pre-frontal cortex, an area associated to **learning and decision-making**. The results show that gratitude has long-term effects on the brain, which can contribute even more to good mental health over time.

Researcher Glenn Fox from The University of Southern California and his colleagues found, in a similar study, that people instructed to feel gratitude showed brain activity in areas related to **empathy**, **understanding others' perspective** and feeling **relief**, which signals that being grateful for others helps in **relaxing the body** and **reducing stress**[7].

Other than being highly beneficial to individuals, gratitude can also be useful in the workplace, according to a study conducted by researchers of four American universities[8]. Participants who practiced gratitude **reduced** their chances of being **aggressive** or seeking **revanche** against those who gave them a negative feedback. Robert Emmons, whom you met a few pages back, also reveals that gratitude leads to **reciprocity**, which increases the possibility of **practicing acts of kindness in the future**—which once again proves the power of mirror neurons and social contagion[9].

To make the benefits of gratitude **even more powerful**, a recent study published by researchers of North Carolina University suggests that, when receiving gratitude, we must then express the feeling **towards the person**, and not talk about how **we** feel for being complimented[10]. This means that when someone does you good, you must express something on the lines of: "You do all you can to brighten people's days" or "You never forget those who help you". Because us humans are egotistical in nature, when we receive someone's gratitude, we tend to express how **we** feel after the act.

Humans **love** to talk about themselves. A finding by Harvard researcher Diana Tamir and her colleague Jason Mitchell confirms this: when we talk about ourselves, areas of **pleasure** in the brain are activated, the same that become active when we **eat or win money**[11]. Talking about ourselves, therefore, is pleasurable! This trait is so ingrained in humans that Tamir and

Mitchell's study participants preferred to **talk about themselves** instead of **winning money**. Yes, this is a **more potent** motivator than the all-powerful financial incentives.

Don't forget to resist that temptation when you show recognition or express gratitude to someone, as Tamir and Mitchell's research warns us that our motivation in helping others comes from our own sense of value—**people want to be admired for their acts of kindness.**

STARTING THE GRATITUDE CYCLE

But it's not because gratitude brings great benefits to your life that you'll act **passively** and only thank those who help you, or worse, think that gratitude means posting a photo of yourself eating lobster in Beverly Hills with *#grateful* and the famous "prayer hands" emoji. Just like with recognition, you must start the gratitude cycle. How? **By helping others**! Yes, gratitude only exists if someone has been helped **first**!

At the time he was a researcher for the University of California, Joseph Chancellor—currently a Facebook executive—made an experiment with Coca-Cola employees in Madrid that shows how, surprisingly, helping others expressively impacts the future behavior of everyone involved[12]. Participants of this experiment were informed that they would take part in a study on happiness, and that, once a week, they should report to researchers: their mood and life satisfaction, their experiences with positive and negative behaviors, how much they helped their colleagues and also how much help they received from them. The trick to this experiment was this: of the participants, 19 were instructed by researchers to be "givers", practicing **acts of kindness** for a group of colleagues (bringing a glass of water or writing a thank you note, for example), but not to a different group—the control.

Knowing the strength of mirror neurons and social contagion, what do you think happened? At the end of four weeks, the group that was graced with acts of kindness started helping their coworkers **278% more** than the control group participants, and their levels of happiness were **significantly higher one month after the study**. You may be thinking that this increase in how much people helped each other is normal, because it's customary to **repay** a favor, but that wasn't exactly what happened: the researcher found that when those who first received help tried to repay the favor, they did it to colleagues who were **not** the "givers". The most surprising revelation of this study, however, was yet to come: for some indicators, scientists observed that **practicing** acts of kindness produced more rewarding impacts than **receiving** them. Compared to their colleagues who **received** acts of kindness, the participants who **practiced** them—the "givers"—reported a more significant reduction of their depression symptoms and an increase in their levels of life and work satisfaction.

Another important discovery comes from researcher Stephanie Brown, from the Stony Brook University's Medical School. When analyzing a sample of 846 couples in their 60s, she and her colleagues detected that people who gave **little help** to friends, family and neighbors, as well as **little emotional support** to their spouse, had **more than double** the chance of dying during the five years of the study[13]. In addition to showing the influence that helping others has on our longevity, this study also reveals how much we can intervene on the health of the elderly in our family. We must not only help them more intensely, because of the several limitations they face after a certain age, but also find ways to make them useful to their friends, family, neighbors, spouses and the community in general. Activities like counseling the young, scheduling a monthly reunion with their best friends, practicing team sports, participating in religious communities, delivering donations to people in need, setting the table for meals and feeding their grandchildren are simple acts that can help them enjoy their **golden years**.

"Helper's high" is how many psychologists call the nice feeling people experience when they help someone[14]. This "high" is caused by the release of **endorphins**, chemical substances that make us feel good. Professor James Fowler of the University of California, one of the world's most prominent references in the study of social network dynamics, showed in a study how a simple act of kindness inspires several other people to act the same[15]. In fact, Fowler and Christakis revealed that every act of kindness carried out by an individual is **tripled** by others in the future.

A 2018 study by researchers of the University of Pennsylvania and the University of Dar es Salaam brought more clarity to the nature of cooperation. This group of scientists analyzed the behavior of 56 tribes of hunter-gatherers in Tanzania for four years, and found that their individual levels of cooperation were directly linked to the level of cooperation of their peers. "Individuals' cooperative behavior is best predicted by the cooperativeness of their neighbors, "the scientists said in the paper published in *Current*

Biology. "The findings highlight the flexible nature of human cooperation and the remarkable capacity of humans to respond adaptively to their social environments"[16]. This is yet another proof of the advantages of starting the gratitude cycle and of your great responsibility in this world—people are more inclined to help **after** seeing someone else helping others. Helping is so beneficial in the long run that a study by researchers from Wharton School and the University of Michigan, published in 2012 in Psychological Science, revealed that simply **remembering** occasions where you helped someone makes you want to help **again**[17].

To reap all the benefits of helping others, we must also learn how to **help right**! The influent researcher Sonja Lyubomirsky led a study in which participants were asked to make five random acts of kindness per week, during six weeks[18]. After being separated into two groups, participants of one group were asked to make **all acts on the same day**, while others had to **divide them over the five weekdays**. Despite having practiced the same number of acts of kindness at the end of the experiment, the level of happiness of both groups after six weeks was drastically different. The group that practiced **all acts of kindness on the same day** had an **increase in happiness**, while the other group had no significant difference in their levels of happiness.

It's important to know that the benefits of choosing one day of the week to practice five acts of kindness can only be felt if this is made **consciously**: remembering **today** that **last Tuesday** you helped an old lady carry her shopping bags **doesn't count**, and it brings no benefits to your happiness. So choose one day of the week and make an **even greater** effort to help your coworker advance in a project, give your place in a crowded elevator to someone else, help someone carry something heavy, let another driver pass in front of you at an intersection, pay the toll for the car behind you, make a nice breakfast for your family, help a charity, donate clothes and other things to the church—any such acts will guarantee an expressive improvement in your happiness after a few weeks. But please, don't forget to help others and be nice on the other days as well. Helping, as opposed to what many people think, is **simple** and doesn't require huge efforts. As much as some of these acts may not be pleasurable at **the moment**, remember that the **sum** of these positive emotions is what can make you reach **eudaimonic happiness.**

In the end, you'll find that recognition really is motivating when you start the cycle of gratitude by helping someone. This act gives you a positive feeling; the person you helped imitates your behavior and helps others; they also get happier and accumulate positive emotions; they proceed to make many other people happy, get recognized by others, promote positive feelings for several individuals and, later, recognize you by expressing how grateful they feel for your action; and so you accumulate positive emotions frequently and enjoy all of their advantages. Why not start right now?

CHAPTER 7

Being Irreplaceable

THE ULTIMATE RECOGNITION IN INTERACTIONS

According to studies on mirror neurons, humans have a tendency to **imitate** each other's body movements, facial expressions, verbal expressions and behaviors[1]. Marvin Simner, researcher of the University of Western Ontario, revealed in his studies that newborn babies, aged two to four days, start crying only after hearing other babies cry; and as incredible as it seems, they can differentiate between **real** cries and **synthetic** ones, and imitate only real cries[2]. For several reasons, this imitation mechanism brought huge benefits to the improvement of communication between our ancestors[3].

Primitive communication through gestures had a fundamental role in survival and the success of our race. When we observed someone in our tribe gesturing to communicate finding a source of water or food, or even as a warning for predators, the fact that we had mirror neurons improved the chances of individuals **copying** that same gesture when it was **their** time to communicate any of these events. Mirror neurons facilitated the **unification** of these gestures, favoring everyone in a tribe to know exactly how to gesture to communicate a given event. If each member of the tribe gestured differently to communicate the **same thing**, our race would probably not exist today.

At a certain point in our evolution, however, our gestures were different. When different tribes started coming together—because we found out that hunting in large groups increased our chances of having lunch—problems started to arise. For one tribe, one gesture could mean "food", while another could see it as "predator". As we can imagine, the person who gestured meaning "food" and made the members of their tribe leave the cave and run into a pack of saber-tooth tigers wouldn't exactly be loved by the few survivors. They would certainly be deeply irritated because that individual **didn't know how to properly communicate**, which put the tribe—and our species—in a risky situation. Because of moments like this, when someone in the tribe had **different gestures from their peers**, they were **expelled** from the group. If this person was lucky enough to not be expelled, the fact that they didn't know how to communicate with others reduced their chances to find a mate to reproduce, or to have good relationships with other people in the group.

Despite the millions of years that separate us from our ancestors and our current use of speech, body language still has a **big impact** on our communication. This is why, even when you're alone talking on the phone, you still **gesture**[4]. As contradictory as it seems, researcher Albert Mehrabian, of the University of California, Los Angeles, reveals that our body language corresponds to 55% of communication[5].

In order to be successful in an interaction, knowing what to *do* may be more important than knowing what to say.

Because of this, a large body of studies reveal that, by **imitating** body postures and gestures of people you interact with, you make them evaluate you **more positively**[6]. Imitating others makes people like you more, because, due to our primitive roots, they'll consider you are from the **"same tribe"**[7]. In many cases, we imitate the postures and gestures of those we talk to without even noticing, completely unaware of such imitation. In a genius study, researchers Clara Cheng and Tanya Chartrand, of Ohio State University, selected a few psychology students for an experiment to analyze their different reactions to a set of photos[8]. When a student entered the lab, they were informed that another student would participate in the experiment with them. In fact, this "other student" was a **member** of the research team (or **confederate**, in scientific language), trained to incite a mimicking behavior in participants.

One part of the students was informed that the other participant was a high school student; another, that they were a graduate student; and a third, that they were a psychology classmate. During every interaction of the confederate with each of the participants, she acted the same: at a certain point, **she crossed her legs and slightly shook her foot**. The real intent of the study was to analyze **in which situations** students would unconsciously mimic her body language. Of the groups informed that the confederate was a high school or graduate student, a very small percentage imitated her gestures. But among participants who thought the confederate was a **classmate**, behavior mimicking increased almost **ten-fold**—they felt they were all **from the same tribe**!

It's even more interesting to note the results of this natural human behavior of imitating each other. It's very common to see couples who start showing a **physical resemblance** after years of imitating each other[9]. By constantly mirroring the other's expressions of happiness, sadness, surprise, anger, excitement and so forth, these couples started having very similar expressions, and their facial muscles started to adopt similar formats.

Have you ever met a couple you thought were siblings? If mimicking the expressions of the person we marry is natural, and if over time our face begins to physically look like that of our spouse, you might want to **choose a partner very carefully**!

Marvin Simner's study on imitation in babies reveals that this trait is rooted in our behavior and actually begins **before** we're even born. When you were in your mother's womb, your heart rate was synchronized with hers[10]. The emotions she felt during pregnancy were passed on to you[11]. Evolution shaped us to be imitation machines, guaranteeing the success of our species.

Some scientists also claim that imitation is a primitive way of **complimenting** the person you're talking to, a way of communicating "**You matter to me**" or "**I like you**"[12].It's not by chance that salespeople who imitate their customers sell more than those who don't[13]. You naturally mimic those with whom you feel a certain similarity, but you also **cause** this feeling when you imitate them—like many other behaviors, imitation also works the other way around.

THE MAGIC OF TOUCH

Literature is vast on the power of imitation, as well as on the power of **touch**, another fundamental trait to improve interactions[14]. Yes, **touching others** during an interaction makes them **like you more**! Before you follow the pattern of many people who say they **don't like being touched**, allow me to present some studies that will change your mind about the importance of this form of expression.

A study by researchers at the University of California, Berkeley found that the **amount of physical touch** among NBA players earlier in the season predicted their performance at the end of the season—the more greetings, hugs, high-fives, chest punches, pats on the head and other "affectionate" ways of touching teammates, the better the performance of individual players and the **team as a whole**[15]. Obviously, these "affectionate" touches among NBA players **are not effective in other situations**. Touching should be done the **right** way—light, short, on the arms, hands, forearms or shoulders. People who say they don't like being touched actually don't like being punched, pinched, held tightly or caressed in other parts of the body, such as the face[16]. Touching the **right** way is key for effective results.

In this sense, there's an experiment whose conclusion is that students touched by professors with pats on the back were almost **twice as likely** to participate in classes when compared to students who were not touched[17]. Likewise, college students lightly touched on the hands by a librarian indicated **liking the library and librarian** more than those who had not been touched[18]. When patients were warmly touched by health professionals during an appointment, they estimated these appointments lasted last **twice as long** as patients who had not been touched[19].

In the early 1980s, researchers at the University of Missouri revealed that people touched during a brief interaction were more likely to agree to a request[20]. In this study, participants were asked to sign a public interest petition: 55% of those who were not touched agreed to the signature; and **81% of those who were slightly touched signed the petition**. Around the same time, researchers at the University of Mississippi and Rhodes College found that patrons lightly touched on the shoulder or hands by a waitress gave larger tips compared to those who weren't touched[21]. In an experiment conducted by James Coan, Hillary Schaefer and Richard Davidson, married women were subjected to a mild shock while their brain activity was monitored by fMRI[22]. In some participants, waiting for the shock triggered the amygdala, which, as you know, is the part of the brain that processes information regarding **threats and stress**. In another group, however, participants showed **no activation** in this part of the brain. The reason? They **held the hands of their husbands** as they waited for the shock—the touch **turned off** the brain circuit responsible for the sense of threat.

Edmund Rolls of the University of Cambridge found that being lightly touched on the arm activates a part of the brain related to **rewards**: the orbitofrontal cortex[23]. Other studies also reveal that touch encourages the release of oxytocin, serotonin, and endorphins—related to feelings of trust, pleasure and pain reduction, respectively—as well as the reduction of the stress hormone cortisol[24].

And it's not just the people **touched** who get the benefits; whoever **touches** them also experiences interesting advantages. One study found that the elderly showed reduced signs of anxiety and depression, and reported greater well-being when they massaged children. Depressed mothers, encouraged to touch and massage their children more often, showed reduced symptoms in their conditions. In this sense, other studies still revealed that a mother's touch made children gain more weight, cry less and be more resilient when facing difficulties[25].

We can see, therefore, that the **right** touch encourages cooperation, makes people evaluate others more positively, increases persuasion, reduces stress, generates confidence, increases pleasure, decreases pain, and, yes, activates the vagus nerve. These characteristics were—and continue to be—fundamental to the survival and development of our species. Did you have any idea that touch was so important in your life? Touching and being touched is part of human nature and provides us with numerous benefits.

THE FUTURE OF INTERACTIONS

Studies on both the power of imitation and the influence of touch give us hints that we can't ignore. Although many "gurus" claim that the future of banks, sales, education and other areas is virtual, **nothing replaces human contact!** Just as you'll have an exponential gain in happiness if you engage in interactions every day, **companies** that invest in improving **personal** contact with customers (when appropriate) will receive greater **loyalty** and better **reviews** from them. Not surprisingly, when Mahdi Roghanizad, of Ivey Business School, and Vanessa Bohns, of Cornell University, studied the difference in persuasion between one request via **email** and another **in person**, the latter turned out to be **34 times more efficient**[26].

In another study already mentioned, in which call center employees significantly increased their performance after talking **in person** with scholarship students who benefited from their work, I purposely failed to mention that Adam Grant also attempted **another** approach to motivate participants[27]. Instead of the face-to-face conversation, one group was given several letters **written** by scholarship students saying how receiving a scholarship was positively impacting their lives. It turns out that, in this condition, one month after reading the letters, call center employees **didn't increase** neither **persistence** (time on the phone) nor **performance** (amount of money collected). The group that had **personal contact** with the students showed an increase in **both variables**.

In addition to the motivational gain, personal interactions can also guarantee an increase in your **happiness**. Martin Seligman, the renowned researcher from the University of Pennsylvania, conducted an experiment in which six groups of participants were to perform **one** task each in order to increase their levels of well-being[28]. One group was assigned to write a **gratitude letter** to someone who helped them, but whom they never thanked. This group should deliver the letter **in person** and wait silently while the person read it. Of all six tasks, the **personal** delivery of the gratitude letter was the one that caused the highest gains in participant **happiness**, in addition to being the one that caused the greatest reductions in depressive symptoms. But the most striking fact of this simple intervention was that the effects of the gratitude letter remained present even **one month after** the experiment. Virtual interactions do not feature touch, imitation or facial expressions—fundamental characteristics for an excellent interaction. Don't get me wrong,

I'm not against technology. I just believe it should be used to **improve** interactions with customers, not to **replace** them.

That is why imitation and touch are the **maximum recognition** one can receive during a conversation. In addition to all these benefits, better personal interactions still satisfy that basic psychological need discovered by Ryan and Deci: **relationships**. To love and to feel loved, to value and to be valued are fundamental factors for motivation. Remember that relationships are not only important to your motivation, but are also the **main predictors of happiness**. Recognizing others, being grateful, helping people and searching for positive interactions are ways to make the most important variable for happiness play in your favor.

Therefore, to get the most out of your interactions, notice the posture of the person you're talking to. Remember, just as we naturally imitate those with whom we feel a certain similarity, intentionally imitating a person **causes** in them the same feeling. How are they positioned? Standing with the right foot in front of the left? If you're facing them, place your left foot in front of the right, giving them the feeling of looking in the **mirror**; this will make them like you more.

Coincidentally, the technique of imitating people is also known as *mirroring*. If they're facing you and gesturing with their left hand, after a while, make the same movement with your right hand. This person will suddenly **love you**! During the interaction, be sure to touch them lightly, preferably on the hand or forearm. Few touches during an interaction are enough to create good harmony, remembering that the **handshake** already has a very special additional characteristic—you and the other person make the **same movement** with your arms when shaking hands, **imitating each other simultaneously**.

Because of the power of these techniques, many people confuse mirroring and touch with **manipulation**. The truth, however, is that mirroring and touching someone during an interaction is nothing more than a way to make the moment **more pleasant**, to **connect** at a deeper level, to create **positive emotions** for you as well as for the other person.

However, two steps are necessary for effective **mirroring**. **First**: be discreet! If the person notices you're imitating them, the benefits are gone[29]. You don't have to make the **same gesture immediately**; wait your turn to speak to reproduce the movement. When they change **posture**, you don't have to do it right away; wait a few seconds and change slowly. Imitating posture is very interesting because **it holds for longer**, generating an increased sense of harmony between the parties. **Second: never** imitate **closed** postures. This includes crossed arms and legs, one arm crossing over the stomach, head tilting down, thumb holding the chin, etc. Closed and shrunken postures can send signs of **stress** to your brain, which have disastrous consequences for your performance and people's feelings, as you're about to discover.

BIOFEEDBACK

In 1984, students at the University of Illinois, divided into two groups, participated in an experiment in which one task consisted of holding a pen in their mouth while assessing how funny some comic strips were[30]. During the analysis of the strips, the participants of one of the groups should hold the pen with their lips, according to the figure below:

In turn, the members of the other group should hold the pen with their teeth:

In that study, the researchers came up with a surprising finding: the students who held the pen with their **teeth** while reading the strips rated them as **funnier** compared to those who held the pen with their lips. Why? Notice that by holding the pen with their teeth, people involuntarily assume a facial expression that resembles a smile, while holding the pen with their lips produces an expression similar to that of **sadness**. So, does that mean that by simply smiling, I'll **start** to feel happier? Exactly!

What Fritz Strack, Leonard Martin, and Sabine Stepper were testing in this experiment was the reliability of the **Facial Feedback Theory**, studied by other scientists, from the father of the Theory of Evolution, Charles Darwin[31], to renowned professor Paul Ekman of the University of California[32]. This theory, validated by a large body of scientific articles at different times, reveals that once you have assumed a certain facial expression, you begin to **feel** the emotion associated with it[33]. After many years, scientists noticed that the most common path of brain signals—from the brain to the muscles—was not the only one. The reverse path was also true—**from the muscles to the brain**[34]!

157

It's not just your brain that tells your body what to do; your body also tells your brain what it should feel.

Neuroscientist Alex Korb of the University of California, Los Angeles explains that the brain analyzes our muscles all the time to understand how we're feeling, and then "delivers" this feeling[35]. Make a sad face and, moments later, you'll become sad. Express joy and, in a moment, you'll feel happy. This phenomenon is called ***biofeedback***. Because of it, it's important to be aware of your facial expressions as they directly affect how you start to feel.

When we relate facial expressions, biofeedback and mirror neurons, your responsibility becomes even clearer. You already know that your expressions are **automatically imitated** by others because of mirror neurons; and also that, consequently, when people's muscles change, their **emotions** also change because of biofeedback. When our ancestors copied their mates' facial expressions of fear, increasing the likelihood of their cortisol levels rising, their bodies were prepared to face a threat, thanks to biofeedback. Facial expressions are also responsible for how people **evaluate** you, whether they'll have a **positive** or negative first impression[36].

One of the most common procedures in current aesthetic medicine is Botox, mostly applied in women. Those who apply Botox to their face seek **greater** self-admiration and admiration **from others**. What few know, however, is that as long as the effects last, Botox will **prevent them from expressing certain emotions**, over time causing others to **lose interest** in interacting with them. It's important to keep in mind that one of the characteristics that we evaluate in someone's smile is the formation of "crow's feet" in the corners of the eyes—they cause the smile to be seen as **sincere**, both by the people we're interacting with and by our own biofeedback.

Let's recall Barbara Fredrickson's study, in which the **joint** activation of the **zygomatic** and **eye orbicular muscles**—the muscle that forms "crow's feet"—predicted greater attention from participants in a task, precisely because this is the information that our brain needs to assess whether the smile is **authentic**[37]. By losing the "crow's feet" in the corner of your eyes because of arbitrary muscle paralysis (Botox), you may pass as "fake" to your brain and the brains of those with whom you interact daily.

Do you think that not being able to express a true smile can **lead** to depression? On the other hand, can injecting Botox on a person **suffering**

from depression make them **get out** of this condition, since the treatment would reduce their chances of expressing negative emotions? Some positive research has already been done on these subjects, and we all hope that more researchers will be interested in the topic[38].

During our conversation, researcher Barbara Fredrickson informed me that those "fake" smiles that people usually give can produce detrimental effects on their feelings and not trigger facial feedback. So, if you want to enjoy the benefits of biofeedback and facial feedback, increasing your well-being and that of people around you, seek **true** happiness by exposing yourself to positive emotions. Any intervention counts!

Few people know that facial and body expressions have a powerful influence on happiness, motivation, and even health[39]. The most interesting thing is that your body has another tool that can improve your performance in any challenge. And this tool is at your disposal 24/7. Let's learn how to use it!

POWER POSTURES

Have you noticed that the moment an athlete wins in a race, their body posture changes? The moment they achieve success, they raise their hands, tilt their head slightly upwards, straighten their spine, line up their shoulders, and stuff out their chest.

Soccer fans will recognize this posture, as it's the same assumed by fans when their team scores. Many soccer players change their posture in a manner similar to that of runners when they score a goal: arms slightly open and pointed upwards, straight spine, shoulders aligned, and chest out.

Changing body posture upon succeeding in any task is a **natural** mechanism in humans. We can say this because, upon observing blind athletes, they showed the same postural behavior when winning a competition, even though they have never **seen** that posture[40]. You change your posture when you close a deal, persuade your boss to approve a project, are recognized in a meeting, or receive a compliment. Any achievement makes your body change! It's important to note that a successful pose is one in which your muscles **expand** and you take up **more space**.

According to the illustration, this postural mechanism works as follows: success comes first, posture comes later. What surprised many scientists, however, was the finding that this mechanism is so deeply rooted in humans that it also works the other way around. When you change your body posture before a challenge, you increase your chances of success.

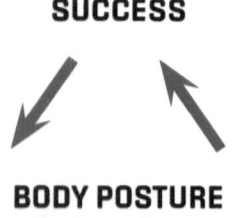

But how does this happen? Harvard researcher Amy Cuddy has been leading a great deal of studies on the subject and making phenomenal breakthroughs. In one experiment, she and other scientists separated two groups of participants: one was to hold two *high power poses* for one minute each; for the same period, the other should maintain two *low power poses*.

HIGH POWER POSES

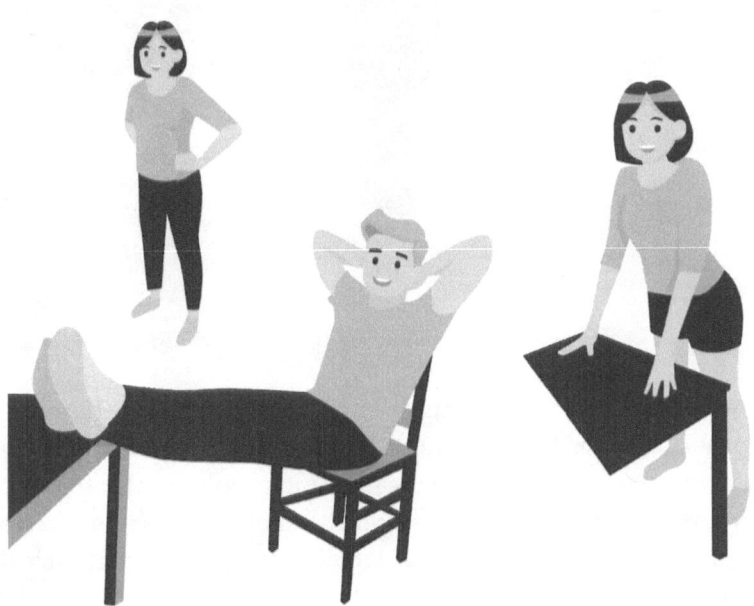

LOW POWER POSES

The researchers measured the levels of two hormones before and after participants maintained their postures. The first hormone was cortisol, which is related to stress and causes the creative and problem-solving part of the brain to partially shut down[41]. The second hormone measured was testosterone, present in both men and women, which is responsible for muscle development and bone strengthening, and also is directly related to behavior[42]. Testosterone is known as the hormone of **dominance**, **power** and **assertiveness**, which means that, when its levels in the bloodstream increase, **courage** and the likelihood of **succeeding** in any challenge also increase. High levels of this hormone cause us to breathe more calmly, which increases oxygen in the brain and makes it work better. Studies confirm that when animals—including humans—achieve higher status in their communities, their testosterone levels **automatically** increase. Likewise, individuals who naturally present higher levels of testosterone are the ones more likely to reach social positions of power[43].

What these scientists found[44] was that a simple postural change can alter the levels of both hormones, cortisol and testosterone. Those who held postures of powerlessness for two minutes had a 17% **increase** in their cortisol levels and a 10% **reduction** in their testosterone levels. On the other hand, participants who maintained **postures of power** during the same period presented a 25% **reduction** in cortisol and a 19% **increase** in testosterone. In other words, people who maintain a power pose become **less stressed and anxious**, while **gaining confidence and creativity**.

This discovery is important because a simple change of posture, even for a short period, can make you **more prepared** for the many challenges of your day, such as an important presentation, a client meeting, a sales visit, asking for a raise, a sports competition or a job interview. Since discovering these studies, whenever I have an important commitment, I come up with a way of expressing a **power pose**. In my classes, trainings and lectures, minutes before the event starts, I'll be in the bathroom, locked in a stall so nobody can see me. I'll put both arms up or on my waist (depending on the privacy of the stall), keep my spine and shoulders straight, stump my chest out, tilt my head about 20 degrees up and breathe deeply for a few minutes. When I go to a meeting in companies that want to hire my training or consulting services, if I can't go to the bathroom, I usually stand there looking at that beautiful wall art that every office displays at their reception, stating their **mission, vision**, and **values**. I stand in front of this wall, put my hands on my waist, stare at my chest, and stand erect for a while, just looking at the words. Of course, everything written on the wall helps me build arguments to close the deal, but at that moment, what I'm really trying to do is **regulate my hormones** so that when I start the meeting, I'm at **the peak of my performance**.

Remember that when you assume a posture with **expanded** muscles, because of biofeedback, your brain can understand that you are **feeling well** and thereby regulate your hormones to make you feel **even better**. It's also important that, before any challenge, you use Barbara Fredrickson's tips and do something to **genuinely** improve your mood. Every time you smile, biofeedback kicks in, and because of the **muscle expansion** and your facial **expression**, you can be even happier. Avoid letting external events change your mood, as might happen if a driver cuts in front of you, honks the horn or yells at you in traffic on the way to work or a meeting. In that case, turn on the radio and listen to something that makes you **smile** or that **inspires** you, instead of getting irritated.

Be very careful, too, with the biggest enemy of body posture: your smartphone! Yes, before any appointment, it's very common for people to sit on a couch—which can deregulate hormones because of the **muscle contraction** and **reduced stature** that position entails—and lean over their phones. I just hope you're not one of those people, because assuming a low power pose, twitching your arm muscles to hold your phone and keeping your head tilted down, is certainly not a smart choice before any major challenge. A valuable tip at times like this is to always **stand** while you wait. As you know, there's a direct relationship between our body posture and the way we begin to feel. Every time we **make ourselves smaller**, sitting on a couch, for example, we become more vulnerable to feeling bad. On the other hand, every time we **stand taller**, assuming an upright posture, for example, we feel better and more confident.

Avoid falling into the temptation of using your phone moments before a major challenge: **put it away** in your briefcase or purse. And if you can keep it **out of reach**, even better. The health damages of using a phone are a subject that's been keeping doctors busy all over the world. One of the most common problems that excessive smartphone use presents is what doctors call text neck[45]. When your posture is erect, the head requires the neck muscles to support about 11.9 lbs., but that weight changes to about 60 lbs. when the head is tilted down. Over time, this overload poses serious problems for your neck. If you work on a laptop, this same problem may occur. So, one of the best investments for your posture is to buy a wireless keyboard and mouse, as well as a laptop support, so that the screen is aligned with your eyes, and your posture while working is upright. Nobody would like to be called in for a surprise meeting by the boss shortly after spending three hours curved over a laptop, right?

It's because of these and other benefits of good body posture that science has been studying the positive health effects of practicing exercises like yoga and pilates[46], because these modalities develop upright posture and muscle expansion. In addition to hormonal advantages, one study also revealed that the practice of meditation drives the brain to age more slowly. An investigation by UCLA, the Australian National University and the Jena University Hospital found that the brain of a person who meditates is, on average, **seven and a half years younger** than that of a person who doesn't keep this habit[47].

Several scientific studies have argued that body posture has connections that go beyond increased confidence, self-control, reduced stress and anxiety. Other benefits are evaluating other people more positively[48], demonstrating leadership even without power[49], increased creativity[50] and confidence[51], as well as greater ease in remembering positive factors[52].

When you increase your amount of positive emotions on a daily basis, avoid negative moments, recognize other people, practice acts of kindness, make an effort in your interactions and take care of your body posture, another fantastic thing happens in your life.

CHAPTER 8

The Results of It All

EXPLANATORY STYLE

Early in his career, Martin Seligman, the father of positive psychology, studied how dogs behaved after being conditioned to understand that they **had no control over future events**, a behavior we have already explored—**learned hopelessness**[1]. Years later, Seligman was called by the insurance company MetLife to study the reasons why the turnover rate of their salespeople was so high. As a former sales executive, I am very familiar with the challenges of this industry. The rejection of salespeople is huge, to the point that one study shows that for every ten visits made, **nine** will receive a **negative** response[2]. At the time, that made half of the new MetLife salespeople resign in the **first year**—and only 20% of them remained in the company for four years or more. As you know, learned hopelessness also happens to human beings when we experience negative events for an **extended time**[3].

After applying some psychological tests to all MetLife insurance brokers, Seligman discovered something important: brokers who were optimistic sold 37% more than their peers, and those ranked among the top 10% of the team had a performance 88% higher. In addition, Seligman found that optimistic brokers were **50% less likely to resign**. This finding was a milestone in the history of positive psychology, which Seligman called *explanatory style*[4], referring to how people **explain past events in their lives**.

What if I ask you what **your** explanatory style is like, how do you think you would do on a test? Well, let's find out!

Imagine that you're at the bank to pay a bill. At the bank, there are 50 more people waiting in line. While you calmly wait your turn, a group of robbers break into the bank. Customers are desperate, some start screaming and running. In the midst of the confusion, one of the robbers gets nervous and fires a **single** shot, which hits your arm. Later, at the hospital, when you're visited by your family and friends, how do you tell the story of what happened to you that day?

An individual who evaluates an event of this sort as **unlucky**—after all, of the 50 people at the bank that day, you were the one who got shot—reveals a *pessimistic explanatory style*. People with this explanatory style explain events with pessimism, believe that they can't succeed at work because they're unlucky and think that the economic crisis will never end. This explanatory style causes people in the robbery situation to say that they had **terrible luck**, because they chose to go to the bank at that moment, or that things like that only happen to them.

Those with an **optimistic explanatory style** exhibit the opposite behavior. They can always see the bright side of things: they believe that they haven't got a promotion at work, for example, because they lack the necessary skills, and therefore see it as an **opportunity** to grow. Those with an **optimistic explanatory style** see an economic crisis as something temporary, and receive a rejection from a customer as natural—perhaps that customer was not in a good place to make a purchase. For someone like that, getting shot in the arm during a robbery is an extremely lucky situation, as the bullet could have hit their **head** or **spine**, or worse, a child.

When MetLife started to analyze the explanatory style of their candidates, something fantastic happened: the turnover rate plummeted, and the company's market share grew by almost 50%[5]. The renowned professor

Tal Ben-Shahar, whom we've met a few pages back, sums up our choice of explanatory style[6].

> "While I do not believe that things necessarily happen for the best, I know that some people are able to make the best of things that happen."

But what's the problem with our **explanatory style**? It's simply that, as you now know, we are **naturally negative**. For us, it's always easier to find the negative than the positive side of things. Remember the advice I gave you to avoid, whenever possible, watching the news and soap operas and talking to negative people? One of the consequences of choosing to have negative moments is developing a **pessimistic explanatory style**, after all, the more tragedies you expose yourself to, the more negative facts you begin to see[7].

When you **choose**, however, to make everyone you interact with smile, when you choose to show others recognition, help your coworkers, watch a comedy series, get away from people who only complain, be mindful of your posture, touch people's lives in a positive way, focus on gratitude instead of greed, practice acts of kindness, buy experiences, invest your money in helping others to have good living conditions and spend it in a prosocial way, replacing selfish behaviors, you are also choosing to **change your explanatory style**. Your explanatory style is **not fixed**, it changes according to what you **expose** yourself to, according to the **choices** you make.

When you change your explanatory style, your brain starts to pay more attention to positive facts. This will consequently increase the frequency of your positive emotions and contribute to your growth and development, as well as improve the quality of your interactions. I would just like to emphasize once again that having an optimistic explanatory style and seeing the good side of things does not mean having unrealistic Pollyanna optimism.

There's also a very big difference between **being positive** and **thinking positive**. Many believe that, to have a more positive life, all we need to do is **think** positive. In fact, the self-help aisle would not be packed of books on that subject if that technique didn't work, would it? Gabriele Oettingen of New York University has a different **secret** to tell.

PART 3

POSITIVE THINKING

CHAPTER 9

Being Positive
×
Thinking Positive

POSITIVE THINKING, NEGATIVE RESULTS

So far, we've explored actions that you can take every day to become a more positive person. But there's great confusion regarding the benefits of **being positive** versus **thinking positive**. In addition to these being different behaviors, their results are also **completely opposite**.

In the beginning of this book, you learned what Yannis Theodorakis, Robert Weinberg and their colleagues found about the relation between athletes and motivational self-talk before a game or test: those who used what the researchers named ***motivational statement***, i.e., phrases like "I can do it!", performed worse than any other group of athletes who used different statements[1]. Football players, for example, had better performance when they said "I can see my goal!" than "I can do it!" The researchers named this sentence model ***instructional self-talk***. In their article, published in 2000, they concluded:

> "[...] instructional self-talk appears to be superior when performing tasks requiring precision, timing and coordination. In addition, both instructional and motivational self-talk produced significantly better performance than a control condition for a strength task."

It's important to emphasize that none of the experiments resulted in a significantly better performance if using motivational self-talk rather than instructional self-talk, which leads us to the conclusion: whenever you use self-talk for motivation, make sure to be instructional.

This research is important if you have trouble getting yourself to exercise, or if your work involves any kind of motor skills. However, when your work involves **cognitive** skills—as do most people's—what should you do to self-motivate? That was the question that researchers Ibrahim Senay and Dolores Albarracín, of the University of Illinois, together with Kenji Noguchi, of the University of Southern Mississippi, wanted to answer[2]. As I mentioned in the beginning of this book, Senay, Albarracín and Noguchi divided the participants of an experiment into two groups, and asked them to solve ten anagrams, following these instructions:

> **Group 1** – Spend one minute wondering whether you can solve the anagrams.
>
> **Group 2** – Spend one minute thinking that you can solve the anagrams.

Unlike what you're instructed to do by the motivational "gurus" of our day—those who are paid big money to "motivate" employees—the first group, led to **question** their ability, solved 50% **more** anagrams than the group instructed to **affirm** their ability to solve them. In a second experiment, instead of asking people to think of something, researchers asked them to **write**. Before solving the anagrams, Group 1 should write "**Will I**" (actually a question), while Group 2 should write "**I will**", "**I**", or "**will**" (actually an affirmation) 20 times each. As a result, the group that wrote "**Will I**" solved practically **100% more** anagrams than the other group.

Until then, no other scientific study had analyzed how **sentence structure** can alter people's motivation and results. The explanation for that behavior change involves understanding that, when you question yourself, your brain requires a response. When you ask yourself, **"Will I get a raise?,"** your brain automatically starts thinking, **"Yes, the last project I coordinated brought high revenues to the company,"** or **"I don't think so, the company is having a hard time and it wouldn't be appropriate to ask for a raise now, I'll wait a little longer."** The answers your brain comes up with help to **prepare** you for the situation, increasing your performance.

On the other hand, when you affirm to yourself, **"I will make it,"** **your brain makes no effort to help you achieve a goal**. This exercise of **questioning** the possibility of reaching a goal, instead of blindly believing you will reach it, is the secret to increasing your chances of success. In science, there's no one better than researcher Gabriele Oettingen to explain to us how this works.

MENTAL CONTRASTING

In the beginning of this book, I presented the results of a study conducted by Gabriele Oettingen in which college seniors informed whether they fantasized about finding a job soon after finishing school[3]. Two years later, Oettingen and her colleague Doris Mayer contacted each of those students to collect more data, and what they found was shocking. Students who reported **frequently fantasizing** about finding a job ended up sending fewer applications and, consequently, receiving **fewer** job offers. Within the same group of "positive thinkers", researchers also observed that those that did have a job earned **lower** salaries in relation to other study participants.

In fact, the other group, which reported **not fantasizing as often**, sent **more** applications, received **more** job offers and, among those already in the market, their salaries were **higher** than those of their colleagues who used to "think positive". But why did students who fantasized less achieve such different results? The answer is in the second stage of the study. In it, the researchers asked students to also report **negative** thoughts, mental images and fantasies. Surprisingly, students with a more balanced ratio between **positive** and **negative** fantasies achieved **far superior** results than those with more prominent "positive thinking" ratios.

Oettingen's research is the first to analyze different types of positive thoughts: those based on **previous experience**, in which despite expecting a positive result, people don't discard the **negative obstacles or facts** that can arise; and those that are **disconnected from reality**, involving thoughts and imaging based on **desires and dreams**. These studies reiterate that when people **fantasize** about a positive result, they understand it has **already happened**[4]. Therefore, they dedicate **less**, make **less** efforts, and, consequently, have **less** chances of achieving their goal. Of course, fantasizing about a positive result makes you feel good and increase your short-term motivation, but the results of this practice can be disastrous to your future.

Oettingen and Mayer, in their article, conclude:

> "[...] our findings imply that positive fantasies can have long-term costs with respect to a person's personality development. [...] For example, the first job is the basis for successive job positions a person holds during his or her life [...], with both status and wages increasing over time. Thus our findings of positive fantasies predicting low success in entering professional life imply that positive fantasies may be problematic not only for the life task of beginning a career. Moreover, an enduring transitional period between academic and professional life should adversely affect relations with parents and friends, financial and living conditions, and the advent of starting a family. Similarly, it should strain well-being, high self-esteem, and professional self-efficacy."

The consequences of positive thinking disconnected from reality don't affect just people, but also companies and other entities. Gabriele Oettingen found, for example, that the **more optimistic** the weekly news were about the oscillations of the Dow Jones, the more it **dropped** the following week and month. When she analyzed the tone of inauguration speeches of American presidents from 1933 to 2009, she saw that the **more optimistic** the speech, the **lower** the GDP and the **higher** the country's unemployment rate[5].

Oettingen found in her research that, after a person fantasized about a future desire, their systolic blood pressure **dropped**[6]. This pressure measures how strongly your heart pumps blood to your body; therefore, the more

relaxed you feel, the **lower** your systolic pressure. On the other hand, when you're excited about practicing any activity, your body uses up more oxygen and nutrients, causing your heart to beat **faster** to distribute the blood and compensate the higher consumption. What researchers know is that there's a **direct** relationship between the **level of systolic pressure** and the **motivation** of an individual[7]. Oettingen's studies confirm that, soon after we fantasize about a future desire, our brain gives us **pleasure** through the feeling that we've **already reached** that goal. Consequently, that feeling of achievement makes us **relax**, which causes our systolic pressure to drop and, with it, our **motivation**. In the beginning of this book, you found that motivation is what makes humans **act**, therefore, **without motivation, there's no action**. This is why people that fantasize often will hardly reach their goals: they **lose** the very motivation that would make them go after these goals.

> **Thinking positive makes you achieve a goal only in your head, causing you to lose motivation and, consequently, not make any efforts to make your goal a reality.**

It would be amazing if the simple act of frequently thinking about something you want, and desiring that with all your heart, could make it come true **effortlessly**. I'm sure you'd love to see a Ferrari parked on your driveway after spending months thinking about owning that car, but unfortunately, **that's not how we write our future**. Many professionals tell people they can have whatever they want, as long as they believe in their dreams, because all that matters is thinking positive. It's easy to sell something **people wish was true**, something that makes them feel **in total control** of their own lives.

The morning I met with Gabriele Oettingen at a café near the New York University campus, in Manhattan, I heard her say that, for a scientist, the choice to spend decades studying a controversial subject that **goes against the expectations of people**—and other researchers—is exhausting. "Still, you must move on", she said, smiling. It seems that, like Ryan and Deci, Oettingen prefers to leave a legacy instead of building instant fame.

Obviously, fantasizing about the future is pleasurable and feeds the ego, but this practice won't help you achieve the goals that require high levels of effort, commitment and energy. Dreaming of a successful future could very well **soothe** your pain in the short term, but the problem is that it'll make it **worse** in the long term. As incredible as it seems, **thinking negative** is what can turn you towards **realistic thinking**. Thinking negative brings you back to Earth. Does this mean you should give up on your dreams? Absolutely not! It means you should stop believing they will happen with just the **power** of positive thinking. Don't stop thinking positive, but face your dreams **differently** if you want them to come true.

By observing that a higher level of success was reached when people thought ***positively and negatively*** about their goals, Gabriele Oettingen named her finding ***mental contrasting***, and started carrying out new experiments to test it. In one of them, students from two German universities were questioned about their most important goal at the moment, and, later, asked to indicate, in a 0% to 100% scale, what they thought was their chance of achieving that goal[8]. Next, participants should write four short sentences about the **positive** results they would have if they achieved that goal (e.g., having more time for friends, going to a renowned graduate school, feeling more confident, etc.), and four more short sentences about the real **obstacles** that could undermine that goal (e.g., being too shy, having too much work to do, not being in shape, etc.). After these exercises, four groups were distributed with the following conditions:

> **Group 1 —** Students should compare two sentences they wrote about the **positive** results of realizing their dreams with two sentences about the **obstacles** that could undermine them. This group was instructed to write details about the obstacles and the positive results, starting with the former
>
> **Group 2 —** Students should **fantasize** using only the four sentences on the **positive** results of realizing their desires, detailing these positive fantasies.

> **Group 3** — Students should **fantasize** using only the four sentences on the **obstacles** that could undermine these desires, detailing these negative fantasies.
>
> **Group 4** — Students should compare two sentences they wrote about the **obstacles** that could undermine their desires with two sentences on the **positive** results of realizing them. This group was instructed to detail positive results and obstacles, **starting with the former**. As you can see, this condition is the opposite of Group 1.

Immediately after this activity, Gabriele Oettingen, Hyeonju Pak, and Karoline Schnetter, the study authors, asked all students to report how **energized** they felt. Two weeks after the experiment, students received a survey about all the actions they had taken to reach their goals. According to the researcher's hypothesis, students who performed mental contrasting (Group 1) would feel **more energized** and, consequently, take **more actions** to reach their goals than students in the other groups. For the research team's surprise, however, **not all students who used mental contrasting had better results**.

Analyzing the data more closely, Oettingen and her team realized that **only** the students who believed they had **good chances** of reaching their goals felt more energized after the exercises and took immediate action. When students that used mental contrasting felt that their goals **would not be reached**—often because they were **disconnected from reality**—they reported feeling **less** energized and, therefore, **took no action** to pursue them. This shows that mental contrasting has **even more advantages** to those who practice it.

> **Comparing a wish to the obstacles to realize it doesn't just make you take more action to achieve it, but also helps you give up on dreams that are too far from reality.**

When I read Gabriele Oettingen's research, I immediately thought of those impacted by stage entrepreneurs, that keep telling you how your company can be the next Google, Uber or Amazon. These professionals show examples of startups that sold for millions, and implore you to think positive, belief in your project and yourself. But after spending hours at events like these, fantasizing about their successful startups and daydreaming about being millionaires, will these spectators take immediate action to fulfill them? Or will they feel relaxed, feeling like they already reached their goals and, therefore, not even visit an accountant to set up a company? What about startup owners that go to these events? Will they make a list of all the difficulties they can find along the way or, after much fantasizing, will they think their dreams can be reached only with the power of positive thinking and no real effort?

Will they leave the event developing plans to improve their products and services, train their employees, fine-tune their processes, adjust sales pitches and schedule more investor meetings, or will they take home the feeling that **there's nothing else to be done**? What do you think?

BIG DREAMS, SMALL ACHIEVEMENTS

Over the last few years, the following quote has become the mantra of many executives and business owners[9]:

"Dreaming big and dreaming small is the same work."

But is it? The author of this quote may have **every** credential of a successful businessman, but from the scientific point of view, this message is **incredibly mistaken**. First, because dreaming small **is not the same work** as dreaming big: Oettingen and other scientists found that dreaming big requires **less** effort from our brain, in addition to being much more **pleasurable**[10]. Second, the quote is unfortunate because dreaming big and dreaming small bring **different results**[11]! When your big dream is unrealistic, it makes you less energized and motivated, making you lose the motivation that would make you act on making this dream a reality. The **small dream** at least makes you **feel that your goal can be reached**, which causes the energy and motivation necessary to go after it.

This doesn't mean that you should always think small, or that it's no use dreaming big, but that you must also think of the **obstacles** that can stop you from getting what you want. Often, when using mental contrasting, you realize that your **big dream** is actually a **nightmare disconnected from reality**—consuming hours of your day, draining your energy, wasting your company's money, keeping you away from friends and family, lowering productivity and keeping you away from smaller, more realistic dreams, which could actually be achieved.

The dangers of the big dream in the corporate world are many. When a businessman's dream is **too** big, making him set unrealistic goals for his team, his employees develop **learned hopelessness**[12]. One danger of learned hopelessness is that, even if the team's goals become realistic and reachable at a certain point in the **future**, because they were **already conditioned** to give up due to the constant failures they faced, people **no longer have** the motivation to dedicate to these goals, which **could be achieved** with their efforts.

> **Scientific findings really are amazing. One of them is that even successful people give bad advice.**

To make sure your dream comes true, however, it can't be **big** or **small**, but **medium**. Renowned researcher Mihaly Csikszentmihalyi, of Claremont Graduate University, conquered the world of psychology by revealing the phenomenon of the **flow state**[13]. Have you ever been so focused on a task that you lost track of time? How did you feel then? How productive were you? This moment of pure focus, productivity, engagement, satisfaction and happiness is precisely the **flow state**: when you're at **peak** performance, developing work that is highly important to you. Since his book on the subject came out, in 1990, Csikszentmihalyi was on the spotlight all over the world, especially because he showed people how to **enter** a flow state. This is one of his tips:

> "The ratio between what one *should* do and *can* do must be perfect. The challenge can't be too big nor too small. It should have a perfect ratio so that, each time one uses their skills, the effort made is the biggest reward."

Mihaly Csikszentmihalyi calls this an *autotelic experience*—when a task is so enjoyable that the **moment** dedicated to performing it is its own **reward**. It's only possible to reach a flow state, then, when the challenge is **moderate**. And how do we know we're **not** in a flow state? When we're **self-conscious** and start paying too much attention to the task we're performing.

Let's recall the research by Roy Baumeister, which shows that financial incentives make people **pay more attention to what they're doing**, causing **poor** performance[14]. This is yet another proof of how much external motivators **undermine** intrinsic motivation, making it hard to even reach a state of **full engagement** in an activity. One of the main contributions of Csikszentmihalyi for the scientific community is the finding that the flow state creates an **ideal**—or optimal—level of motivation. This means that this state develops intrinsic motivation.

Back to moderate goals, Csikszentmihalyi shows that when the "dream" is too big, people **give up**, because they think they'll never be able to reach it—an understanding that's completely consistent with Gabriele Oettingen's findings

> **"Research shows that if goals are unrealistic, but you can achieve them by cheating, then people will cheat. They will commit fraud to obtain the incentive," said researcher George Loewenstein in an article for the journal *Psychology Today*, warning us of yet another danger of establishing impossible goals for ourselves and our teams**[15]**.**

In the ideal scenario, therefore, you should not determine your goals in terms of big dreams, but of **several** medium and achievable dreams. By achieving one medium goal at a time, your chances of success can increase considerably.

WOOP: A TOOL FOR SUCCESS

Despite all the positive results of her research, Gabriele Oettingen still wasn't satisfied. She wanted her work to have an **even bigger** impact on people's lives, and her solution was literally DIY.

Peter Gollwitzer, professor and researcher at the New York University whose research also focuses on what people can do to reach goals, along with his colleagues, found that when we commit to a goal, the most effective way to reach it is to make a **plan** immediately. This plan should focus on a **behavior** to be followed every time a given situation is presented. For example, if you're always too tired to exercise in the morning, Gollwitzer suggests establishing a plan like this: **if the alarm goes off tomorrow at 6:30 a.m., I'll get up** (behavior) and **take a walk in the park** (goal). Gollwitzer made several studies about this method and found that, for example, when he asked his students to write a report two days after Christmas, 71% of those who had set a plan describing **where, when and how** they would do the assignment turned it in before the deadline[16]. Of the other share of students, who wasn't instructed to create a plan, only 32% turned in the report. Gollwitzer named his method *implementation intentions*: when a person makes a **plan in advance** of how they'll **behave** at the time of **facing** a given situation, they are **more prepared** to act.

In analyzing Gollwitzer's studies, Gabriele Oettingen realized that **mental contrasting** and **implementation intentions** had in common the ability to make people aware of their thoughts and mental images, which psychology calls *metacognitive strategy*[17]. Oettingen noted that joining both strategies could be the key to finally creating an easy-to-use tool. Good for Oettingen, she's **married** to Peter Gollwitzer!

The couple decided to compare the effectiveness of their tools **separately**, and then **together**. Which would be most effective in getting people to achieve their goals? The results were exciting! Both the group that used **mental contrasting** and the one that used **implementation intentions** progressed further in their objectives. However, the third group tested by the pair of researchers, this time using both tools **together**, made much more significant progress[18].

At first, Oettingen and Gollwitzer decided to call their tool **MCII** (Mental Contrasting Implementation Intentions), but came to realize that the name was not very attractive. It was then that **WOOP** (Wish, Outcome, Obstacle, Plan) emerged as a revolutionary tool. WOOP works in a very simple way:

> On a piece of paper, write your wish using three to six words. Then, write down the best possible result of fulfilling your wish, also using three to six words. Then, write down the main obstacle that can stop you from fulfilling it. Remember that the obstacle must be something within your control, something that depends only on you. Set your imagination free and let it guide you on this; write down everything that comes to mind. Finally, develop a plan to overcome this obstacle, describe a specific action that will make you overcome it. Write the time and place where the obstacle will appear, then develop your plan using an IF-THEN statement: IF obstacle X occurs (moment and location), THEN I will do Y. Repeat this plan out loud to yourself, just once.

Extremely simple, isn't it? You can apply WOOP to any type of wish, as it's a totally flexible tool. If your greatest wish for the next two weeks, for example, is to lose weight, then you can develop a WOOP plan as follows:

> **Wish:** To lose 5 lbs.
>
> **Outcome:** Greater self-confidence.
>
> **Obstacle:** Pastry shop on the way home.
>
> **Plan:** **If** I leave the office at 6:00 pm and feel like getting a pastry, **then** I'll take another route.

But isn't thinking of a wish and then an obstacle a natural human behavior? Unfortunately, no! Oettingen and her colleague A. Timur Sevincer found in a series of experiments that **only 16%** of people use mental contrasting

spontaneously—when they're not led to think of an obstacle, 40% of them only think positive[19]. Certainly, this is because positive thinking is much more **pleasurable** than **mental contrasting**, and it requires **less effort** from the brain, as I explained.

Decades of research using WOOP guaranteed great success for people with goals such as exercising more[20], eating better[21], recovering from back pain[22], reducing the amount of stress in life after a heart attack[23], improving their love live[24], and doing better at school[25]. When I spoke to Gabriele Oettingen in New York, I learned that there are many ongoing studies using WOOP. She found that, in order for it to be the most effective, you should use WOOP **daily** to make it a **habit**.

If you're new to WOOP, it's important that you initially focus on small wishes that you want to fulfill in the next 24 hours—examples range from not fighting your spouse to spending a day without exposing yourself to negative news. If you make a WOOP plan every morning, it will allow you to constantly **adjust** your goals, which will make your wish **more likely** to occur. If, for example, you want to make more calls to customers and set a goal of **15** calls per day, and by midday you find that you've already made **10** calls, you can adjust your goal to **18** or **20.**

To ensure that this becomes a daily exercise, Oettingen did us one more favor: she launched the WOOP **app**. It allows you to WOOP at any time, avoiding losing opportunities to fulfill your wishes. The feature also guarantees you'll WOOP the **right** way, not skipping any of the stages or doing it in a hurry.

WOOP is a fantastic tool for two more reasons. In the first place, it works **unconsciously**[26]. When WOOPing, your mind begins to work to attain your wish **without you noticing**. Soon, you reach your goal **without even realizing it**. Second, WOOP is a tool that works on what psychologists call *integrative solutions*: results that **spread** and affect **other areas of your life**. If you want to lose weight, for example, when using WOOP, you will not only lose weight, but also **exercise** more, **eat** healthier, **perform** better at work, **sleep** better, feel more **attractive**, have more **confidence**, **lose the fear** of speaking in public, etc.

Oettingen's studies show that there's a very big difference between **being positive** and **thinking positive**. While **thinking positive** is the false belief that your wishes can be attained only with the **power of thought** and no effort, **being positive** is something else. You **become** a positive person when you seek to increase your number of positive emotions, avoid unnecessary negative emotions, invest your money in others, enhance your interactions, change your explanatory style, and accept that you will face difficulties in life. So you have a **positive outlook** on the future, but it's **realistic**.

The illusion of positive thinking brings terrible consequences, so it would be extremely beneficial to **get rid** of this habit, if you have it. Instead of positive thinking, use your time to wonder: What is my greatest wish? What is the personal **obstacle** that can keep me from attaining it?

WOOP is undoubtedly a spectacular way to achieve goals, but our motivation and ability to reach these goals are often met with an even greater obstacle: **our beliefs**

CHAPTER 10

The Happiness Mentality

THE GIFT OF PRACTICE

Think of the greatest expert in your field of work: what made them **better** than the others? What does this expert have that is different? What differentiated Mozart from other musicians? What characteristics of Ayrton Senna led him to be one of the best pilots in the world? And what does the best salesperson you know have that others don't?

When I'm introduced to someone, I often hear the question, "What do you do for work?" When I say that I'm a professor of several disciplines, including some in the field of **sales**, I immediately hear something like, **"Wow, being good at sales is a real gift**!" You've probably already heard this about your profession, and probably already **said** it about someone else's.

Because it's **difficult** for us to explain why some professionals are far better than others in their careers, we attribute their success to their having **something special**: a gift, a skill, genetics, some **"superpower"**. Therefore, we think we can **never** be equal to them, since we don't have that attribute. Many people say that Pelé was **born** to play soccer, and that the best salesman in the company where you work was born to sell. But when science sets out to analyze why some individuals have extreme success in their fields, the answers we find are quite different from that.

Wolfgang Amadeus Mozart possessed a skill called ***perfect pitch***[1]. Because of it, as a kid, when he heard a piano or any other instrument, he could say with absolute accuracy what the musical note was—even from another room, far from the source of the sound. This ability was not limited to detecting musical notes; Mozart could hear and differentiate **any** sound—from a train whistle to a kettle whistle—and accurately say what was the musical note in question. For many years, scientists believed that **perfect pitch** was a genetic skill, granted only to a few lucky ones. Until, in 2014, Japanese psychologist Ayako Sakakibara trained a group of children between the ages of two and six for a few months, and made them **all** learn to identify any note played on a piano[2].

Some neuroscientists who studied the brain of Albert Einstein found that his lower parietal lobe was **larger** and had a different shape compared to other people, which led them to believe that this was what made Einstein so successful in performing abstract mathematical calculations[3]. But years of research revealed that **the longer an individual worked as a mathematician, the more gray matter he had in that part of the brain**[4].

Another example of this phenomenon comes from an article published by Edward Taub, a researcher at the University of Alabama. Taub studied the brain of nine musicians and found that **the part responsible for controlling their left hand**—used extensively to play the violin, cello or guitar—was **significantly larger** than that of non-musicians[5]. In addition, the part of the musicians' brains intended for controlling the fingers of the left hand was so large that it invaded another region of the brain, responsible for touch in the palm of the hand. Has **nature** determined at birth that these people would be musicians and gifted them with special brains to use their left hands with speed and precision? Or has the fact that they played their musical instruments **daily** and used their left hand intensively made their brains **change and adapt**?

These and several other studies demystify the belief of many that some individuals were **born** with special abilities, that only a few win the **genetic lottery**. This is not to say that all are born equal, for there are, indeed, initial differences[6]. What these studies reveal is that, whatever the initial differences in people's skills, practice can make them disappear in the long run. It means that an individual's initial abilities **don't give them any advantage throughout their life**, since anyone can develop them through practice. But the practice that makes genetic advantages go away with time is not just any practice.

Professor Karl Anders Ericsson of Florida State University, the world's leading expert in the study of experts, has been studying the habits of specialists in the most diverse fields for more than 40 years. Many people believe that simply practicing an activity for many years makes a professional an expert in their field, which is refuted by science. The most curious fact about professional experience is that, in fact, in many cases it makes the professional **worse**. Often, a physician with 20 years of experience is more likely to be **worse** than another with 5 years of experience[7]. A driver with 30 years of experience may be worse than another with 7 years of practice.

Ericsson names the "experience" that many people claim to have as *naive practice*, an activity that you do every day, but in which you don't challenge yourself to do **better** or try anything **new**. Ericsson's studies point out that simply repeating an activity doesn't make a person better at it, mainly because, after reaching an "acceptable" level of performance and developing "automated" skills, additional years of experience will gradually **deteriorate these skills** if no conscious efforts are made to improve them.

According to Ericsson's findings, what actually improves professional performance is what's called *purposeful practice*, that is, the activity in which a person makes constant efforts to **improve, regardless of their current performance level**. Purposeful practice consists of four elements: **specific purpose, intense focus, immediate feedback**, and **frequent discomfort**.

Early in his career, Anders Ericsson's interest was to study the possibility of making a person **increase their short-term memory capacity**. He recruited Steve Faloon, a student at Carnegie Mellon University, and trained him for two years to memorize sequences of numbers[8]. In the early sessions, Steve could not memorize more than eight digits, achieving a performance similar to anyone else's. A few sessions later, Steve seemed not to have improved, until, in a specific session, he memorized **nine** digits. Ericsson noted that this was achieved because of the way he conducted the study, not because the student suddenly had an improvement in memory. In the same session, Ericsson asked Steve to memorize a **five-digit** sequence. If he succeeded, the researcher would give him a new sequence with **six** digits, dictating

one digit per second, and so on—just as Steve memorized a sequence, the researcher **added a digit**. By contrast, whenever Steve missed the sequence, Ericsson **removed two digits**.

This way, Ericsson kept the student feeling **challenged all the time**, but in a rate that Steve could cope with—the process created a **flow state** in Steve, because of its moderate difficulty. And so Steve gradually and slowly improved his performance. Shortly after the **hundredth** training session, he was able to memorize **40** digits, a better result than that of some **professionals** in the field. The student worked with Ericsson for more than 200 sessions, achieving the incredible result of memorizing **82** digits!

In addition to the way in which Ericsson led the study to help Steve achieve this impressive mark, **Steve himself developed a training technique during the sessions**. He told Ericsson that his secret was to memorize **several** sequences of three or four digits, leaving **one** sequence of up to six digits to be memorized at the end. This technique developed by Steve proved to be fundamental to the success of the study, something that Ericsson noticed only when he tried to replicate the method with student Reneé Elio. Ericsson recruited Reneé to memorize a sequence of numbers, but the student **didn't achieve the same success as Steve**, managing to memorize only **twenty digits**—which is equally impressive.

As he sought to better understand why Steve had been able to memorize so many digits and Reneé hadn't, despite the identical manner in which he conducted both studies, Ericsson, along with Bill Chase, his research partner, discovered something impressive. By recruiting another student for the study, Dario Donatelli, and using the **same method**—dictating one number per second, starting with a five-digit sequence, increasing one digit each time the current sequence was memorized or removing two digits if not—this time the scientists added **Steve's help** to teach Dario what he had done to memorize the sequences. With the **right training method** and the **help of someone who had already succeeded in the task**, Dario memorized **more than 100 digits**—about 20 more than Steve[9]. Just so you have an idea, this is a random sequence of 100 digits:

0976241760840814322609883501092783174852348572941581851735800348692734047642957254972364502916459715971

The difference between Reneé and Dario was that, while Reneé developed his own strategy to memorize the digits through wrongs and rights, Dario used the **same** technique that worked for Steve. At that point, Ericsson found that in addition to the way the study was conducted, the **kind of training** used to improve a person's performance also made a difference. It was in this context that the concept of ***purposeful practice*** arose. Note how Steve always had a ***specific purpose***: each time he memorized a sequence of numbers, his next goal was to memorize a sequence with **one more digit**. This practice also made Steve never reach a "comfort zone", ensuring a position of frequent discomfort. During the sessions, Steve was deeply involved in the activity, not distracting himself with other tasks, ensuring ***intense focus*** on the task. As Steve memorized a new, larger sequence, Ericsson warned him that he had succeeded by ensuring that he had ***immediate feedback*** on his performance.

Anders Ericsson has made an incredible contribution to science by proving that **how** a person trains can ensure their success. By dictating one digit per second, adding one digit at each correct sequence and removing two digits at each mistake, Ericsson succeeded in **increasing the capacity** of Steve's short-term memory. The study with Steve also shows that by using the four elements of ***purposeful practice***, chances of success increase dramatically. Also, the study with Dario Donatelli proves that, when trained by someone who **knows the most efficient way to achieve progress**, success is even more likely. The combination of **purposeful practice** and **effective training** results in what Anders Ericsson calls ***deliberate practice***, which will truly make you an expert in your field.

THE MAGIC OF MENTAL REPRESENTATION

Ericsson asserts that **deliberate practice** allows people to form **mental representations** that facilitate performance[10]. For you to better understand what mental representation is, let's think of a blindfold chess game between chess grandmasters. In this modality, the match is not only against one opponent, but against **tens** of players at the same time. As the name says, in these matches **the player is not allowed to look at the boards**, that is, they must play dozens of simultaneous games using **only the memory** of where the pieces are, which for any of us is a huge challenge. The feat of playing blindfold chess against several opponents at the same time, a century-old practice, has German Marc Lang as his current champion: he faced **46 opponents, won 25 games, drew 19 and lost only 2**[11].

Lang, however, is not the only player with this ability. Scientists William Chase and Herbert Simon conducted an experiment with other chess players and concluded that when an experienced player watched a moved board for five seconds, representing a real game situation, they later **remembered the position of approximately two-thirds of the pieces**[12]. Beginner players performed far worse, remembering the position of only **four pieces** in arrangements ranging from 12 to 24 pieces. Similarly, soccer players watching videos of matches that were suddenly paused could more successfully describe **what would happen next**[13].

For years, deliberate practice has made both chess and soccer players have complex and sophisticated mental representations that could help them **know in advance** what could happen in a game according to the position of the pieces or players—something that creates a **huge advantage**. These **mental representations** cause these players to make moves that seem **magical** to other people, but which to them are **extremely simple** because they have seen those situations **thousands of times**.

An interesting example of the power of mental representations is the TV show *Property Brothers*, presented by twin brothers Drew and Jonathan Scott. If you've never seen it, it works like this: the twin brothers are always tasked with finding a new home for a participating couple to renovate and decorate, with Drew being an expert real estate buyer, and Jonathan being in charge of renovation and decoration. One constant in the program is that the couple finds the interior of the house ugly and unlikely to improve, while Jonathan can visualize exactly what he'll do in the rooms to turn the house into something fantastic—which he **always** does. After so many renovations aimed at transforming the interior of the property into something amazing, having immediate feedback on the progress of the work and facing the most uncomfortable contingencies possible, Jonathan already has several mental representations that allow him to envision the **renovated** room before anyone else.

One of the biggest misconceptions about the studies of Anders Ericsson is to interpret that simply practicing an activity for many years results in better performance, which was made popular by author Malcolm Gladwell as the ***10,000 hours rule***[14]. But Anders Ericsson's studies point out that such a rule **doesn't exist**, because 10,000 hours of **naive practice** create the exact opposite result: people become **worse** at what they do. A lot of people have a lot more than 10,000 hours of experience driving cars, but that doesn't give them the advantage of being better than a novice Formula 1 pilot. The type of practice and the coaching of a mentor give the Formula 1 pilot a huge advantage in this case. Now, if the practice in question is ***deliberate*** or ***purposeful***, the years of experience will truly make that person an expert. In some fields, people become experts with less than 10,000 hours of practice; in others, they reach this level after more than 20,000 hours.

While science is solid on the great amount of effort required for someone to become an expert and reap the fruits of their achievements, many continue to believe in easy solutions to success—many, indeed, are **desperate** for these solutions. You must surely know someone who invests exorbitant amounts on coaching, immersion, seminars, workshops, online courses, or joining multilevel marketing companies for believing in the miraculous promises of wealth and daily success that these institutions sell. Watch out!

Just to end any discussion of the existence or not of a gift, in our conversation at Florida State University's campus, Anders Ericsson contended that in all his years of research he found **no** experts that had achieved success without a **great deal of effort**. This confirms that no one is **born** to do anything, that there's no one who doesn't need to **make an effort** to have a great performance, or who only needs **a little** effort to perform well. When we believe in a gift, this is precisely what we assume: **that some individuals don't have to work hard, or at least not as hard as others to succeed**.

One of the topics of my conversation with Ericsson was soccer, a sport in which we clearly notice some players are more skilled than others from the beginning. I asked him why there are cases of children who show a higher skill than others in the sport, and his response was nothing short of genius: "We see only the **phenomenon as it's happening**, that boy out there on the field, playing much better than the others at that moment. What we don't see is what happens **before** or **after** the game. That boy may have a father who is crazy about soccer and practices with him every day, or he can practice in one of the best soccer schools in town. After the game, after all the fans have left, he may have continued to practice to correct the mistakes he made in that game, or he may have used the time to improve on some basics, or sought feedback from his coach on his performance." In life, it's no different: we only see our **present** reality, not what we could have done to improve our condition or, more importantly, what we can do to be better.

THE GIFT OF ADAPTATION

After more than 40 years of research, Anders Ericsson has found that **we all have the same gift**, that of ***adaptation***. Our brain has an incredible ability to develop and adapt to any reality we can imagine. This means that **you can be better at everything you do**, perform similarly or better than many people in your field, as long as you're never satisfied with your current performance and practice your activity **deliberately** or **purposefully**. In some activities, however, the age at which you started your practice can also make a difference. But the amazing thing is that being better at what you do is a natural human trait of, as Edward Deci and Richard Ryan have discovered. In fact, being better at what you do corresponds to one of the basic human needs found by the two scientists: **competence**. By realizing that each day you get better at your work, sport or hobby, you experience an increase in your sense of competence, which consequently motivates you to work harder and harder.

A study held by Harvard researcher Teresa Amabile and her colleague Steven Kramer, sought to find what was the most significant factor in motivating people during their working hours, and revealed that it was a feeling of making progress[15]. And notice how strong is the link between motivational factors: the progress that this study participants reported as motivating was that achieved by doing meaningful work, that is, **purposeful** work. To make matters even more interesting, one of Abraham Maslow's few achievements was observing that **self-actualization** is one of the pillars of psychological health, so much so that this item is almost at the top of his pyramid[16]. Self-actualization is nothing more than a state of mind motivated by **growth**, **purpose**, and **appreciation of beauty**. Is there a better way to achieve self-actualization than to know that **it's possible to grow in everything you do**, to find a **purpose** for your life and work, to pursue a life in which you can **focus on the present** and to **appreciate the beauty of things**? I doubt it.

Knowing you can be better at everything you do is of great importance to your happiness and motivation. Believing in **gifts**, however, has consequences unknown to most people.

A DANGEROUS BELIEF

Professors Carol Dweck of Stanford University and Carol Diener of the University of Illinois have conducted a scientific experiment that reveals the dangers of believing people can have a gift or natural talent[17]. Many scientists, in fact, use this experiment model, which guides participants to try to solve something difficult, or even impossible, to analyze how they behave when faced with **difficulties**. The researchers applied 12 conceptual problems to children in sixth and seventh grades (ages 10-13): the first 8 could be **easily** solved, but the last 4 were **too advanced** for them. The problems chosen were designed so that the researchers could easily follow each strategy that the children used in their resolution. Thus, it was possible to analyze the differences in the children's strategies when they were **successful** in solving the first 8 problems; and also whether the strategies underwent any changes as they attempted to solve the 4 last, more difficult problems. In this experiment, Dweck and Diener also encouraged children to say what they were thinking out loud while doing the task, which would allow the scientists to understand their feelings in times of success and difficulty.

After the exercises, the researchers asked the children a series of questions about the difficult problems—how they felt they would do if they needed to solve the problems **again**, how many questions they believed to have gotten **right** and **wrong**, for example. The catch of the experiment, however, happened **before** the children solved the exercises. Dweck and Diener made all of them answer to the **Crandall Intellectual Achievement Responsibility Questionnaire**, designed to examine what factors the child attributes to her successes and failures: Is her success obtained from her **effort** in solving a task or from the fact that **the teacher likes her**? Does she claim to have failed a test because she **isn't smart enough** or because she **hasn't studied properly**? With these data, researchers could know in advance what answers each student would give in the experiment to justify their failures in solving the difficult problems.

Later, this experiment helped Carol Dweck name these differences in mentality as *fixed intelligence* and *flexible intelligence*[18]. People who believe in **fixed intelligence** think it's **immutable**: either you are smart or you aren't. These individuals believe that they **can't become better at what they do**, for they have their beliefs directed towards gift, special abilities, or IQ (intelligence quotient). On the other hand, those who believe in **flexible**

intelligence know that, despite the initial differences in performance between one person and another in any area of life, **they can develop, be better at what they do, and become smarter over time**. The questionnaire applied by the scientists could clearly define which students believed in which model of intelligence and how the differences between these beliefs influenced the way they faced difficult problems. Which children would persist while experiencing difficulties? Which would give up?

As you can imagine, as soon as they began to face difficulties, many children who believed in **fixed intelligence** immediately began to **denigrate their intelligence**, saying things like "I think I'm not very smart" or "I've never had a good memory", or even "I'm not good at these things". **None** of the children in the group who believed in **flexible intelligence** presented this type of behavior[19]. It's important to remember that, a few moments **before** facing the difficult problems, the children with **fixed intelligence succeeded** in resolving the first eight problems, but once they encountered **difficulties**, they began to **lose faith in their own capacity**. And that faith was lost so intensely that when the researchers asked if they could solve the first eight problems **again**, many of them **denied it**. In addition to losing faith in the future, these children also lost **faith in the past**—especially because when asked how many problems they thought they had solved, on average they remembered **five** correct answers and **six** mistakes, when they actually had **eight** correct answers and **four** mistakes. The belief in **fixed intelligence** made them **maximize mistakes** and **minimize right answers**. Children in the **flexible intelligence** group reported their numbers of mistakes and right answers more accurately.

By believing in fixed intelligence, you run the risk of being influenced by one of the biggest enemies of your personal development: ***impostor syndrome***[19]. We have all manifested this syndrome at some point in our lives—in a college presentation, work meeting or relationship. Impostor syndrome is the feeling that, although you are prepared for a challenge, at some point other people will notice that **you're not so good** at what you're doing, that there may be someone there better than you, that eventually everyone will find out that you're an **impostor**. And believe me, this feeling happens even to professors of renowned universities.

This is exactly what happened to some students in Dweck's experiment: when confronted with a more advanced exercise, they began to denigrate their own abilities by saying phrases such as "I think I'm not very smart"—something that undermined their performance, made them lose the belief that they were able to solve the exercises again and also led them to believe that their past (good) performance had been bad.

In the study by Dweck and Diener, the fact that researchers can clearly analyze the students' strategies for solving problems has generated other relevant findings. In dealing with difficult problems, the group of students who believed in **fixed intelligence** showed a serious **decline** in the effectiveness of their strategies, which proved to be excellent in solving the easier problems. In addition, these children have quickly **given up** solving difficult problems, which proves that when you believe that your intelligence is fixed, that is, that you can't get better at what you do, **you lose the resilience to face more complicated situations.**

THE VICTORY MENTALITY

The contrast between these results and those of the students in the **flexible intelligence** group is simply fantastic. When faced with difficult problems, a large part of that group of children started to say things like "I love a challenge" or "Mistakes are our friends", and more than 80% of them have **maintained or improved** the strategies used to solve the problems[20]. Unlike the other group, these students tried to solve the problems for a longer time, and **some of them succeeded even though they were above their level of knowledge**. This experiment shows something that few people can see:

The things you believe in eventually become your reality.

In my travels to every corner of Brazil, I often encounter frightening situations. As traveling for work is a frequent part of many people's jobs, airport terminals and the inside of planes are interesting places for people like me, who are interested in psychology and like to analyze the behavior of an audience I am also a part of: parents who are away from their children. To remember their little ones during a week away, many parents carry their children's drawings, paintings and other expressions of art, as well as photos and videos stored on their smartphones.

One of the most common scenes in airports and airplanes is parents showing off their children's art to coworkers or seat neighbors. When this happens, I notice a pattern in their behavior. They say things like "He's only five!" or "She's so smart!" or even the funniest, most biased phrase of all, "It's not because he's my son, but he's much smarter than the children his age". Of course, it's important for parents to be proud of their children, but we must know that we're **highly biased** in evaluating our little (or big) ones' pieces of art.

Many parents show off their children's paintings as if they were the next Picasso or Leonardo da Vinci, while in other people's eyes, the child's drawing is nothing more than a series of meaningless scribbles. In fact, we ourselves see pictures of famous artists and make similar evaluations—for many adults, certain paintings are far from being works of art. The problem with this behavior in parents is that, if they have a habit of over-valuing their children's work to other people, they'll certainly behave the same way with the children themselves. I've seen lots of parents tell their kids things like "You're so smart" or "Look at how smart you are!" But does this kind of phrase really help them have more self-confidence?

In praising your children this way, you're creating in them the belief of fixed intelligence: **either you are smart, or you aren't**! And, as you now know, this kind of mentality will disrupt your child's development, leading them to become less than what they could[21]. If you really love your children and want them to have a happy life, don't praise them that way. One of your primary goals as a parent is to make the happy choice to develop in your child a mentality of **flexible intelligence**, of **possibilities**, of **evolution**, of **constant challenge**, of **not giving up** easily when facing difficulties, of failures and mistakes as **opportunities to move forward**—not as shameful situations.

In addition, other studies have shown that having a higher than average IQ **doesn't** mean having an advantage for life, since people can **develop** through either **purposeful or deliberate practice**[22]. There aren't **any** positive effects in telling your child they're smarter than others or smarter than average. In fact, several scientists have found that there's **absolutely no** relation between good grades and success in life, so don't worry if your child is not the best or the smartest or even if they have bad grades: you can help them **build** a flexible mindset for life and reduce these differences in performance in their teens and adult life[23].

Also, don't be overly proud if your kid has high grades at school, as that doesn't mean that they'll **always** succeed or that they **don't need their parents' help to be even better**. Next time your kid proudly shows you a new painting or drawing, praise them like this: **"Good job! You're getting better at drawing every day! Remember that a few years ago you colored outside the lines and didn't know how to match the colors? Now you're coloring so much better than before, and you know what? If you continue to make this kind of effort, you'll make even better drawings!"** This type of praise encourages **flexible intelligence**, which encourages a **growth mindset**.

In the corporate environment, it's the same. If you hold a leadership position, learn to praise your team members by showing them their evolution over the months or years they've been in the company. Use examples that remind them that their past performance **wasn't as good as today**, always leaving the final message that **if they continue to make an effort, they'll be even better**. This kind of praise arouses in people the feeling of **competence**, activating the motivational mechanisms studied by Ryan and Deci.

It's important to remember that there's no magical moment in your personal or professional life in which you won't have to improve anymore. Your development **never** reaches the top, you can be better at what you do at **any point in life**. No matter how many years you've spent dedicating yourself, **there's always something new to learn**.

WHERE WOULD YOU BE TODAY?

If, like many people, you believe that your intelligence is fixed, that without a high IQ you can't succeed and that certain individuals are **born** with special abilities that give them advantages for the rest of their lives, what will become of you? If in early life, children with a **fixed mindset** are already beginning to suffer the consequences of this belief, what could **several decades** of this mentality have done to your life? **Where could you be today if it wasn't for that?**

As you have seen, countless scientists agree, in their studies, that **becoming better at what you do is critical to your motivation**, as this enhances your sense of **competence**. So, don't feel frustrated if **today** you don't have the performance you'd like in a task that's important to you; don't think it's too late to start an activity you enjoy, like learning to speak a new language, playing a musical instrument or even changing careers—you can be better at everything you already do or **haven't started yet**, just practice the activity purposefully and remember that intelligence is flexible.

The afternoon I went to Stanford to visit scientist Carol Dweck at the wonderful facilities of Jordan Hall, a question I asked her was precisely whether there's an age when a person **can no longer change mentality**. The great news I got was: Dweck and a group of scientists have succeeded in changing the mindset of **elderly** people, which reinforces the scientific findings that our brains truly are **amazing**, and can **transform** and **adapt** even as we reach more advanced ages.

The rule holds true for your current job as well. Don't get frustrated with your performance **today**, and never think that your colleague who's the star of the company will occupy this position forever—**you can become better than him, as long as you work hard, practice the right way and have the counseling of a qualified mentor/teacher You can be better at what you do!** In helping and recognizing others, in your gratitude, in your praise; you can be better at finding purpose in your work; you can be better in your interactions, your relationships, your mood, your beliefs, your pursuit of positive emotions, your marriage; you can be better as a leader, in your empathy, your body posture, in interpreting the events of life, in your mentality, in reducing negative emotions in your daily life, in evaluating what motivates people, in positive thinking, in negative thinking, in defining your values.

And now you know that these statements are not cheap motivation or incentives to positive thinking—they are pure science.

CONCLUSION

A Dance of Motivation and Happiness

IT ALL STARTS WITH A CHOICE

By understanding the negative impact of the pursuit of money and material goods, and letting go of the false belief that these factors bring greater motivation and happiness, you automatically become less materialistic and stop comparing with those who have more money and goods. This way, you gain greater life satisfaction and a more positive self-image, which reduces your chances of becoming a victim of stress-related diseases caused by materialism. Once you're satisfied with your life, you begin to really value the things you already have, rather than wanting to accumulate resources that don't bring you happiness or long-term motivation.

In addition, life satisfaction causes you to stop looking for motivation and happiness in the recognition of others. When you find that you don't need recognition nor more money than necessary to be happy, you increase your likelihood of having prosocial behaviors and invest your money in experiences, thus reducing the speed of the hedonic treadmill and increasing your happiness and that of several other people.

By implementing these changes in your way of thinking and acting, you'll begin to reap the true fruits of happiness and motivation, and realize that there are other variables more important than money in that equations. On this path, you begin to strive for motivation and happiness in all your daily actions and understand the true purpose of your work, which you begin to see as a calling, not a job. By modeling the purpose of your own work, you begin to enjoy a greater sense of autonomy, of having control over your destiny, which exponentially increases your motivation.

When you begin to understand that people have a misguided notion of the factors that motivate them, you change your way of looking at recognition, as you discover that its true power comes about when **you** recognize others. So you start making more effort in your daily interactions, learning that recognizing others is not just giving compliments, prizes and financial incentives, but making people feel that they **exist**, they are perceived, they are important.

You also begin to understand that one of the best forms of recognition is to be thankful to those who helped you through life—after all, in order for people to have someone to be grateful for, they must first have been helped by someone else. So **you** begin the cycle of gratitude, helping others and practicing conscious acts of kindness. By knowing the influence of social contagion and the mirror neuron system on our behavior, you come to understand that your responsibility in the world is much greater than you think, and that all your actions will make your network of contacts imitate your behavior, spreading the benefit of your actions to people you may never even meet, contributing to the happiness of many.

When you understand the impact that all of these positive emotions have on your life and your success, you begin to increase their frequency through your behavior. So you stop choosing to feel negative emotions, increasing your chances of reaching the ratio of three positive moments for each negative moment in a day. That way, your mind expands, you see more options and become more creative and resilient. You realize that happiness is truly the cause of success. When you become aware that your behavior makes a difference in your success, you stop suffering from learned hopelessness, you no longer have the feeling that success depends only on factors beyond your control and you stop being a victim of current circumstances. By doing this, you further reduce the amount of negative emotions in your day and teach your brain to pay more attention to the positive things in the world, which changes your explanatory style.

By choosing to increase your positive charge and make an effort to remember, each night, the positive things that happened to you that day, writing them down in a gratitude journal, you make your brain focus on the present—and so you begin to find more joy in the small pleasures of life. Having a gratitude journal makes you relive the positive emotions of your day, which increases your chances of reaching the ideal ratio between positive and negative emotions. When you're focused on enjoying the present, you stop fantasizing about the future and gain a more realistic view of the world as you discover that negative moments and obstacles are inevitable but surmountable. As you become aware that there'll always be obstacles in your life, you'll determine what challenges you'll need to face in order to achieve each of your goals, and what will be your plan to overcome them. This prevents your energy from being drained by the pleasure of positive thinking and gives you the motivation to act toward your goals, which increases your chances of achieving what you want.

When you discover that there's a tool to help you achieve your personal and professional goals more efficiently, you realize that much of your success is under your control, and you stop believing that success is a privilege of those lucky enough to have a gift or superior intelligence. You come to understand that gifts aren't real, that our brains constantly develop and adapt to new situations, which gives you the possibility to become better in everything you do. As long as you're strongly committed and never comfortable with your current performance, you begin to develop a growth mindset. And when your mentality is of growth, when you're aware that intelligence is flexible and that, although there are initial differences in performance between individuals, they're not guaranteed for life, you begin to develop a higher drive, not give up on challenges so easily, seek personal growth constantly, trust your future capacity, and recognize others, which in turn will realize that they can always be better at what they do.

Everything is connected in the beautiful dance of motivation and happiness. Remember that the sequence of events I just described begins with **one** choice. This choice sets in motion a number of other benefits that can change your life and the life of those around you. All that matters is making that **first** choice. Regardless of the happy choice you choose to prioritize, this

sequence of events will happen, not necessarily in the order I've described, but in the end, the dance of motivation and happiness will circle the entire hall, completing its cycle.

Remember that you have a **limited amount of days** to complete this cycle and leave your mark on the world. The choice of how **you'll use these days** is all yours! By applying science to your everyday life, you'll increasingly feel that **happiness is not sought, but built**. This construction takes place with your **decisions**.

What will you choose today to start taking control of your success?

ACKNOWLEDGMENTS

While reading several scientific articles and talking to researchers to write this book, I've changed many of my concepts and thought deeply about the factors that have helped me shape the story of my life. As I thought of those who helped me write *Happy Choices*, I looked back on 1996, when I met my great friend Marcelo Sabbag. We hit it off quickly because we liked the same kind of music, and soon we were together almost every day having fun and jamming to our favorite punk rock bands.

The years went by and our friendship became stronger and stronger until, in 2000, when we were about to graduate, Marcelo came up with the crazy idea—at the time, my family was facing financial difficulties—of studying in the USA. I immediately dismissed the plan, but he insisted and went to pick me up at my house to take the obligatory English test. We took the test and were approved, and the next step would be to start paying for the trip—which was totally out of my family's possibilities. Once again, my friend Marcelo insisted and asked his mother, Maria Amélia Sabbag, to pay the first installments for my part of the trip. Dona Maria Amélia, who treated me like a son, made that great effort, and so in December of 2000, we set off for the United States, towards the dream destination of any punk rock fan: California.

I was selected to work at Big Bear Lake, near Los Angeles, and Marcelo went to work in Lakeshore, near Fresno. A few days after starting work, I realized that my workload would not allow me to pay my bills and, as always, doing what only best friends do, Marcelo decided to pick me up at Big Bear to work with him in Lakeshore.

It was because of all of Marcelo's persistence and friendship, besides the affection of Dona Maria Amélia, that I had the opportunity to learn to speak English, read scientific articles, to do an MBA in the United States, study in England, talk with scientists and, therefore, write this book. The punk rock times are gone, and adulthood took my friend Marcelo to live by the coast with his wife and children. I continued to live in Curitiba with my wife and children. But despite time and distance, my thoughts and gratitude will never go away. Without the efforts of my friend Marcelo and Dona Maria Amélia, I certainly wouldn't be writing this sentence—and you would never have read this book.

Obviously, there are other important characters in this story. My parents, Juarez and Maria Aparecida, are no doubt two of them. My father and mother educated me, loved me, didn't let me study at just any university, and, yes, they paid the other installments of the trip! Without their sacrifice for my future, I wouldn't have had the opportunities I had during my executive career, and my story would have been very different.

During the trip I made to write this book, I had the happiness of spending a week in the company of the most important teacher I ever had: my dear father, Juarez. Eighteen years after my parents had made it possible for me to live in California, my father and I met in Los Angeles, one of my first destinations in 2000. We stayed in Hollywood and had a weekend like one of those father and son movies, sharing very special moments that I'll never forget. After that, we still went to Irvine, San Francisco, Stanford, Raleigh, Chapel Hill, Tallahassee and Miami. Seven cities in five days, an intense and tiresome schedule that only a loving (and proud) parent can stand.

This story has another hero—actually, a Wonder Woman! Her name is Mariana, and I'm so lucky to call her my wife! For the last 15 years, Mariana has been the greatest positive example I have in my life. A partner who helped me make profound changes in my way of seeing the world. Without her, I wouldn't be half of who I am today. From the moment I chose not to be an executive anymore, Mariana supported me and built a dream with me, even in the difficult times we faced. Years before my choice, Mariana had already traced the same path, leaving her executive career to become an academic. Years later, she founded a sustainability consulting firm, and is doing work that inspires her every day and makes her fully realized professionally. Although our fields are different—I'm a business administrator, and she's a forest engineer—the path we followed was the same. We both chose to leave the corporate world, our important positions and fat salaries for a common goal: to make companies apply strategies that generate social transformation.

Another reason for our choice was the birth of our first child, Leonardo, an infinite source of positive emotions in our family. A few years later, our little princess, Victoria, arrived, which multiplied these positive emotions and brought our family even closer together. Without the power of these three heroes, I could never have found the strength to devote myself to this book.

I'm also grateful for the love of my dear brothers, Marcel and Letícia, my sisters-in-law, Angela and Carolina, my brothers-in-law, Rafael and Paulo, my super nephews and nieces, Nicolas, Carolina, Maria Fernanda, André, Tiago, Lucas, Alexandre and Clara, and, of course, my in-laws, Rita and José Luiz, who make every effort to bring our family together every week. May the barbeques continue!

My literary agent, Felipe Colbert, had a very important role in getting this book to your hands. Felipe has a rare knowledge of the publishing market and a huge connection with publishers. Always humorous, working with super-dedication and supporting me during all our negotiations with publishers, Felipe turned the three years of coming up with this book into a reality a few months after we started our partnership. Every author deserves an agent like Felipe, and I feel honored to have him by my side in the battle that is being a writer in Brazil. Thank you, Felipe!

Through Felipe, I met Pedro Almeida, editor of this book. If Felipe made this project possible, it was Pedro who made it happen. I'm very grateful for Pedro for believing in the contents of this book and for having granted me the privilege of having it published by Faro Editorial. For those who don't know, it was Pedro who brought the bestseller *Marley & Me* to Brazil when the book was just a gamble. *Marley & Me* sold more than six million copies in our country. Imagine the pride (and the nerves!) I felt when Felipe told me that "the man" who brought *Marley & Me* to Brazil had liked my book and wanted to meet me! The tension was gone in just a few minutes of conversation with Pedro, who's a true gentleman, but my pride will remain forever. Pedro is a professional who's truly concerned about the impact that Faro Editorial books have on society. Faro Editorial wants to leave a legacy, and I hope this book will contribute to that.

I'm very grateful to professors Gabriele Oettingen, Edward Deci, Richard Ryan, Nina Mazar, Grant Donnelly, Paul Piff, Carol Dweck, Barbara Fredrickson and Anders Ericsson for having welcomed me wonderfully during my visit to the United States. The insights these great researchers gave me during our conversations were priceless in finding the links that were missing in this book.

Many thanks also to professors Adam Grant, Dan Ariely, Sonja Lyubomirsky, Lalin Anik, Elizabeth Dunn, Lara Aknin, Marco Iacoboni, Minah Jung, Emily Powell, Francesca Gino, Alan Cowen, Chip Heath, Lamar Pierce, Tim Kasser, Ken Sheldon, Tal Ben-Shahar, Shawn Achor, Bob Sutton, Lisa Feldman Barrett, Dan Gilbert, Eric Barker, Ed Diener, Richard Shell, Sheena Iyengar, Max Bazerman, Jonathan Haidt, Sam Bowles and Paul Green for having kindly—and some, often—replied to my emails and provided me with new articles, insights and tips that helped me in my activities as a teacher, author and entrepreneur. The work of these researchers and many others has changed my life and my values radically. The work of some of them even saved my life. I very much thank the writer Daniel Pink—a great inspiration—for always responding to my emails, encouraging my work as a writer and solving all my doubts quickly and simply.

Thanks also to my friend Raul Candeloro for all the support and advice he gave me during my new career. Raul, in addition to always being ready to help, does much more than this by making every effort to enable Brazilian sales professionals to keep on developing as they read the content of *VendaMais* magazine, which he has been leading for over 20 years.

Without the work of the amazing Maria Thereza Moss, who translated this book into English, I wouldn't have received the beautiful comments made by the scientists who read this book before its release. Each review gave me more confidence that this book really could change the lives of many people. Besides, Maria Thereza's work made it possible for a big personal dream of mine to come true — "Happy Choices" will be released internationally. Thanks a ton, Maria Thereza!

The dear Sandra Beraldo, from the Commercial Association of Paraná, is another person who deserves special thanks for being on the mission to provide quality education to the small and medium business owners of Paraná. I'm extremely proud to be by her side on this goal.

Fortunately, a lot of other people should be acknowledged here, but as I have limited space in this book, I apologize for the lack of formal thanks and make myself available to everyone I've ever had contact with in life to help them at any time.

Hoping that the people recognized here can start another cycle of gratitude, I say goodbye!

Luiz Gaziri

REFERENCES

INTRODUCTION

1. Gneezy, U., & Rustichini, A. (2000). Pay enough or don't pay at all. *The Quarterly Journal of Economics*, *115*(3), 791-810.
2. Ariely, D., Gneezy, U., Loewenstein, G., & Mazar, N. (2009). Large stakes and big mistakes. *The Review of Economic Studies*, *76*(2), 451-469.
3. Global Emotions Report (2018). *Gallup*.
4. Aknin, L. B., Norton, M. I., & Dunn, E. W. (2009). From wealth to well-being? Money matters, but less than people think. *The Journal of Positive Psychology*, *4*(6), 523-527.
5. Lepper, M. R., Greene, D., & Nisbett, R. E. (1973). Undermining children's intrinsic interest with extrinsic reward: A test of the "overjustification" hypothesis. *Journal of Personality and social Psychology*, *28*(1), 129.
6. Deci, E. L. (1971). Effects of externally mediated rewards on intrinsic motivation. *Journal of Personality and Social Psychology*, *18*(1), 105.

7. Theodorakis, Y., Weinberg, R., Natsis, P., Douma, I., & Kazakas, P. (2000). The effects of motivational versus instructional self-talk on improving motor performance. *The Sport Psychologist, 14*(3), 253-271.
8. Senay, I., Albarracín, D., & Noguchi, K. (2010). Motivating goal-directed behavior through introspective self-talk: The role of the interrogative form of simple future tense. *Psychological Science, 21*(4), 499-504.
9. Oettingen, G., & Mayer, D. (2002). The motivating function of thinking about the future: expectations versus fantasies. *Journal of Personality and Social Psychology, 83*(5), 1198.
10. Lyubomirsky, S., Sheldon, K. M., & Schkade, D. (2005). Pursuing happiness: The architecture of sustainable change. *Review of General Psychology, 9*(2), 111.
11. Weiner, B. (1985). An attributional theory of achievement motivation and emotion. *Psychological Review, 92*(4), 548.

CHAPTER 1

1. Easterlin, R. A. (2001). Income and happiness: Towards a unified theory. *The Economic Journal, 111*(473), 465-484.
2. Myers, D. G. (2015). *Psychology, 11th Ed*. Worth Publishers, 479-487.
Diener, E., & Biswas-Diener, R. (2002). Will money increase subjective well-being? *Social Indicators Research, 57*(2), 119-169.
3. Diener, E., & Suh, E. M. (Eds.). (2000). *Culture and Subjective Well-Being*. MIT press, 185-218.
4. Seligman, M. E. (2007). *The Optimistic Child: A Proven Program to Safeguard Children Against Depression and Build Lifelong Resilience*. Houghton Mifflin Harcourt.
Seligman, M. E., Walker, E. F., & Rosenhan, D. L. (2001). *Abnormal Psychology* (pp. 248-299). New York: Norton.
5. World Health Organization. (2017). Depression and other common mental disorders: global health estimates.
6. Kasser, T., & Ryan, R. M. (1993). A dark side of the American dream: Correlates of financial success as a central life aspiration. *Journal of Personality and Social Psychology, 65*(2), 410.
Kasser, T., & Ryan, R. M. (1996). Further examining the American dream: Differential correlates of intrinsic and extrinsic goals. *Personality and Social Psychology Bulletin, 22*(3), 280-287.
7. Layard, R. (2011). *Happiness: Lessons from a New Science*. Penguin UK.
Diener, E., & Seligman, M. E. (2004). Beyond money: Toward an economy of well-being. *Psychological Science in the Public Interest, 5*(1), 1-31.
Frey, B. S., & Stutzer, A. (2010). *Happiness and Economics: How the Economy and Institutions Affect Human Well-Being*. Princeton University Press.

Blanchflower, D. G., & Oswald, A. J. (2004). Well-being over time in Britain and the USA. *Journal of Public Economics, 88*(7-8), 1359-1386.
8. Kahneman, D., & Deaton, A. (2010). High income improves evaluation of life but not emotional well-being. *Proceedings of the National Academy of Sciences, 107*(38), 16489-16493.
9. Borger, J., & Campbell, D. (2003). The Governator. *The Guardian, Aug 8.*
10. Deci, E. L. (1971). Effects of externally mediated rewards on intrinsic motivation. *Journal of Personality and Social Psychology, 18*(1), 105.
11. Quoidbach, J., Dunn, E. W., Petrides, K. V., & Mikolajczak, M. (2010). Money giveth, money taketh away: The dual effect of wealth on happiness. *Psychological Science, 21*(6), 759-763.
12. Diener, E., Horwitz, J., & Emmons, R. A. (1985). Happiness of the very wealthy. *Social Indicators Research, 16*(3), 263-274.
13. Catalano, R. (1991). The health effects of economic insecurity. *American Journal of Public Health, 81*(9), 1148-1152.
14. Clingingsmith, D. (2016). Negative emotions, income, and welfare: Causal estimates from the PSID. *Journal of Economic Behavior & Organization, 130,* 1-19.
15. Dew, J., Britt, S., & Huston, S. (2012). Examining the relationship between financial issues and divorce. *Family Relations, 61*(4), 615-628.
Little, S. (2018). Money worries biggest reason for marriages ending, survey finds. *Independent*, Jan 8.
16. Kushlev, K., Dunn, E. W., & Lucas, R. E. (2015). Higher income is associated with less daily sadness but not more daily happiness. *Social Psychological and Personality Science, 6*(5), 483-489.
17. Sheldon, K. M., Elliot, A. J., Kim, Y., & Kasser, T. (2001). What is satisfying about satisfying events? Testing 10 candidate psychological needs. *Journal of Personality and Social Psychology, 80*(2), 325.
18. Keegan, P. (2015). Here's what really happened at that company that set a $ 70,000 minimum wage, Inc. Slate, October 23.
19. McGraw, K. O., & McCullers, J. C. (1979). Evidence of a detrimental effect of extrinsic incentives on breaking a mental set. *Journal of Experimental Social Psychology, 15*(3), 285-294.
20. Kasser, T., Ryan, R. M., Zax, M., & Sameroff, A. J. (1995). The relations of maternal and social environments to late adolescents' materialistic and prosocial values. *Developmental Psychology,31*(6), 907.
21. Jensen, M. C., & Meckling, W. H. (1976). Theory of the firm: Managerial behavior, agency costs and ownership structure. *Journal of Financial Economics, 3*(4), 305-360.
22. Larkin, I., Pierce, L., & Gino, F. (2012). The psychological costs of pay-for-performance: Implications for the strategic compensation of employees. *Strategic Management Journal, 33*(10), 1194-1214.

23. Deci, E. L., Koestner, R., & Ryan, R. M. (1999). A meta-analytic review of experiments examining the effects of extrinsic rewards on intrinsic motivation. *Psychological Bulletin, 125*(6), 627.
24. Heath, C. (1999). On the social psychology of agency relationships: Lay theories of motivation overemphasize extrinsic incentives. *Organizational Behavior and Human Decision Processes, 78*(1), 25-62.
25. Goethals, G. R., Messick, D. M., & Allison, S. T. (1991). The uniqueness bias: Studies of constructive social comparison.
26. Gallup (2017). State of the Global Workplace. *Gallup.*
27. Yerkes, R. M., & Dodson, J. D. (1908). The relation of strength of stimulus to rapidity of habit-formation. *Journal of Comparative Neurology, 18*(5), 459-482.
28. Gneezy, U., & Rustichini, A. (2000). A fine is a price. *The Journal of Legal Studies, 29*(1), 1-17.
29. Baumeister, R. F. (1984). Choking under pressure: self-consciousness and paradoxical effects of incentives on skillful performance. *Journal of Personality and Social Psychology, 46*(3), 610.
30. Baumeister, R. F., & Showers, C. J. (1986). A review of paradoxical performance effects: Choking under pressure in sports and mental tests. *European Journal of Social Psychology, 16*(4), 361-383.
31. Bengtsson, S. L., Lau, H. C., & Passingham, R. E. (2008). Motivation to do well enhances responses to errors and self-monitoring. *Cerebral Cortex, 19*(4), 797-804.
32. Dandy, J., Brewer, N., & Tottman, R. (2001). Self-consciousness and performance decrements within a sporting context. *The Journal of Social Psychology, 141*(1), 150-152.
33. McGraw, K. O., & McCullers, J. C. (1979). Evidence of a detrimental effect of extrinsic incentives on breaking a mental set. *Journal of Experimental Social Psychology, 15*(3), 285-294.
34. Kasser, T., Ryan, R. M., Couchman, C. E., & Sheldon, K. M. (2004). Materialistic values: Their causes and consequences. *Psychology and Consumer Culture: The Struggle for a Good Life in a Materialistic World, 1*(2), 11-28.
    Belk, R. W. (1985). Materialism: Trait aspects of living in the material world. *Journal of Consumer Research, 12*(3), 265-280.
    Kasser, T., & Ahuvia, A. (2002). Materialistic values and well-being in business students. *European Journal of Social Psychology, 32*(1), 137-146.
35. Fromm, E. (1976). To Have or to Be. London. *Abacus.*
    Rogers, C. R. (1964). Toward a modern approach to values: The valuing process in the mature person. *The Journal of Abnormal and Social Psychology, 68*(2), 160.
36. Kasser, T., & Ryan, R. M. (2001). Be careful what you wish for: Optimal functioning and the relative attainment of intrinsic and extrinsic goals. *Life Goals and Well-Being: Towards a Positive Psychology of Human Striving, 1*, 116-131.
    Kasser T., & Kasser V. G. The dreams of people high and low in materialism. *Journal of Economic Psychology.* 2001 Dec 1;22(6):693-719.
    Cohen P., Cohen J. 1996. Life values and adolescent mental health. Erlbaum: Mahwah, NJ.

37. Donnelly, G. E., Zheng, T., Haisley, E., & Norton, M. I. (2018). The amount and source of millionaires' wealth (moderately) predict their happiness. *Personality and Social Psychology Bulletin*, 0146167217744766.
38. Festinger, L. (1954). A theory of social comparison processes. *Human relations*, *7*(2), 117-140.
39. Boyce, C. J., Brown, G. D., & Moore, S. C. (2010). Money and happiness: Rank of income, not income, affects life satisfaction. *Psychological Science*, *21*(4), 471-475.
40. Rahtz, D. R., Sirgy, M. J., & Meadow, H. L. (1988). Elderly life satisfaction and television viewership: An exploratory study. *ACR North American Advances*.
41. Braun, O. L., & Wicklund, R. A. (1989). Psychological antecedents of conspicuous consumption. *Journal of Economic Psychology*, *10*(2), 161-187.
42. Bodner, R., & Prelec, D. (2003). Self-signaling and diagnostic utility in everyday decision making. *The Psychology of Economic Decisions*, *1*, 105-26.
43. Gino, F., Norton, M. I., & Ariely, D. (2010). The counterfeit self: The deceptive costs of faking it. *Psychological Science*, *21*(5), 712-720.
44. Vohs, K. D., Mead, N. L., & Goode, M. R. (2006). The psychological consequences of money. *Science*, *314*(5802), 1154-1156.
45. Gino, F., & Pierce, L. (2009). The abundance effect: Unethical behavior in the presence of wealth. *Organizational Behavior and Human Decision Processes*, *109*(2), 142-155.
46. Piff, P. K., Kraus, M. W., & Martinez, A. (2017). The social consequences of a rigged game. *Unpublished Results*.
47. Piff, P. K., Stancato, D. M., Côté, S., Mendoza-Denton, R., & Keltner, D. (2012). Higher social class predicts increased unethical behavior. *Proceedings of the National Academy of Sciences*, *109*(11), 4086-4091.
48. Kraus, M. W., Côté, S., & Keltner, D. (2010). Social class, contextualism, and empathic accuracy. *Psychological Science*, *21*(11), 1716-1723.
49. Szalavitz, M. (2010). The rich are different: more money, less empathy. *Time*, Nov 24.
50. Keltner, D., Gruenfeld, D. H., & Anderson, C. (2003). Power, approach, and inhibition. *Psychological Review*, *110*(2), 265.
51. Frederick, S., & Loewenstein, G. (1999). 16 hedonic adaptation. *Well-Being. The Foundations of Hedonic Psychology/Eds. D. Kahneman, E. Diener, N. Schwarz. NY: Russell Sage*, 302-329.
52. Brickman, P., Coates, D., & Janoff-Bulman, R. (1978). Lottery winners and accident victims: Is happiness relative? *Journal of Personality and Social Psychology*, *36*(8), 917.
53. Diener, E., Suh, E. M., Lucas, R. E., & Smith, H. L. (1999). Subjective well-being: Three decades of progress. *Psychological Bulletin*, *125*(2), 276.
    Lucas, R. E., Clark, A. E., Georgellis, Y., & Diener, E. (2003). Reexamining adaptation and the set point model of happiness: reactions to changes in marital status. *Journal of Personality and Social Psychology*, *84*(3), 527.
54. Wengle, H. P. (1986). The psychology of cosmetic surgery: a critical overview of the literature 1960-1982 — Part I. *Annals of Plastic Surgery*, *16*(5), 435-443.

55. Schkade, D. A., & Kahneman, D. (1998). Does living in California make people happy? A focusing illusion in judgments of life satisfaction. *Psychological Science, 9*(5), 340-346.
56. Calhoun, L. G., & Tedeschi, R. G. (Eds.). (2014). *Handbook of Posttraumatic Growth: Research and Practice*. Routledge.
    Peterson, C., Park, N., Pole, N., D'Andrea, W., & Seligman, M. E. (2008). Strengths of character and posttraumatic growth. *Journal of Traumatic Stress, 21*(2), 214-217.
57. Kasser, T. (2003). *The High Price of Materialism*. MIT press.
58. Brickman, P. (1971). Hedonic relativism and planning the good society. *Adaptation-Level Theory*.
59. Peterson, C., Ruch, W., Beermann, U., Park, N., & Seligman, M. E. (2007). Strengths of character, orientations to happiness, and life satisfaction. *The Journal of Positive Psychology, 2*(3), 149-156.
60. Lyubomirsky, S., King, L., & Diener, E. (2005). The benefits of frequent positive affect: Does happiness lead to success? *Psychological Bulletin, 131*(6), 803.
61. Diener, E., Nickerson, C., Lucas, R. E., & Sandvik, E. (2002). Dispositional affect and job outcomes. *Social Indicators Research, 59*(3), 229-259.
62. Smith, S. M., Nichols, T. E., Vidaurre, D., Winkler, A. M., Behrens, T. E., Glasser, M. F., ... & Miller, K. L. (2015). A positive-negative mode of population covariation links brain connectivity, demographics and behavior. *Nature Neuroscience, 18*(11), 1565.
63. Ben-Shahar, T. (2007). *Happier: Learn the Secrets to Daily Joy and Lasting Fulfillment*. McGraw-Hill Companies.
64. Goldberg, C. (2006). Harvard's crowded course to happiness: 'Positive psychology' draws students in droves, The Boston Globe. Retrieved March 21, 2006.
65. Shimer, D. (2018). Yale's most popular class ever: happiness. *The New York Times*. Retrieved January 26, 2018.
66. Kahneman, D., & Deaton, A. (2010). High income improves evaluation of life but not emotional well-being. *Proceedings of the National Academy of Sciences, 107*(38), 16489-16493.
67. Wilson, T. D., Wheatley, T., Meyers, J. M., Gilbert, D. T., & Axsom, D. (2000). Focalism: A source of durability bias in affective forecasting. *Journal of Personality and Social Psychology, 78*(5), 821.

CHAPTER 2

1. Carrig, D. (2017). Warren Buffett gave away this much of his wealth in the past 10 years. CNBC, Jul 13.
2. Clifford, C. (2017). Billionaire Warren Buffet says the 'real problem' with the US economy is people like him. CNBC, Jun 27.
3. Woodruff, J. (2017). America shoud stand for more than just wealth, says Warren Buffett. PBS, Jun 26.

4. Aknin, L. B., Barrington-Leigh, C. P., Dunn, E. W., Helliwell, J. F., Burns, J., Biswas-Diener, R., ... & Norton, M. I. (2013). Prosocial spending and well-being: Cross-cultural evidence for a psychological universal. *Journal of Personality and Social Psychology, 104*(4), 635.
5. Piper, W. T., Saslow, L. R., & Saturn, S. R. (2015). Autonomic and prefrontal events during moral elevation. *Biological Psychology, 108*, 51-55.
6. Oveis, C., Horberg, E. J., & Keltner, D. (2010). Compassion, pride, and social intuitions of self-other similarity. *Journal of Personality and Social Psychology, 98*(4), 618.
7. Oveis, C., Cohen, A. B., Gruber, J., Shiota, M. N., Haidt, J., & Keltner, D. (2009). Resting respiratory sinus arrhythmia is associated with tonic positive emotionality. *Emotion, 9*(2), 265.
8. Brooks, A. C. (2007). Does giving make us prosperous? *Journal of Economics and Finance, 31*(3), 403-411.
9. Dunn, E. W., Aknin, L. B., & Norton, M. I. (2008). Spending money on others promotes happiness. *Science, 319*(5870), 1687-1688.
10. Anik, L., Aknin, L. B., Norton, M. I., Dunn, E. W., & Quoidbach, J. (2013). Prosocial bonuses increase employee satisfaction and team performance. *PloS one, 8*(9), e75509.
11. Dunn, E. W., Ashton-James, C. E., Hanson, M. D., & Aknin, L. B. (2010). On the costs of self-interested economic behavior: How does stinginess get under the skin? *Journal of Health Psychology, 15*(4), 627-633.
12. Mogilner, C., Chance, Z., & Norton, M. I. (2012). Giving time gives you time. *Psychological Science, 23*(10), 1233-1238.
13. Pchelin, P., & Howell, R. T. (2014). The hidden cost of value-seeking: People do not accurately forecast the economic benefits of experiential purchases. *The Journal of Positive Psychology, 9*(4), 322-334.
14. Lyubomirsky, S. (2010). 11 Hedonic adaptation to positive and negative experiences. *The Oxford Handbook of Stress, Health, and Coping*, 200.
15. Van Boven, L. (2005). Experientialism, materialism, and the pursuit of happiness. *Review of General Psychology, 9*(2), 132.
16. Matz, S. C., Gladstone, J. J., & Stillwell, D. (2016). Money buys happiness when spending fits our personality. *Psychological science, 27*(5), 715-725.
17. Whillans, A. V., Weidman, A. C., & Dunn, E. W. (2016). Valuing time over money is associated with greater happiness. *Social Psychological and Personality Science, 7*(3), 213-222.
18. Mitchell, T. R., Thompson, L., Peterson, E., & Cronk, R. (1997). Temporal adjustments in the evaluation of events: The "rosy view". *Journal of Experimental Social Psychology, 33*(4), 421-448.
19. Emmons, R. A., & McCullough, M. E. (2003). Counting blessings versus burdens: an experimental investigation of gratitude and subjective well-being in daily life. *Journal of Personality and Social Psychology, 84*(2), 377.

20. Krause, N., Emmons, R. A., Ironson, G., & Hill, P. C. (2017). General feelings of gratitude, gratitude to god, and hemoglobin A1c: Exploring variations by gender. *The Journal of Positive Psychology, 12*(6), 639-650.
21. Pennebaker, J. W., & Susman, J. R. (1988). Disclosure of traumas and psychosomatic processes. *Social Science & Medicine, 26*(3), 327-332.
22. Demerouti, E., & Cropanzano, R. (2017). The buffering role of sportsmanship on the effects of daily negative events. *European Journal of Work and Organizational Psychology, 26*(2), 263-274.
23. Mischel, W., Ebbesen, E. B., & Raskoff Zeiss, A. (1972). Cognitive and attentional mechanisms in delay of gratification. *Journal of Personality and Social Psychology, 21*(2), 204.
24. Hyman, M. (2018). *Food: What the Heck Should I Eat?* Hachette UK.
25. Woolley, K., & Fishbach, A. (2017). Immediate rewards predict adherence to long-term goals. *Personality and Social Psychology Bulletin, 43*(2), 151-162.
26. Godwin, M. (2016). Humans are great at arguing but bad at reasoning. Julia Galef Explains Why. *Heleo, Oct 10*.
27. Gilead, M., Sela, M., & Maril, A. (2018). That's my truth: evidence for involuntary opinion confirmation. *Social Psychological and Personality Science*, 1948550618762300.
28. Nickerson, R. S. (1998). Confirmation bias: A ubiquitous phenomenon in many guises. *Review of General Psychology, 2*(2), 175.
29. Craig, A. D. (2002). How do you feel? Interoception: the sense of the physiological condition of the body. *Nature Reviews Neuroscience, 3*(8), 655.
30. Loewenstein, G. (1999). Experimental economics from the vantage-point of behavioural economics. *The Economic Journal, 109*(453), 25-34.
31. Partington, R. (2017). Nobel prize in economics awarded to Richard Thaler. *The Guardian*.
32. Pfeffer, J. (2016). Why the assholes are winning: Money trumps all. *Journal of Management Studies, 53*(4), 663-669.

CHAPTER 3

1. Wrzesniewski, A., & Dutton, J. E. (2001). Crafting a job: Revisioning employees as active crafters of their work. *Academy of Management Review, 26*(2), 179-201.
2. Bellah, R. N., Madsen, R., Sullivan, W. M., & Swidler, A. (6). A., & Tipton, SM (1985). *Habits of the Heart: Individualism and Commitment in American Life*.
    Wrzesniewski, A., McCauley, C., Rozin, P., & Schwartz, B. (1997). Jobs, careers, and callings: People's relations to their work. *Journal of Research in Personality, 31*(1), 21-33.
3. Rath, T., & Harter, J. (2010). The economics of wellbeing. *Omaha, NE: Gallup Press*.
4. Gallup (2017). State of the global workplace. *Gallup Press*.

5. Grant, A. M., Campbell, E. M., Chen, G., Cottone, K., Lapedis, D., & Lee, K. (2007). Impact and the art of motivation maintenance: The effects of contact with beneficiaries on persistence behavior. *Organizational Behavior and Human Decision Processes, 103*(1), 53-67.
6. Buell, R. W., Kim, T., & Tsay, C. J. (2016). Creating reciprocal value through operational transparency. *Management Science, 63*(6), 1673-1695.
7. Gneezy, U., & Rustichini, A. (2000). Pay enough or don't pay at all. *The Quarterly Journal of Economics, 115*(3), 791-810.
8. Drevitch, G. (2017). The mystery of motivation. *Psychology Today*, Jan 3.
9. Lepper, M. R., Greene, D., & Nisbett, R. E. (1973). Undermining children's intrinsic interest with extrinsic reward: A test of the "overjustification" hypothesis. *Journal of Personality and social Psychology, 28*(1), 129.
10. Vansteenkiste, M., Lens, W., & Deci, E. L. (2006). Intrinsic versus extrinsic goal contents in self-determination theory: Another look at the quality of academic motivation. *Educational Psychologist, 41*(1), 19-31.

    Vansteenkiste, M., Simons, J., Lens, W., Sheldon, K. M., & Deci, E. L. (2004). Motivating learning, performance, and persistence: The synergistic effects of intrinsic goal contents and autonomy-supportive contexts. *Journal of Personality and Social Psychology, 87*(2), 246.

    Vansteenkiste, M., Simons, J., Lens, W., Soenens, B., & Matos, L. (2005). Examining the impact of extrinsic versus intrinsic goal framing and internally controlling versus autonomy-supportive communication style upon early adolescents' academic achievement. *Child Development, 76*(2), 483-501.

    Vansteenkiste, M., Simons, J., Soenens, B., & Lens, W. (2004). How to become a persevering exerciser? Providing a clear, future intrinsic goal in an autonomy-supportive way. *Journal of Sport and Exercise Psychology, 26*(2), 232-249.

    Vansteenkiste, M., Simons, J., Lens, W., Soenens, B., Matos, L., & Lacante, M. (2004). Less is sometimes more: Goal content matters. *Journal of Educational Psychology, 96*(4), 755.
11. Boyle, P. A., Buchman, A. S., Wilson, R. S., Yu, L., Schneider, J. A., & Bennett, D. A. (2012). Effect of purpose in life on the relation between Alzheimer disease pathologic changes on cognitive function in advanced age. *Archives of General Psychiatry, 69*(5), 499-504.
12. Hill, P. L., & Turiano, N. A. (2014). Purpose in life as a predictor of mortality across adulthood. *Psychological Science, 25*(7), 1482-1486.
13. Fredrickson, B. L., Grewen, K. M., Coffey, K. A., Algoe, S. B., Firestine, A. M., Arevalo, J. M., ... & Cole, S. W. (2013). A functional genomic perspective on human well-being. *Proceedings of the National Academy of Sciences, 110*(33), 13684-13689.
14. Wheeler, M. (2013). Be happy: your genes might thank you for it. *UCLA Newsroom*, Jul 29.
15. Tonin, M., & Vlassopoulos, M. (2014). Corporate philanthropy and productivity: Evidence from an online real effort experiment. *Management Science, 61*(8), 1795-1811.

16. Langer, E. J., & Rodin, J. (1976). The effects of choice and enhanced personal responsibility for the aged: A field experiment in an institutional setting. *Journal of Personality and Social Psychology, 34*(2), 191.

    Rodin, J., & Langer, E. J. (1977). Long-term effects of a control-relevant intervention with the institutionalized aged. *Journal of Personality and Social Psychology, 35*(12), 897.

17. Glass, D. C., Reim, B., & Singer, J. E. (1971). Behavioral consequences of adaptation to controllable and uncontrollable noise. *Journal of Experimental Social Psychology, 7*(2), 244-257.

    Glass, D. C., & Singer, J. E. (1973). Experimental studies of uncontrollable and unpredictable noise. *Representative Research in Social Psychology*.

18. Seligman, M. E., & Maier, S. F. (1967). Failure to escape traumatic shock. *Journal of Experimental Psychology, 74*(1), 1.

19. Maier, S. F., & Seligman, M. E. (2016). Learned helplessness at fifty: Insights from neuroscience. *Psychological Review, 123*(4), 349.

20. Trougakos, J. P., Hideg, I., Cheng, B. H., & Beal, D. J. (2014). Lunch breaks unpacked: The role of autonomy as a moderator of recovery during lunch. *Academy of Management Journal, 57*(2), 405-421.

21. Wheatley, D. (2017). Autonomy in paid work and employee subjective well-being. *Work and Occupations, 44*(3), 296-328.

22. Warr, P. (2003). 20 Well-being and the workplace. *Well-Being: Foundations of Hedonic Psychology*, 392.

23. Collins, C. J., Allen, M. R. (2006). Research report on phase 4 of Cornell University/Gevity Institute study Human resource management practices and firm performance in small businesses: A look at the effects of HR practices on financial performance and turnover (CAHRS Working Paper #06-10). Ithaca, NY: Cornell University, School of Industrial and Labor Relations, Center for Advanced Human Resource Studies.

24. Maslow, A. H. (1943). A theory of human motivation. *Psychological Review, 50*(4), 370.

    Maslow, A. M. (1962). Toward a psychology of being. Princeton, NJ: D. Nostrand Co.

    Maslow, A. H. (1971). *The Farther Reaches of Human Nature*. Arkana/Penguin Books.

25. Wahba, M. A., & Bridwell, L. G. (1976). Maslow reconsidered: A review of research on the need hierarchy theory. *Organizational Behavior and Human Performance, 15*(2), 212-240.

26. Clark, J. V. (1960). Motivation in work groups: A tentative view. *Human Organization, 19*(4), 199-208.

    Cofer, C. N., & Appley, M. H. (1964). Motivation: Theory and research.

    Berkowitz, L. (1969). Social motivation. *The Handbook of Social Psychology, 3*, 50-135.

    Hall, D. T., & Nougaim, K. E. (1968). An examination of Maslow's need hierarchy in an organizational setting. *Organizational Behavior and Human Performance, 3*(1), 12-35.

    Vroom, V. H. (1964). Work and motivation.

Salancik, G. R., & Pfeffer, J. (1977). An examination of need-satisfaction models of job attitudes. *Administrative Science Quarterly*, 427-456.
27. Rasskazova, E., Ivanova, T., & Sheldon, K. (2016). Comparing the effects of low-level and high-level worker need-satisfaction: A synthesis of the self-determination and Maslow need theories. *Motivation and Emotion, 40*(4), 541-555.
28. Deci, E. L., & Ryan, R. M. (2011). Self-determination theory. *Handbook of Theories of Social Psychology, 1*(2011), 416-433.
29. Deci, E. L. (1971). Effects of externally mediated rewards on intrinsic motivation. *Journal of Personality and Social Psychology, 18*(1), 105.
30. Deci, E., & Ryan, R. M. (1985). *Intrinsic Motivation and Self-Determination in Human Behavior*. Springer Science & Business Media.
31. Deci, E. L., & Ryan, R. M. (1985). The general causality orientations scale: Self-determination in personality. *Journal of Research in Personality, 19*(2), 109-134.
32. Deci, E. L., & Ryan, R. M. (2011). Self-determination theory. *Handbook of Theories of Social Psychology, 1*(2011), 416-433.
33. Peterson, C., & Seligman, M. E. (1984). Causal explanations as a risk factor for depression: Theory and evidence. *Psychological Review, 91*(3), 347.
34. Iyengar, S. S., & Lepper, M. R. (2000). When choice is demotivating: Can one desire too much of a good thing? *Journal of Personality and Social Psychology, 79*(6), 995.
Schwartz, B. (2004). *The Paradox of Choice: Why More is Less*(Vol. 6). New York: HarperCollins.

CHAPTER 4

1. Cannon, W. B. (1929). Bodily changes in pain hunger, fear and rage. New York: Appeleton; cited from O'Brien JD et al., 1987. *Gut, 28*, 960-969.
2. Gabrielsen, G. W., & Smith, E. N. (1995). Physiological responses of. *Wildlife and Recreationists: Coexistence through Management and Research*, 95.
3. Levenson, R. W. (1994). Human emotion: A functional view. *The Nature of Emotion: Fundamental Questions, 1*, 123-126.
4. Ekman, P. E., & Davidson, R. J. (1994). *The Nature of Emotion: Fundamental Questions*. Oxford University Press.
5. Baker, S. M., Bennett, P., Bland, J. S., Galland, L., Hedaya, R. J., Houston, M., ... & Vasquez, A. (2010). Textbook of functional medicine. *Gig Harbor, WA: The Institute for Functional Medicine*.
6. Arnsten, A. F. (2009). Stress signalling pathways that impair prefrontal cortex structure and function. *Nature Reviews Neuroscience, 10*(6), 410.
7. Davis, M. (1992). The role of the amygdala in fear and anxiety. *Annual Review of Neuroscience, 15*(1), 353-375.
Ressler, K. J. (2010). Amygdala activity, fear, and anxiety: modulation by stress. *Biological Psychiatry, 67*(12), 1117-1119.

8. Rozin, P., & Royzman, E. B. (2001). Negativity bias, negativity dominance, and contagion. *Personality and Social Psychology Review, 5*(4), 296-320.
9. Ellsworth, P. C., & Smith, C. A. (1988). Shades of joy: Patterns of appraisal differentiating pleasant emotions. *Cognition & Emotion, 2*(4), 301-331.
10. Nicolson, N. A. (2008). Measurement of cortisol. *Handbook of Physiological Research Methods in Health Psychology, 1*, 37-74.
11. Ludwig, M., & Leng, G. (2006). Dendritic peptide release and peptide-dependent behaviours. *Nature Reviews Neuroscience, 7*(2), 126.

    Schneiderman, N., Ironson, G., & Siegel, S. D. (2005). Stress and health: psychological, behavioral, and biological determinants. *Annu. Rev. Clin. Psychol., 1*, 607-628.

    American Psychological Association. (2012). Stress in America: Our health at risk. *Washington DC, American Psychological Association*.

    Schoorlemmer, R. M. M., Peeters, G. M. E. E., Van Schoor, N. M., & Lips, P. T. A. M. (2009). Relationships between cortisol level, mortality and chronic diseases in older persons. *Clinical Endocrinology, 71*(6), 779-786.

    Walker, B. R. (2007). Glucocorticoids and cardiovascular disease. *European Journal of Endocrinology, 157*(5), 545-559.

    Thaker, P. H., Lutgendorf, S. K., & Sood, A. K. (2007). The neuroendocrine impact of chronic stress on cancer. *Cell Cycle, 6*(4), 430-433.

    Marcovecchio, M. L., & Chiarelli, F. (2012). The effects of acute and chronic stress on diabetes control. *Sci. Signal., 5*(247), 10-10.
12. Epel, E. S., Blackburn, E. H., Lin, J., Dhabhar, F. S., Adler, N. E., Morrow, J. D., & Cawthon, R. M. (2004). Accelerated telomere shortening in response to life stress. *Proceedings of the National Academy of Sciences of the United States of America, 101*(49), 17312-17315.
13. Cherkas, L. F., Aviv, A., Valdes, A. M., Hunkin, J. L., Gardner, J. P., Surdulescu, G. L., ... & Spector, T. D. (2006). The effects of social status on biological aging as measured by white-blood-cell telomere length. *Aging Cell, 5*(5), 361-365.
14. Arana, G. (2015). The benefits of positive news ripple far beyond the first smile. Huffington Post, Aug 19.
15. Berger, J., & Milkman, K. (2010). Social transmission, emotion, and the virality of online content. *Wharton Research Paper,106*.
16. Yi, Y. (1990). Cognitive and affective priming effects of the context for print advertisements. *Journal of Advertising, 19*(2), 40-48.
17. Przybylski, A. K., Murayama, K., DeHaan, C. R., & Gladwell, V. (2013). Motivational, emotional, and behavioral correlates of fear of missing out. *Computers in Human Behavior, 29*(4), 1841-1848.

CHAPTER 5

1. Barraza, J. A., & Zak, P. J. (2009). Empathy toward strangers triggers oxytocin release and subsequent generosity. *Annals of the New York Academy of Sciences, 1167*(1), 182-189.
2. Psychology Today. (2018). What is oxytocin?
3. Glaser, J. E., & Glaser, R. D. (2014). The neurochemistry of positive conversations. *Harvard Business Review.* http://blogs. hbr. org/2014/06/the-neurochemistry-of-positive-conversations.
4. Fredrickson, B. L., & Branigan, C. (2005). Positive emotions broaden the scope of attention and thought-action repertoires. *Cognition & emotion, 19*(3), 313-332.
5. Johnson, K. J., Waugh, C. E., & Fredrickson, B. L. (2010). Smile to see the forest: Facially expressed positive emotions broaden cognition. *Cognition and Emotion, 24*(2), 299-321.
6. Wadlinger, H. A., & Isaacowitz, D. M. (2006). Positive mood broadens visual attention to positive stimuli. *Motivation and Emotion, 30*(1), 87-99.
7. Rowe, G., Hirsh, J. B., & Anderson, A. K. (2007). Positive affect increases the breadth of attentional selection. *Proceedings of the National Academy of Sciences, 104*(1), 383-388.
8. Isen, A. M., Rosenzweig, A. S., & Young, M. J. (1991). The influence of positive affect on clinical problem solving. *Medical Decision Making, 11*(3), 221-227.
9. Staw, B. M., & Barsade, S. G. (1993). Affect and managerial performance: A test of the sadder-but-wiser vs. happier-and-smarter hypotheses. *Administrative Science Quarterly*, 304-331.
10. Sy, T., Côté, S., & Saavedra, R. (2005). The contagious leader: impact of the leader's mood on the mood of group members, group affective tone, and group processes. *Journal of Applied Psychology, 90*(2), 295.
11. Fredrickson, B. L., & Joiner, T. (2002). Positive emotions trigger upward spirals toward emotional well-being. *Psychological Science, 13*(2), 172-175.
12. Fredrickson, B. L., Tugade, M. M., Waugh, C. E., & Larkin, G. R. (2003). What good are positive emotions in crisis? A prospective study of resilience and emotions following the terrorist attacks on the United States on September 11th, 2001. *Journal of Personality and Social Psychology, 84*(2), 365.
13. Peterson, C., & Seligman, M. E. (1984). Causal explanations as a risk factor for depression: Theory and evidence. *Psychological Review, 91*(3), 347.
14. Cohn, M. A., Fredrickson, B. L., Brown, S. L., Mikels, J. A., & Conway, A. M. (2009). Happiness unpacked: positive emotions increase life satisfaction by building resilience. *Emotion, 9*(3), 361.
    Fredrickson, B. L., Cohn, M. A., Coffey, K. A., Pek, J., & Finkel, S. M. (2008). Open hearts build lives: positive emotions, induced through loving-kindness meditation, build consequential personal resources. *Journal of Personality and Social Psychology, 95*(5), 1045.

15. Hejmadi, A., Waugh, C. E., Otake, K., & Fredrickson, B. L. (2008). Cross-cultural evidence that positive emotions broaden views of self to include close others. *Manuscript in Preparation*.
    Aron, A., Aron, E. N., & Smollan, D. (1992). Inclusion of other in the self scale and the structure of interpersonal closeness. *Journal of Personality and Social Psychology*, 63(4), 596.
16. Csikszentmihalyi, M., Rathunde, K., & Whalen, S. (1997). *Talented Teenagers: The Roots of Success and Failure*. Cambridge University Press.
17. Lyubomirsky, S., & Ross, L. (1997). Hedonic consequences of social comparison: a contrast of happy and unhappy people. *Journal of Personality and Social Psychology*, 73(6), 1141.
18. Fredrickson, B. L., Cohn, M. A., Coffey, K. A., Pek, J., & Finkel, S. M. (2008). Open hearts build lives: positive emotions, induced through loving-kindness meditation, build consequential personal resources. *Journal of Personality and Social Psychology*, 95(5), 1045.
19. Fredrickson, B. L., Tugade, M. M., Waugh, C. E., & Larkin, G. R. (2003). What good are positive emotions in crisis? A prospective study of resilience and emotions following the terrorist attacks on the United States on September 11th, 2001. *Journal of Personality and Social Psychology*, 84(2), 365.
20. Steptoe, A., Wardle, J., & Marmot, M. (2005). Positive affect and health-related neuroendocrine, cardiovascular, and inflammatory processes. *Proceedings of the National academy of Sciences of the United States of America*, 102(18), 6508-6512.
21. Davidson, R. J., Kabat-Zinn, J., Schumacher, J., Rosenkranz, M., Muller, D., Santorelli, S. F., ... & Sheridan, J. F. (2003). Alterations in brain and immune function produced by mindfulness meditation. *Psychosomatic Medicine*, 65(4), 564-570.
22. Fredrickson, B. L., Mancuso, R. A., Branigan, C., & Tugade, M. M. (2000). The undoing effect of positive emotions. *Motivation and Emotion*, 24(4), 237-258.
23. Gil, K. M., Carson, J. W., Porter, L. S., Scipio, C., Bediako, S. M., & Orringer, E. (2004). Daily mood and stress predict pain, health care use, and work activity in African American adults with sickle-cell disease. *Health Psychology*, 23(3), 267.
24. Cohen, S., Doyle, W. J., Turner, R. B., Alper, C. M., & Skoner, D. P. (2003). Emotional style and susceptibility to the common cold. *Psychosomatic Medicine*, 65(4), 652-657.
25. Bardwell, W. A., Berry, C. C., Ancoli-Israel, S., & Dimsdale, J. E. (1999). Psychological correlates of sleep apnea. *Journal of Psychosomatic Research*, 47(6), 583-596.
26. Richman, L. S., Kubzansky, L., Maselko, J., Kawachi, I., Choo, P., & Bauer, M. (2005). Positive emotion and health: going beyond the negative. *Health Psychology*, 24(4), 422.
27. Ostir, G. V., Markides, K. S., Peek, M. K., & Goodwin, J. S. (2001). The association between emotional well-being and the incidence of stroke in older adults. *Psychosomatic Medicine*, 63(2), 210-215.
28. Danner, D. D., Snowdon, D. A., & Friesen, W. V. (2001). Positive emotions in early life and longevity: findings from the nun study. *Journal of Personality and Social Psychology*, 80(5), 804.

29. Fredrickson, B. L. (2001). The role of positive emotions in positive psychology: The broaden-and-build theory of positive emotions. *American Psychologist, 56*(3), 218.
30. Wrzesniewski, A., & Dutton, J. E. (2001). Crafting a job: Revisioning employees as active crafters of their work. *Academy of Management Review, 26*(2), 179-201.
31. Losada, M. (1999). The complex dynamics of high performance teams. *Mathematical and Computer Modelling, 30*(9-10), 179-192.
32. Achor, S. (2011). *The Happiness Advantage: The Seven Principles of Positive Psychology that Fuel Success and Performance at Work*. Random House.
33. Lorenz, E. (1972). *Predictability: Does the Flap of a Butterfly's Wing in Brazil Set off a Tornado in Texas?* na.
34. Fredrickson, B. L., & Losada, M. F. (2005). Positive affect and the complex dynamics of human flourishing. *American Psychologist, 60*(7), 678.
35. Keyes, C. L. (2002). The mental health continuum: From languishing to flourishing in life. *Journal of Health and Social Behavior*, 207-222.
36. Baumeister, R. F., Bratslavsky, E., Finkenauer, C., & Vohs, K. D. (2001). Bad is stronger than good. *Review of General Psychology, 5*(4), 323.
37. Diener, E., & Diener, C. (1996). Most people are happy. *Psychological Science, 7*(3), 181-185.
38. Fredrickson, B. L., & Losada, M. F. (2005). Positive affect and the complex dynamics of human flourishing. *American Psychologist, 60*(7), 678.
39. Gottman, J. M. (2014). *What Predicts Divorce?: The Relationship Between Marital Processes and Marital Outcomes*. Psychology Press.
40. Schwartz, R. M., Reynolds III, C. F., Thase, M. E., Frank, E., Fasiczka, A. L., & Haaga, D. A. (2002). Optimal and normal affect balance in psychotherapy of major depression: Evaluation of the balanced states of mind model. *Behavioural and Cognitive Psychotherapy, 30*(4), 439-450.
41. Elwert, F., & Christakis, N. A. (2008). The effect of widowhood on mortality by the causes of death of both spouses. *American Journal of Public Health, 98*(11), 2092-2098.
42. Christakis, N. A., & Fowler, J. H. (2013). Social contagion theory: examining dynamic social networks and human behavior. *Statistics in Medicine, 32*(4), 556-577.
43. Woolley, A. W., Chabris, C. F., Pentland, A., Hashmi, N., & Malone, T. W. (2010). Evidence for a collective intelligence factor in the performance of human groups. *Science, 330*(6004), 686-688.
44. Christakis, N. A., & Fowler, J. H. (2008). The collective dynamics of smoking in a large social network. *New England Journal of Medicine, 358*(21), 2249-2258.
45. Fowler, J. H., & Christakis, N. A. (2008). Dynamic spread of happiness in a large social network: longitudinal analysis over 20 years in the Framingham Heart Study. *Bmj, 337*, a2338.
46. Powdthavee, N. (2008). Putting a price tag on friends, relatives, and neighbours: Using surveys of life satisfaction to value social relationships. *The Journal of Socio-Economics, 37*(4), 1459-1480.

47. Diener, E., & Sandvik, E. (86). Pavot, W.(1991). Happiness is the frequency, not the intensity, of positive versus negative affect. *Subjective Well-Being: An Interdisciplinary Perspective*, 119-139.
48. Wrzesniewski, A., & Dutton, J. E. (2001). Crafting a job: Revisioning employees as active crafters of their work. *Academy of Management Review, 26*(2), 179-201.
49. Trougakos, J. P., Hideg, I., Cheng, B. H., & Beal, D. J. (2014). Lunch breaks unpacked: The role of autonomy as a moderator of recovery during lunch. *Academy of Management Journal, 57*(2), 405-421.
50. Misra, S., Cheng, L., Genevie, J., & Yuan, M. (2016). The iPhone effect: the quality of in-person social interactions in the presence of mobile devices. *Environment and Behavior, 48*(2), 275-298.
51. Nadler, R. T., Rabi, R., & Minda, J. P. (2010). Better mood and better performance: Learning rule-described categories is enhanced by positive mood. *Psychological Science, 21*(12), 1770-1776.
52. Rath, T., & Harter, J. (2010). Your friends and your social wellbeing. *The Gallup Management Journal*.
53. Gonzales, A. L., Hancock, J. T., & Pennebaker, J. W. (2010). Language style matching as a predictor of social dynamics in small groups. *Communication Research, 37*(1), 3-19.
54. Parkinson, C., Kleinbaum, A. M., & Wheatley, T. (2018). Similar neural responses predict friendship. *Nature Communications, 9*(1), 332.
55. McPherson, M., Smith-Lovin, L., & Cook, J. M. (2001). Birds of a feather: Homophily in social networks. *Annual Review of Sociology, 27*(1), 415-444.
56. Giles, L. C., Glonek, G. F., Luszcz, M. A., & Andrews, G. R. (2005). Effect of social networks on 10 year survival in very old Australians: the Australian longitudinal study of aging. *Journal of Epidemiology & Community Health, 59*(7), 574-579.
57. Holt-Lunstad, J., Smith, T. B., & Layton, J. B. (2010). Social relationships and mortality risk: a meta-analytic review. *PLoS Medicine, 7*(7), e1000316.
58. Owens, B. P., Baker, W. E., Sumpter, D. M., & Cameron, K. S. (2016). Relational energy at work: Implications for job engagement and job performance. *Journal of Applied Psychology, 101*(1), 35.
59. Gallese, V., Fadiga, L., Fogassi, L., & Rizzolatti, G. (1996). Action recognition in the premotor cortex. *Brain, 119*(2), 593-609.
60. Alibali, M. W., Heath, D. C., & Myers, H. J. (2001). Effects of visibility between speaker and listener on gesture production: Some gestures are meant to be seen. *Journal of Memory and Language, 44*(2), 169-188.
61. Whiten, A., & Brown, J. (1998). Imitation and the reading of other minds: Perspectives from the study of autism, normal children and non-human primates. *Intersubjective Communication and Emotion in Early Ontogeny*, 260-280.
62. Carr, L., Iacoboni, M., Dubeau, M. C., Mazziotta, J. C., & Lenzi, G. L. (2003). Neural mechanisms of empathy in humans: a relay from neural systems for imitation to limbic areas. *Proceedings of the National Academy of Sciences, 100*(9), 5497-5502.

63. Piper, W. T., Saslow, L. R., & Saturn, S. R. (2015). Autonomic and prefrontal events during moral elevation. *Biological Psychology, 108*, 51-55.
64. Oveis, C., Horberg, E. J., & Keltner, D. (2010). Compassion, pride, and social intuitions of self-other similarity. *Journal of Personality and Social Psychology, 98*(4), 618.
65. Bargh, J. A., Chen, M., & Burrows, L. (1996). Automaticity of social behavior: Direct effects of trait construct and stereotype activation on action. *Journal of Personality and Social Psychology, 71*(2), 230.
66. Friedman, H. S., & Riggio, R. E. (1981). Effect of individual differences in nonverbal expressiveness on transmission of emotion. *Journal of Nonverbal Behavior, 6*(2), 96-104.

CHAPTER 6

1. Lepper, M. R., Greene, D., & Nisbett, R. E. (1973). Undermining children's intrinsic interest with extrinsic reward: A test of the "overjustification" hypothesis. *Journal of Personality and social Psychology, 28*(1), 129.
2. Ariely, D., Gneezy, U., Loewenstein, G. & Mazar, N. (2009). Large stakes and big mistakes. *The Review of Economic Studies, 76*(2), 451-469.
3. Grant, A. M., & Gino, F. (2010). A little thanks goes a long way: Explaining why gratitude expressions motivate prosocial behavior. *Journal of Personality and Social Psychology, 98*(6), 946.
4. Deci, E. L. (1971). Effects of externally mediated rewards on intrinsic motivation. *Journal of Personality and Social Psychology, 18*(1), 105.
5. Amabile, T., & Kramer, S. (2012). How leaders kill meaning at work. *McKinsey Quarterly, 1*(2012), 124-131.
6. Wong, Y. J., Owen, J., Gabana, N. T., Brown, J. W., McInnis, S., Toth, P., & Gilman, L. (2018). Does gratitude writing improve the mental health of psychotherapy clients? Evidence from a randomized controlled trial. *Psychotherapy Research, 28*(2), 192-202.
7. Henning, M., Fox, G. R., Kaplan, J., Damasio, H., & Damasio, A. (2017). A potential role for mu-opioids in mediating the positive effects of gratitude. *Frontiers in Psychology, 8*, 868.
8. DeWall, C. N., Lambert, N. M., Pond Jr, R. S., Kashdan, T. B., & Fincham, F. D. (2012). A grateful heart is a nonviolent heart: Cross-sectional, experience sampling, longitudinal, and experimental evidence. *Social Psychological and Personality Science, 3*(2), 232-240.
9. Vozza, S. (2016). The science of gratitude and why it's important in your workplace. Fast Company, Nov. 24.
10. Algoe, S. B., Kurtz, L. E., & Hilaire, N. M. (2016). Putting the "You" in "Thank You" examining other-praising behavior as the active relational ingredient in expressed gratitude. *Social Psychological and Personality Science, 7*(7), 658-666.

11. Tamir, D. I., & Mitchell, J. P. (2012). Disclosing information about the self is intrinsically rewarding. *Proceedings of the National Academy of Sciences, 109*(21), 8038-8043.
12. Chancellor, J., Margolis, S., Jacobs Bao, K., & Lyubomirsky, S. (2017). Everyday prosociality in the workplace: The reinforcing benefits of giving, getting, and glimpsing.
13. Brown, S. L., Nesse, R. M., Vinokur, A. D., & Smith, D. M. (2003). Providing social support may be more beneficial than receiving it: Results from a prospective study of mortality. *Psychological Science, 14*(4), 320-327.
14. Carter, S.B. (2014). Helper's high: the benefits (and risks) of altruism. *Psychology Today*, Sep. 4.
15. Fowler, J. H., & Christakis, N. A. (2010). Cooperative behavior cascades in human social networks. *Proceedings of the National Academy of Sciences, 107*(12), 5334-5338.
16. Smith, K. M., Larroucau, T., Mabulla, I. A., & Apicella, C. L. Hunter-gatherers maintain assortativity in cooperation despite high-levels of residential change and mixing. *Current Biology, 28*(19), 3152-3157.
17. Grant, A., & Dutton, J. (2012). Beneficiary or benefactor: Are people more prosocial when they reflect on receiving or giving? *Psychological Science, 23*(9), 1033-1039.
18. Lyubomirsky, S., Sheldon, K. M., & Schkade, D. (2005). Pursuing happiness: The architecture of sustainable change. *Review of General Psychology, 9*(2), 111.

CHAPTER 7

1. Chartrand, T. L., & Van Baaren, R. (2009). Human mimicry. *Advances in Experimental Social Psychology, 41*, 219-274.
Prochazkova, E., & Kret, M. E. (2017). Connecting minds and sharing emotions through mimicry: A neurocognitive model of emotional contagion. *Neuroscience & Biobehavioral Reviews, 80*, 99-114.
2. Simner, M. L. (1971). Newborn's response to the cry of another infant. *Developmental Psychology, 5*(1), 136.
3. Lakin, J. L., Jefferis, V. E., Cheng, C. M., & Chartrand, T. L. (2003). The chameleon effect as social glue: Evidence for the evolutionary significance of nonconscious mimicry. *Journal of Nonverbal Behavior, 27*(3), 145-162.
   Gueguen, N., Jacob, C., & Martin, A. (2009). Mimicry in social interaction: Its effect on human judgment and behavior. *European Journal of Social Sciences, 8*(2), 253-259.
4. Rizzolatti, G., & Arbib, M. A. (1998). Language within our grasp. *Trends in Neurosciences, 21*(5), 188-194.
5. Mehrabian, A. (1971). *Silent Messages* (Vol. 8). Belmont, CA: Wadsworth.
6. Chartrand, T. L., & Bargh, J. A. (1999). The chameleon effect: the perception-behavior link and social interaction. *Journal of Personality and Social Psychology, 76*(6), 893.
7. Bailenson, J. N., & Yee, N. (2005). Digital chameleons: Automatic assimilation of nonverbal gestures in immersive virtual environments. *Psychological Science, 16*(10), 814-819.

8. Cheng, C. M., & Chartrand, T. L. (2003). Self-monitoring without awareness: using mimicry as a nonconscious affiliation strategy. *Journal of Personality and Social Psychology, 85*(6), 1170.
9. Zajonc, R. B., Adelmann, P. K., Murphy, S. T., & Niedenthal, P. M. (1987). Convergence in the physical appearance of spouses. *Motivation and Emotion, 11*(4), 335-346.
10. Van Leeuwen, P., Geue, D., Thiel, M., Cysarz, D., Lange, S., Romano, M. C., ... & Grönemeyer, D. H. (2009). Influence of paced maternal breathing on fetal-maternal heart rate coordination. *Proceedings of the National Academy of Sciences, 106*(33), 13661-13666.
11. Radtke, K. M., Ruf, M., Gunter, H. M., Dohrmann, K., Schauer, M., Meyer, A., & Elbert, T. (2011). Transgenerational impact of intimate partner violence on methylation in the promoter of the glucocorticoid receptor. *Translational Psychiatry, 1*(7), e21.
12. Bavelas, J. B., Black, A., Lemery, C. R., & Mullett, J. (1990). 14 Motor mimicry as primitive empathy. *Empathy and its Development*, 317.
13. Jacob, C., Guéguen, N., Martin, A., & Boulbry, G. (2011). Retail salespeople's mimicry of customers: Effects on consumer behavior. *Journal of Retailing and Consumer Services, 18*(5), 381-388.
    Kulesza, W., Szypowska, Z., Jarman, M. S., & Dolinski, D. (2014). Attractive cameleons sell: The mimicry-attractiveness link. *Psychology & Marketing, 31*(7), 549-561.
14. Hertenstein, M. J., Verkamp, J. M., Kerestes, A. M., & Holmes, R. M. (2006). The communicative functions of touch in humans, nonhuman primates, and rats: a review and synthesis of the empirical research. *Genetic, Social, and General Psychology Monographs, 132*(1), 5-94.
15. Kraus, M. W., Huang, C., & Keltner, D. (2010). Tactile communication, cooperation, and performance: An ethological study of the NBA. *Emotion, 10*(5), 745.
16. Walker, D. N. (1970). *Openness to Touching: A Study of Strangers in Nonverbal Interaction* (Doctoral dissertation, University of Connecticut).
17. Keltner, D. (2009). *Born to be Good: The Science of a Meaningful Life*. WW Norton & Company.
18. Fisher, J. D., Rytting, M., & Heslin, R. (1976). Hands touching hands: Affective and evaluative effects of an interpersonal touch. *Sociometry*, 416-421.
19. Aguilera, D. C. (1967). Relationship between physical contact and verbal interaction between nurses and patients. *Journal of Psychiatric Nursing and Mental Health Services, 5*(1), 5.
20. Willis, F. N., & Hamm, H. K. (1980). The use of interpersonal touch in securing compliance. *Journal of Nonverbal Behavior, 5*(1), 49-55.
21. Crusco, A. H., & Wetzel, C. G. (1984). The Midas touch: The effects of interpersonal touch on restaurant tipping. *Personality and Social Psychology Bulletin, 10*(4), 512-517.
22. Coan, J. A., Schaefer, H. S., & Davidson, R. J. (2006). Lending a hand: Social regulation of the neural response to threat. *Psychological Science, 17*(12), 1032-1039.
23. Rolls, E. T. (2000). The orbitofrontal cortex and reward. *Cerebral Cortex, 10*(3), 284-294.

24. Keltner, D. (2009). *Born to be Good: The Science of a Meaningful Life*. WW Norton & Company.
25. Ibid.
26. Roghanizad, M. M., & Bohns, V. K. (2017). Ask in person: You're less persuasive than you think over email. *Journal of Experimental Social Psychology, 69*, 223-226.
27. Grant, A. M., Campbell, E. M., Chen, G., Cottone, K., Lapedis, D., & Lee, K. (2007). Impact and the art of motivation maintenance: The effects of contact with beneficiaries on persistence behavior. *Organizational Behavior and Human Decision Processes, 103*(1), 53-67.
28. Seligman, M. E., Steen, T. A., Park, N., & Peterson, C. (2005). Positive psychology progress: empirical validation of interventions. *American Psychologist, 60*(5), 410.
29. Kavanagh, L. C., Suhler, C. L., Churchland, P. S., & Winkielman, P. (2011). When it's an error to mirror: The surprising reputational costs of mimicry. *Psychological Science, 22*(10), 1274-1276.
30. Strack, F., Martin, L. L., & Stepper, S. (1988). Inhibiting and facilitating conditions of the human smile: a nonobtrusive test of the facial feedback hypothesis. *Journal of Personality and Social Psychology, 54*(5), 768.
31. Darwin, C., & Prodger, P. (1998). *The expression of the emotions in man and animals*. Oxford University Press, USA.
32. Ekman, P. (2007). *Emotions Revealed: Recognizing Faces and Feelings to Improve Communication and Emotional Life*. Macmillan.
33. Dimberg, U., & Söderkvist, S. (2011). The voluntary facial action technique: A method to test the facial feedback hypothesis. *Journal of Nonverbal Behavior, 35*(1), 17-33.
34. Peper, E., & Lin, I. M. (2012). Increase or decrease depression: How body postures influence your energy level. *Biofeedback, 40*(3), 125-130.
35. Korb, A. (2015). *The Upward Spiral: Using Neuroscience to Reverse the Course of Depression, one Small Change at a Time*. New Harbinger Publications.
36. Bar, M., Neta, M., & Linz, H. (2006). Very first impressions. *Emotion, 6*(2), 269.
37. Johnson, K. J., Waugh, C. E., & Fredrickson, B. L. (2010). Smile to see the forest: Facially expressed positive emotions broaden cognition. *Cognition and Emotion, 24*(2), 299-321.
38. Davis, J. I., Senghas, A., Brandt, F., & Ochsner, K. N. (2010). The effects of BOTOX injections on emotional experience. *Emotion, 10*(3), 433.
39. Rosenberg, E. L., Ekman, P., Jiang, W., Babyak, M., Coleman, R. E., Hanson, M., ... & Blumenthal, J. A. (2001). Linkages between facial expressions of anger and transient myocardial ischemia in men with coronary artery disease. *Emotion, 1*(2), 107.
40. Tracy, J. L., & Matsumoto, D. (2008). The spontaneous expression of pride and shame: Evidence for biologically innate nonverbal displays. *Proceedings of the National Academy of Sciences, 105*(33), 11655-11660.
41. Hamilton, L. D., Carré, J. M., Mehta, P. H., Olmstead, N., & Whitaker, J. D. (2015). Social neuroendocrinology of status: a review and future directions. *Adaptive Human Behavior and Physiology, 1*(2), 202-230.

42. Mehta, P. H., & Josephs, R. A. (2010). Testosterone and cortisol jointly regulate dominance: Evidence for a dual-hormone hypothesis. *Hormones and Behavior*, *58*(5), 898-906.
43. Sapolsky, R. M. (1991). Testicular function, social rank and personality among wild baboons. *Psychoneuroendocrinology*, *16*(4), 281-293.
   De Waal, F., & Waal, F. B. (2007). *Chimpanzee Politics: Power and Sex among Apes*. JHU Press.
44. Carney, D. R., Cuddy, A. J., & Yap, A. J. (2010). Power posing: Brief nonverbal displays affect neuroendocrine levels and risk tolerance. *Psychological Science*, *21*(10), 1363-1368.
45. Gustafsson, E., Thomée, S., Grimby-Ekman, A., & Hagberg, M. (2017). Texting on mobile phones and musculoskeletal disorders in young adults: a five-year cohort study. *Applied Ergonomics*, *58*, 208-214.
46. Evans, S., Tsao, J. C., Sternlieb, B., & Zeltzer, L. K. (2009). Using the biopsychosocial model to understand the health benefits of yoga. *Journal of Complementary and Integrative Medicine*, *6*(1).
   Reddy, S., Dick, A. M., Gerber, M. R., & Mitchell, K. (2014). The effect of a yoga intervention on alcohol and drug abuse risk in veteran and civilian women with posttraumatic stress disorder. *The Journal of Alternative and Complementary Medicine*, *20*(10), 750-756.
   Seppälä, E. M., Nitschke, J. B., Tudorascu, D. L., Hayes, A., Goldstein, M. R., Nguyen, D. T., ... & Davidson, R. J. (2014). Breathing-based meditation decreases posttraumatic stress disorder symptoms in US Military veterans: A randomized controlled longitudinal study. *Journal of Traumatic Stress*, *27*(4), 397-405.
47. Luders, E., Cherbuin, N., & Gaser, C. (2016). Estimating brain age using high-resolution pattern recognition: younger brains in long-term meditation practitioners. *Neuroimage*, *134*, 508-513.
48. Cuddy, A. J., Wilmuth, C. A., Yap, A. J., & Carney, D. R. (2015). Preparatory power posing affects nonverbal presence and job interview performance. *Journal of Applied Psychology*, *100*(4), 1286.
49. Arnette, S. L., & Ii, T. F. P. (2012). The effects of posture on self-perceived leadership. *International Journal of Business and Social Science*, *3*(14).
50. Galinsky, A. D., Magee, J. C., Gruenfeld, D. H., Whitson, J. A., & Liljenquist, K. A. (2008). Power reduces the press of the situation: implications for creativity, conformity, and dissonance. *Journal of Personality and Social Psychology*, *95*(6), 1450.
51. Kwon, J., & Kim, S. Y. (2015, September). The Effect of Posture on Stress and Self-Esteem: Comparing Contractive and Neutral Postures. In *Proceedings of International Academic Conferences* (No. 2705176). International Institute of Social and Economic Sciences.
52. Wilson, V. E., & Peper, E. (2004). The effects of upright and slumped postures on the recall of positive and negative thoughts. *Applied Psychophysiology and Biofeedback*, *29*(3), 189-195.

CHAPTER 8

1. Seligman, M. E., & Maier, S. F. (1967). Failure to escape traumatic shock. *Journal of Experimental Psychology, 74*(1), 1.
2. Ryals, L. J., & Davies, I. A. (2010). Do you really know who your best sales people are?
3. Seligman, M. E., & Schulman, P. (1986). Explanatory style as a predictor of productivity and quitting among life insurance sales agents. *Journal of Personality and Social Psychology, 50*(4), 832.
4. Peterson, C., & Seligman, M. E. (1984). Causal explanations as a risk factor for depression: Theory and evidence. *Psychological Review, 91*(3), 347.
5. Seligman, M. E. (2006). *Learned Optimism: How to Change Your Mind and Your Life*. Vintage.
6. Ben-Shahar, T. (2010). *Even Happier: A Gratitude Journal for Daily Joy and Lasting Fulfillment*. McGraw-Hill.
7. Garrett, N., González-Garzón, A., Foulkes, L., Levita, L., & Sharot, T. (2018). Updating Beliefs Under Perceived Threat.
   Ortiz de Gortari, A. B., & Griffiths, M. D. (2014). Altered visual perception in Game Transfer Phenomena: An empirical self-report study. *International Journal of Human-Computer Interaction, 30*(2), 95-105.

CHAPTER 9

1. Theodorakis, Y., Weinberg, R., Natsis, P., Douma, I., & Kazakas, P. (2000). The effects of motivational versus instructional self-talk on improving motor performance. *The Sport Psychologist, 14*(3), 253-271.
2. Senay, I., Albarracín, D., & Noguchi, K. (2010). Motivating goal-directed behavior through introspective self-talk: The role of the interrogative form of simple future tense. *Psychological Science, 21*(4), 499-504.
3. Oettingen, G., & Mayer, D. (2002). The motivating function of thinking about the future: expectations versus fantasies. *Journal of Personality and Social Psychology, 83*(5), 1198.
4. Kappes, H. B., & Oettingen, G. (2011). Positive fantasies about idealized futures sap energy. *Journal of Experimental Social Psychology, 47*(4), 719-729.
5. Sevincer, A. T., Wagner, G., Kalvelage, J., & Oettingen, G. (2014). Positive thinking about the future in newspaper reports and presidential addresses predicts economic downturn. *Psychological Science, 25*(4), 1010-1017.
6. Kappes, H. B., & Oettingen, G. (2011). Positive fantasies about idealized futures sap energy. *Journal of Experimental Social Psychology, 47*(4), 719-729.

7. Wright, R. A., & Kirby, L. D. (2001). Effort determination of cardiovascular response: An integrative analysis with applications in social psychology. *Advances in Experimental Social Psychology, 33*, 255-307.
8. Oettingen, G., Pak, H., & Schnetter, K. (2001). Self-regulation of goal-setting: Turning free fantasies about the future into binding goals. *Journal of Personality and Social Psychology, 80*(5), 736.
9. Correa, C. (2013). *Sonho Grande*. Rio de Janeiro: Sextante.
10. Sevincer, A. T., & Oettingen, G. (2013). Spontaneous mental contrasting and selective goal pursuit. *Personality and Social Psychology Bulletin, 39*(9), 1240-1254.
11. Oettingen, G., Pak, H., & Schnetter, K. (2001). Self-regulation of goal-setting: Turning free fantasies about the future into binding goals. *Journal of Personality and Social Psychology, 80*(5), 736.
12. Seligman, M. E., & Maier, S. F. (1967). Failure to escape traumatic shock. *Journal of Experimental Psychology, 74*(1), 1.
13. Csikszentmihalyi, M. (1990). Flow: The psychology of optimal performance. *NY: Cambridge UniversityPress, 40*.
14. Baumeister, R. F. (1984). Choking under pressure: self-consciousness and paradoxical effects of incentives on skillful performance. *Journal of Personality and Social Psychology, 46*(3), 610.
15. Drevitch, G. (2017). The mystery of motivation. *Psychology Today*, Jan 3.
16. Gollwitzer, P. M., & Brandstätter, V. (1997). Implementation intentions and effective goal pursuit. *Journal of Personality and Social Psychology, 73*(1), 186.
17. Flavell, J. H. (1979). Metacognition and cognitive monitoring: A new area of cognitive-developmental inquiry. *American Psychologist, 34*(10), 906.
18. Adriaanse, M. A., Oettingen, G., Gollwitzer, P. M., Hennes, E. P., De Ridder, D. T., & De Wit, J. B. (2010). When planning is not enough: Fighting unhealthy snacking habits by mental contrasting with implementation intentions (MCII). *European Journal of Social Psychology, 40*(7), 1277-1293.
19. Sevincer, A. T., & Oettingen, G. (2013). Spontaneous mental contrasting and selective goal pursuit. *Personality and Social Psychology Bulletin, 39*(9), 1240-1254.
20. Stadler, G., Oettingen, G., & Gollwitzer, P. M. (2009). Physical activity in women: Effects of a self-regulation intervention. *American Journal of Preventive Medicine, 36*(1), 29-34.
21. Stadler, G., Oettingen, G., & Gollwitzer, P. M. (2010). Intervention effects of information and self-regulation on eating fruits and vegetables over two years. *Health Psychology, 29*(3), 274.
22. Christiansen, S., Oettingen, G., Dahme, B., & Klinger, R. (2010). A short goal-pursuit intervention to improve physical capacity: A randomized clinical trial in chronic back pain patients. *Pain, 149*(3), 444-452.
23. Marquardt, M. K., Oettingen, G., Gollwitzer, P. M., Sheeran, P., & Liepert, J. (2017). Mental contrasting with implementation intentions (MCII) improves physical activity and weight loss among stroke survivors over one year. *Rehabilitation Psychology, 62*(4), 580.

24. Houssais, S., Oettingen, G., & Mayer, D. (2013). Using mental contrasting with implementation intentions to self-regulate insecurity-based behaviors in relationships. *Motivation and Emotion, 37*(2), 224-233.
25. Duckworth, A. L., Grant, H., Loew, B., Oettingen, G., & Gollwitzer, P. M. (2011). Self-regulation strategies improve self-discipline in adolescents: Benefits of mental contrasting and implementation intentions. *Educational Psychology, 31*(1), 17-26.
26. Ouellette, J. A., & Wood, W. (1998). Habit and intention in everyday life: The multiple processes by which past behavior predicts future behavior. *Psychological Bulletin, 124*(1), 54.

CHAPTER 10

1. Deutsch, D., Henthorn, T., & Dolson, M. (2004). Absolute pitch, speech, and tone language: Some experiments and a proposed framework. *Music Perception: An Interdisciplinary Journal, 21*(3), 339-356.
2. Sakakibara, A. (2014). A longitudinal study of the process of acquiring absolute pitch: A practical report of training with the 'chord identification method'. *Psychology of Music, 42*(1), 86-111.
3. Witelson, S. F., Kigar, D. L., & Harvey, T. (1999). The exceptional brain of Albert Einstein. *The Lancet, 353*(9170), 2149-2153.
4. Aydin, K., Ucar, A., Oguz, K. K., Okur, O. O., Agayev, A., Unal, Z., ... & Ozturk, C. (2007). Increased gray matter density in the parietal cortex of mathematicians: a voxel-based morphometry study. *American Journal of Neuroradiology, 28*(10), 1859-1864.
5. Elbert, T., Pantev, C., Wienbruch, C., Rockstroh, B., & Taub, E. (1995). Increased cortical representation of the fingers of the left hand in string players. *Science, 270*(5234), 305-307.
6. Bilalić, M., McLeod, P., & Gobet, F. (2007). Does chess need intelligence? — A study with young chess players. *Intelligence, 35*(5), 457-470.
7. Choudhry, N. K., Fletcher, R. H., & Soumerai, S. B. (2005). Systematic review: the relationship between clinical experience and quality of health care. *Annals of Internal Medicine, 142*(4), 260-273.
8. Ericcson, K. A., Chase, W. G., & Faloon, S. (1980). Acquisition of a memory skill. *Science, 208*(4448), 1181-1182.
9. Chase, W. G., & Ericsson, K. A. (1982). Skill and working memory. In *Psychology of Learning and Motivation* (vol. 16, pp. 1-58). Academic Press.
10. Ericsson, K. A., & Kintsch, W. (1995). Long-term working memory. *Psychological Review, 102*(2), 211.
11. Hearst, E. (2011). After 64 years: new world blindfold record set by Marc Lang playing 46 games at once. Blindfoldchess, Dec 16.
12. Chase, W. G., & Simon, H. A. (1973). Perception in chess. *Cognitive Psychology, 4*(1), 55-81.

13. Ward, P., Ericsson, K. A., & Williams, A. M. (2013). Complex perceptual-cognitive expertise in a simulated task environment. *Journal of Cognitive Engineering and Decision Making, 7*(3), 231-254.
14. Gladwell, M. (2008). *Outliers: The story of success*. Hachette UK.
15. Amabile, T., & Kramer, S. (2011). *The Progress Principle: Using Small Wins to Ignite Joy, Engagement, and Creativity at Work*. Harvard Business Press.
16. Maslow, A. (1965). Self-actualization and beyond.
17. Diener, C. I., & Dweck, C. S. (1980). An analysis of learned helplessness: II. The processing of success. *Journal of Personality and Social Psychology, 39*(5), 940.
18. Dweck, C. S., & Leggett, E. L. (1988). A social-cognitive approach to motivation and personality. *Psychological Review, 95*(2), 256.
19. Clance, P. R. (1985). *The Impostor Phenomenon: Overcoming the Fear that Haunts Your Success*. Peachtree Pub Ltd.
20. Diener, C. I., & Dweck, C. S. (1980). An analysis of learned helplessness: II. The processing of success. *Journal of Personality and Social Psychology, 39*(5), 940.
21. Mueller, C. M., & Dweck, C. S. (1998). Praise for intelligence can undermine children's motivation and performance. *Journal of Personality and Social Psychology, 75*(1), 33.
22. Bilalić, M., McLeod, P., & Gobet, F. (2007). Does chess need intelligence? — A study with young chess players. *Intelligence, 35*(5), 457-470.
23. Elert, G. (1992). The SAT: Aptitude or demographics. *E-World*. Retrieved.

Stanley, T. J. (2000). *The Millionaire Mind*. Andrews McMeel Publishing.

ABOUT THE AUTHOR

LUIZ GAZIRI approaches subjects of interest in the corporate world and our daily lives **based 100% on scientific proof**. He is constantly in contact with scientists from many different countries and has visited researchers at the most renowned institutions in the world.

Gaziri offers **lectures**, **workshops** and **consulting**, and is a professor at **FAE Business School, ISAE/FGV** and **PUC-PR**. He studied in the United States, England and Brazil, and worked as an executive for 16 years, occupying leadership positions in companies of many different sizes and industries. He also wrote *The Incredible Science of Sales*. His work has been featured in the most prominent media outlets in Brazil.

In addition to working in the happiness and motivation field, Gaziri also helps companies in matters of leadership, people management, sales and marketing. His purpose is to empower people and organizations to make better decisions based on science.

info@luizgaziri.com
www.luizgaziri.com
Facebook, LinkedIn, Instagram, Twitter: Luiz Gaziri

www.ingramcontent.com/pod-product-compliance
Lightning Source LLC
Chambersburg PA
CBHW021812170526
45157CB00007B/2560